WordPerfect 6.0

for Wimps

Becky J. Campbell

Bruce Hallberg

NRP
NEW RIDERS
PUBLISHING

New Riders Publishing, Carmel, Indiana

WordPerfect 6.0 for Wimps

By Becky J. Campbell and Bruce Hallberg

Published by
New Riders Publishing
11711 N. College Ave., Suite 140
Carmel, IN 46032 USA

Copyright © 1993 by New Riders Publishing

Printed in the United States of America 1 2 3 4 5 6 7 8 9 0

Library of Congress Cataloging-in-Publication Data

Hallberg, Bruce A., 1964-
WordPerfect 6.0 for Wimps / by Bruce Hallberg, Becky J. Campbell.
    p.   cm.
    Includes index.
    ISBN 1-56205-188-1 : $16.95
    1. WordPerfect (Computer file) 2. Word Processing. I. Campbell,
Becky. II. Title.
Z52.5.W65H324   1993
652.5'536--dc20   93-5368
                                                  CIP

Publisher
  Lloyd J. Short

Associate Publisher
  Tim Huddleston

Acquisitions Manager
  Cheri Robinson

Acquisitions Editor
  Rob Tidrow

Managing Editor
  Matthew Morrill

Marketing Manager
  Brad Koch

Developmental Editor
  Pete J. Kuhns

Editors
  John Kane
  Steve Weiss
  Phil Worthington

Technical Editor
  Sharon Heafey

Book Design and Production
  Roger S. Morgan
  Lisa Daugherty
  Dennis Clay Hager
  Carla Hall
  Mike Mucha
  Juli Pavey
  Angela M. Pozdol
  Michelle Self
  Barbara Webster
  Alyssa Yesh

Indexer
  Caroline Roop

Proofreaders
  Mitzi Foster Gianakos
  Sean Meadlock
  Tonya Simpson
  Marcella Thompson
  Donna Winter

Acquisitions Coordinator
  Stacey Beheler

Editorial Secretary
  Karen Opal

Publishing Assistant
  Melissa Keegan

About the Authors

Becky J. Campbell is an unbelievably adequate person and a system operator on ZiffNet forums on CompuServe. Becky has worked for the last ten years in computer programming design and networking. In that capacity she has served on the Board of Directors for NUI (NetWare Users International). She was a word processor in a past life and has spent countless hours supporting users of WordPerfect in the Real World. Becky wrestles gorillas in her spare time.

Bruce Hallberg is a real big shot at a biotechnology company located in Redwood City, California. He has been heavily involved with PCs since 1980 and has specialized in accounting and business control systems for the past seven years. He has consulted with a large number of local and national companies in a variety of areas and has expertise in networking, programming, and system implementations. He works with a wide variety of PC computer platforms, including DOS, Windows, OS/2, Unix, and the Macintosh as well as more computer programs than you can shake a banana at.

Dedication

Bruce: For Bruce and Cheryl Hallberg.

Becky: This book is dedicated to Joe and Marybeth Higuera who provided their support, as they always have.

Acknowledgments

Becky and Bruce would like to acknowledge the following people:

Peter Kuhns at New Riders Publishing, who is a really good editor, and who was very dedicated to this project. He also has us snowed that he is really fun to work with.

Cheri Robinson, Tim Huddleston, and the other fine folks at New Riders Publishing. Also to Lloyd Short for giving us work.

The really helpful, friendly, and knowledgeable folks who tirelessly answer questions at the WordPerfect support lines.

The real Orville E. Fudpucker, originator of the best TSJD (Texas Sized Jelly Doughnut), for letting us use his name in examples.

The WordPerfect author support folks, Sandi Hetzel and Lesa Carter.

In addition, Becky would like to acknowledge:

Bruce Hallberg who is an okay sort of guy.

Conni Gallo, for her insight and support.

Starbuck's Coffee, without whose excellent products this book would not have been written in time.

Trademark Acknowledgments

New Riders Publishing has made every attempt to supply trademark information about company names, products, and services mentioned in this book. Trademarks indicated below were derived from various sources. New Riders Publishing cannot attest to the accuracy of this information.

WordPerfect 6.0 is a registered trademark of WordPerfect Corporation.

Trademarks of other products mentioned in this book are held by the companies producing them.

Warning and Disclaimer

This book is designed to provide information about the WordPerfect 6.0 program. Every effort has been made to make this book as complete and as accurate as possible, but no warranty or fitness is implied.

The information is provided on an "as is" basis. The authors and New Riders Publishing shall have neither liability nor responsibility to any person or entity with respect to any loss or damages arising from the information contained in this book or from the use of the disks or programs that may accompany it.

Contents at a Glance

Contents

INTRODUCTION

Introduction
(or, Important Stuff
No One Ever Reads)

Everybody knows that computers are scary and intimidating, at least at first. The same is true of WordPerfect. And it probably doesn't help that your neighbors' six-year-old brat knows more about computers than you do.

This book is perfect for you if you are new to WordPerfect—and especially if you are new to computers. This book translates computerese into plain-English explanations and helps you become a WordPerfect master through step-by-step instructions. You might even find it a little humorous along the way (even though our editors didn't, but that's OK; editors are a little slow at times).

(Editor's Note: Huh?)

WordPerfect for Wimps leads you through the basics of the world's most powerful word processor: WordPerfect. This book takes you through the steps of writing, editing, and printing with this program, and builds on those skills so that you can produce a professional-looking document with tables, graphics, and all sorts of cool stuff.

Sure, WordPerfect is huge, and powerful. (Why else would it be so expensive?) It has dozens of features that only rocket scientists care about. If you're just starting out, that stuff just gets in the way (you can learn it later). For now, let's just cover the basics. Hey, some day you may write your own masterpiece with WordPerfect. (After all, we did!) So, whether you aspire to be the next Gore Vidal or just want to write a letter to Mom, this book is for you.

What Makes WordPerfect So Great?

Despite the fact that it's so big, WordPerfect is such a neat program that you can use it for everything from writing your grocery list to making your morning coffee. Well, OK, maybe it won't make your coffee or even get your morning paper (darn!), but you can actually do a lot with it:

 Manage all your files without actually using ugly DOS commands.

 Change your mind—frequently. WordPerfect has all sorts of editing features and toys that let you change the way your documents look. You can try out different styles and formats *before* you ever print anything.

 Make your computer do stuff automatically. This is great if you have to do certain tasks over and over. You can automate anything from frequently repeated keystrokes to commonly used letters and forms. This is one of the main reasons we use computers rather than typewriters.

 Write anything you want—from a letter to a form to a book to a professional newsletter—with ease.

These are just a few of the reasons why WordPerfect is the most popular word processing program on the planet.

What Ain't So Great about WordPerfect?

Powerful programs—like WordPerfect—have so many features that new users sometimes have difficulty getting "up and running" easily. It also means that:

 WordPerfect offers so many choices and so many ways of accomplishing the same task that new users can get lost trying to accomplish a simple task!

 It can be easy to get lost among the "jungle" of menus, submenus, and subsubmenus.

This book helps you carve out a route through the myriad menus and choices with clear, step-by-step instructions along the way. You will learn the direct route to take to accomplish the tasks you want to—while learning that there are other paths that you can explore on your own.

How This Book Is Organized

You can read this book from front to back, from back to front (but don't reveal the surprise ending to your friends), or from the middle out. It's arranged so that you can read it from front to back as a tutorial, or so you can just skip to the interesting parts.

Chapter 0: Don't Be A Wimp, Read This First

This chapter is just like Ground Zero; everything starts here. You should read Chapter 0 before you read anything else. It covers the minimum basics you need to know before you start using WordPerfect and before you read any other part of the book.

Chapter 1: Installing WordPerfect 6.0 (No Bananas Necessary)

Chapter 1 takes you through installing WordPerfect 6.0 on your computer. Included are the steps you need to take to prepare yourself—and your computer—for the Big Day! Refer back to this chapter when you want to add a printer or otherwise change your installation.

Chapter 2: Setting Up for Success: Changing WordPerfect's Default Settings

WordPerfect's Setup program has all sorts of nifty settings. Some of them are fun, but some are pretty serious! Be sure to read this chapter so that you can set yourself up to use some of WordPerfect's really great features right from the start.

Chapter 3: Setting Up a Document

Chapter 3 tells you how to set up your WordPerfect document to take the most advantage of WordPerfect's formatting functions. No need to struggle with formats as you go along; get your document set up right before you type anything.

Chapter 4: The Basics of Entering and Formatting Text

Start exploring the wonderful world of different types of fonts and formats that will give your documents that professional look and make people sit up and take notice (arf arf)! Learn the editing tricks the professionals use and how to save your work for posterity.

Chapter 5: Whoops! (The Basics of Editing)

In Chapter 5, you build on your basic letter-writing abilities to polish up your presentation.

Chapter 6: Nagging Details

Chapter 6 tells you how to use some of WordPerfect's nifty features—including the spell checker, the thesaurus, and the grammar checker—to polish up your writing.

Chapter 7: Printing Your Letter

Chapter 7 tells you how to get perfect printouts of your documents so you can spring your composition onto an unsuspecting world.

Chapter 8: A Word about Files

Now you can be the life of the party by sharing your knowledge of file management! Chapter 8 shows you how to move, copy, and view your files by using WordPerfect's file-management tools.

Chapter 9: Get Serious with Styles and Other Fancy Stuff

Chapter 9 delves into the fashionable document—showing how you can be working with Styles and Outlines in a jiffy!

Chapter 10: What Is a Macro and How Much Weight Will I Lose?

Shed those unsightly keystrokes with WordPerfect macros. In this chapter, you'll remember why you bought a computer instead of a typewriter!

Chapter 11: Caution: Rated PG (Perfect Graphics)

Include great-looking graphics in your documents and contour the text to your liking.

Chapter 12: Mighty Columns

Build up your work with columns by learning how to create the perfect newsletter or shopping list with this terrific WordPerfect feature.

Chapter 13: Data on the Table

Don't wait to present your information in tables! You hold the keys to each of the cells in a table. Learn how to add, subtract, multiply, and do even more here.

Chapter 14: Caution: Merge Ahead

Learn how to create a letter, envelope, and Rolodex card from one magic file with the WordPerfect merge functions.

Glossary

Don't get tangled up in nerdy terms, learn what they mean right here! This glossary defines nerdy terms about computers in general, as well as some nerdy words you will come across while you use WordPerfect (or any word processor, for that matter).

Appendix A: (Im)perfect Computers

If you really think your computer can do scary things such as explode or start World War III, you may want to read this chapter first. It will make you feel more comfortable about tackling WordPerfect instead of feeling like WordPerfect or your computer might tackle you.

Strange Type You Will See in This Book

Just so you know what's going on, this book uses special typefaces and shows certain keystrokes in a special way. Even if these special formatting characters are confusing, at least you'll be confused consistently (which is what the editors insisted on, darn them). Be prepared for these special characters:

 Bold. If the book tells you to type something (such as a command or some text), the actual words you must type appear in **bold**. Here's an example:

Type **THIS BOOK IS A GREAT WORK OF ART** and press Enter.

 Italic. When a new term or phrase is introduced, it appears in *italic*.

 Special type. Sometimes DOS or WordPerfect may show you a message. When this book shows you one of those messages, it appears in a special typeface, like this:

```
This computer will self-destruct in five seconds.
```

Hot keys. Like many other computer programs, WordPerfect lets you choose commands from menus. In the menu, the commands often have a special highlighted character, called a *shortcut key* or a *hot key*. The highlighted letter is a key you can press on the keyboard instead of using the mouse to click on the menu item. Shortcut keys for menus appear in bold and are underlined, as in this example:

Open the **F**ile menu, and then select **O**pen.

Some people like to use shortcut keys because this is faster than lifting your hand off the keyboard to use the mouse.

When you see a shortcut key, you can choose that option from the menu simply by pressing that key. Sometimes, when using a menu for the first time, you also have to hold down the Alt key on the keyboard. This is demonstrated in the next chapter, so don't worry about it now.

 Key combinations. You also need to know the following two types of key combinations:

Key1,Key2. When you see two keys separated by a comma, you should press the first key, release it, and then press the second key. Here's an example:

Type **A,Tab** and make a noise like a duck.

In this example, you press the A key (and then let go of it, of course) and then press the Tab key (and then say "quack").

Key1-Key2. When keys are separated by a dash, you press the first key and hold it down *while* you press the second key. Then release them. Here's an example:

Press **Alt-F8**.

Here you press and hold Alt (short for Alternate) and then press the F8 key (F is short for "function"). After you press F8, you can let go of both keys (this is one of those things that takes longer to describe than to do).

Asides

Along with the exciting text in this book, you will see little asides to help you on your guided tour of WordPerfect. Look for these interesting and useful items as you read:

TRICK

A **TRICK** usually contains a nifty shortcut. These little asides might make your life easier; you can also show off for your friends and neighbors. Very impressive.

STOP!

STOP! Halt! Pay attention here! If you skip a **STOP!**, not only will Guido come to your house to break your knees, but you risk endangering Western civilization as we know it. At the very least, reading a **STOP!** might keep you from drop-kicking your monitor through your living room window. This icon is meant to keep you from making a mistake that you (and we) might regret.

FOOD FOR THOUGHT

Hmmmm... I'm hungry. **FOOD FOR THOUGHT** notes are the perfect appetizer if you're hungry for knowledge. These notes contain information that you don't necessarily have to read to understand something, but is provided in case you're interested. Whatever the topic—WordPerfect's merge codes, creating styles, or something more interesting like creating the perfect banana split—**FOOD FOR THOUGHT** notes are the perfect snack for a gorilla-sized appetite.

SAVE THE DAY

A **SAVE THE DAY** can help you out of a sticky situation. We may even throw in a **SAVE THE DAY** just in case you might have ignored a **STOP!** icon. But don't count on it, because you were supposed to pay attention to the STOP! in the first place!

Other Things You Should Take into Consideration as You Work

Here are the rest of the trifling details of an Introduction that the editors made us put in:

Marketing Spiel

The staff of New Riders Publishing is committed to bringing you the very best in computer reference material. Each New Riders book is the result of months of work by the authors and staff (but mostly the authors—really!), who research and refine the information contained within its covers.

As part of this commitment to you, New Riders invites your input. Please let us know if you enjoy this book, if you have trouble with the information and examples presented, if you have a suggestion for the next edition, or if you would like us to send Guido out to pay the authors a little visit.

If you have a question or comment about any New Riders book, please write to NRP at the following address. We will respond to as many readers as we can. Your name, address, or phone number will never become a part of a mailing list or be used for any purpose other than to help us continue to bring you the best books possible.

New Riders Publishing
Attn: Associate Publisher
11711 N. College Avenue
Carmel, IN 46032
FAX: (317) 571-3484

If you prefer, you can contact the product director for *WordPerfect for Wimps* via CompuServe at {70031,2231}.

Legal Stuff

The legal folks, not to be outdone by the Marketing Department, have demanded that this little tidbit be inserted here (they are, after all, lawyers):

> Please note that the New Riders staff cannot serve as a technical resource for WordPerfect or WordPerfect-related questions, including hardware- or software-related problems. Refer to the documentation that accompanies your hardware or software package for help with specific problems.

Now, Something We Really Do Want to Say...

Thank you very much for selecting *WordPerfect for Wimps*. A lot of people have worked very hard to bring this book to you, and we sincerely hope you enjoy reading it as much as we enjoyed producing it. We're just glad that they let us out long enough to do it. Right after this is done, it's back to the special room for us.

CHAPTER O

Don't Be a Wimp, Read This First

"One of the hallmarks of true wimps is they invariably bypass all instructions, hints, and advice. I used to do that all the time. Then one day I threw my glasses across the room in frustration and had to repair them with electrical tape. It was then that I knew I was a hopeless wimp. It was awful."—Confessions of a Former Wimp

Don't let this happen to you! Read this chapter first! Why? Because WordPerfect and this book use terms and keys that you may have never seen. Before you can take charge of WordPerfect, you need to be familiar with the most common keys and terms WordPerfect uses. This chapter quickly introduces you to these terms and shows you:

 That Help is always at your fingertips

 Words you will need to know

 Ways to navigate WordPerfect without a compass

 A quick lesson in creating, saving, and reopening a WordPerfect document

Buzz through these pages and expose yourself to the words and keys you'll encounter in this book. Afterward, dive into WordPerfect in a super quick tutorial.

Instant Help: A Guide to Happy WordPerfecting

WordPerfect wants you to enjoy using their program; some aids have been thoughtfully included to guide you.

 Help. WordPerfect includes an online Help feature in the program, shown in figure 0.1. *Online* means that you can access the Help files at any time you are working in the program. Just press the F1 key (or F3, depending on how you have WordPerfect set up) to access Help.

There is even a Help on how to use and understand Help!

Figure 0.1:

Help is just a button away.

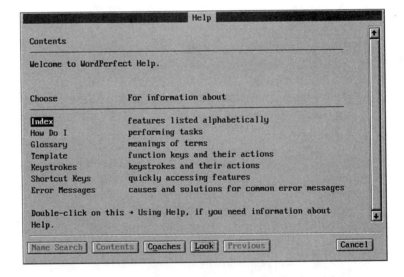

 Coach. Unlike Mr. Simmons, the high school football coach, WordPerfect's coach shows you, step-by-step, how to do something properly. If you run into a function that doesn't seem clear on the Help screen, click on the <u>C</u>oach button and a little mini-tutorial illustrates how to use the function properly (see fig. 0.2). Not every function has a Coach; to find out if the one you want has a Coach, click on the <u>C</u>oach button.

Figure 0.2:

More coaches than you
can shake a coed at!

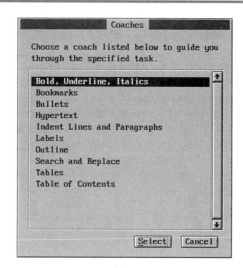

Lessons. Interactive tutorials are also included with WordPerfect.
Figure 0.3 shows a lesson for indenting text.

Figure 0.3:

A lesson on indenting.

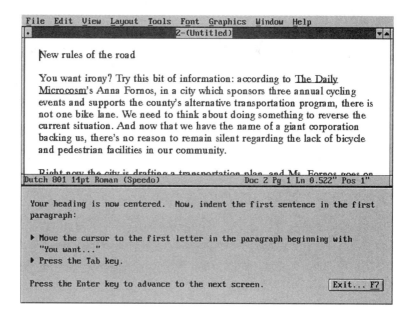

Start Off with WordPerfect's Default Configuration

This book uses WordPerfect's *default configuration*. In other words, WordPerfect has set up its installation program so that the program installs a set of files and settings with preconceived names and settings.

TRICK

Ask the person who installed WordPerfect on your computer if he or she used the default installation. If not, find out which directory names were used for the WordPerfect program and the shared WordPerfect files. In a standard installation, WordPerfect is installed in \WP60 and the shared files are found in \WPC60DOS.

If a later chapter in the book discusses customizing WordPerfect (several do), you will be shown how you can change the defaults and how settings are configured.

Nowhere in this book will you find information on changing the directory or file names that WordPerfect has set up to be installed on your computer. If your program was installed with different names, you will need to make those adjustments for yourself. In one case, however, you learn how to change the names of a file.

Important Words You'll See in This Book

Here are some terms that will make you the life of the party. Figures 0.4 and 0.5 show you where these parts and pieces are found.

Figure 0.4:

WordPerfect-ese
visualized on-screen in
Text Mode.

Cursor —

Window —

Pull-down
menu

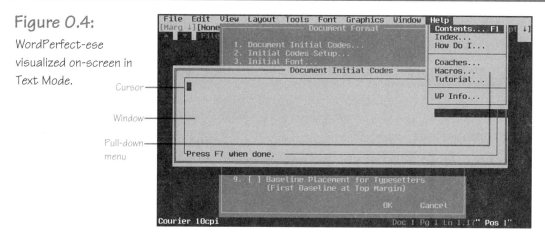

Figure 0.5:

The more appealing
components in
Graphics Mode.

Button —

Cursor —

Window —

Entry field —

Pull-down
menu

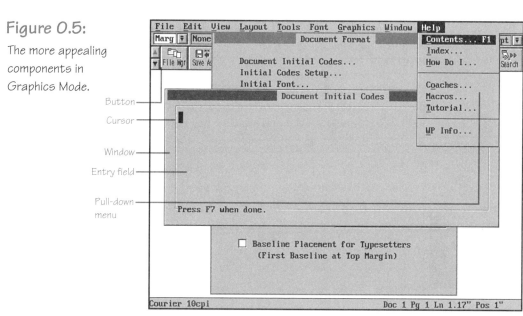

Table 0.1
WordPerfect Dissected

"What's that?"	"What's it for?"
Cursor	Usually a slowly flashing rectangle that can be many other different shapes and sizes. In the Graphics and Page modes in WordPerfect, the cursor appears as a narrow vertical bar.
Pull-down menus	WordPerfect's functions are often accessed through *pull-down menus*. The entire menu isn't on-screen all the time; you have to pull the complete menu down with your mouse or two keystrokes. The words <u>F</u>ile, <u>E</u>dit, <u>V</u>iew, and others across the top of the screen indicate the type of commands in each pull-down menu. The <u>V</u>iew pull-down menu, for example, displays commands that affect what you view on-screen. To open these menus, click on the word with your mouse. Simple!
Window	WordPerfect usually asks you for settings and other information in boxes called dialog boxes. When you select a command from a pull-down menu, a dialog box usually appears asking for more information. Also, when you work with more than one document in WordPerfect, each document is displayed in a separate window.

FOOD FOR THOUGHT

Do not confuse windows in WordPerfect with the program *Windows 3.1* from Microsoft Corporation. They are two entirely different things.

Button	After you enter information in a dialog box, you often need to accept the changes by clicking on a button—a little box with the words OK, Cancel, Detonate, or something else. Click on the button with the left mouse button.
Active window	Occasionally you may have more than one window shown on-screen at one time. The *active window* is the one that you are actually working in at that time.

"What's that?"	"What's it for?"
Mouse	A mouse is NOT REQUIRED in order to use WordPerfect. WordPerfect can be operated just fine without a mouse. Some people find that using a mouse is a nuisance (just like real mice!).

FOOD FOR THOUGHT

You do not need a mouse to use this book.

Pointer	If you use a mouse to operate the WordPerfect program, you will see a *pointer* on-screen.
	If you are running WordPerfect in text mode, the pointer will be appear as a small rectangle on your screen. If you are running WordPerfect in graphics or page mode, the pointer is shaped like a little arrow.
Click	A click is a quick press and release of one of the buttons. This will signal to the computer that you want to take a specific action.
	Most mice have two buttons, but some have three and some only have one. The left mouse button is used by right handed people. IF you are left handed, one of the first things you will learn how to do is switch mouse buttons so that the right button is the clicker.
Double-click	Some selections require that you double-click the mouse button. This is a click-click in rapid succession on the same mouse button.
Scroll bars	A scroll bar appears on the right side of a window that contains too much information to fit in the window. The small moving box in the scroll bar gives a rough position of the current screen in relation to the whole document. To see more information in the window, move your pointer right over the box, hold down the left mouse button, drag the box down (or up) a little, and let go of the mouse button..
	Another method is to click in the bar *outside* of the box. This will cause the screen to move by an entire "screenful." The Page Up, Page Down, and arrow keys also move the scroll bar.

Table 0.1
continued

"What's that?"	"What's it for?"
Entry field	Some of the windows that appear on-screen contain a rectangle with a slowly flashing cursor. These are entry fields that eagerly await information from you. In WordPerfect, an entry field might ask you to type a file name, a number, or some other selection.

A Keyboard Tour

Besides the normal alphabetical, numerical, and punctuation keys on your keyboard, a number of other keys operate the WordPerfect program (see fig. 0.6). WordPerfect takes advantage of the function keys considerably, as explained in table 0.2, and even has special uses for the traditional keyboard keys (see table 0.3). The more you know about using these keys in WordPerfect, the easier your life will be when you are using this program.

Figure 0.6:

A typical PC keyboard with all the trimmings.

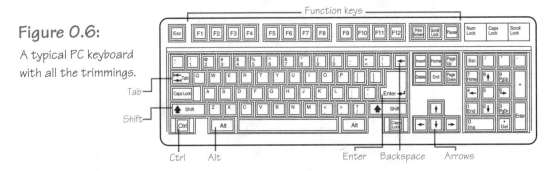

Table 0.2
Special PC Keys You May Need To Use

Funky Key	What it Does
Arrows	The arrow keys help you navigate your way around both your screen and some of the windows.
	Use either the arrow keys on your keyboard's keypad (make sure Num Lock is off) or dedicated arrow keys if you have them.

Funky Key	What it Does
Function kjeys	Another special group of keys, the function keys (F1, F2, F3, and so on) are important for operating WordPerfect, especially if you do not have a mouse.

In WordPerfect, the function keys are almost always shortcut keys. By learning some of the function key operations, you can access commands from pull-down menus that would normally require several keystrokes or the mouse.

Familiar Keys that Serve Special Purposes

The familiar keys you used back in the stone age on a typewriter are even more useful in WordPerfect. Each of the keys in table 0.3 serves more than its intended purpose in WordPerfect 6.0. Take a gander:

Table 0.3
Ordinary Keys with New Responsibilities

The Key	Its Responsibilities in WordPerfect
Shift	Aside from its normal responsibilities of accessing uppercase letters and the symbols over the number keys, the Shift key is also used to modify the action of the function keys. If you press Shift-F1, for example, you get completely different results from pressing F1 alone.
Ctrl	The Control key also modifies the action of the function keys, and enables you to access certain items more quickly from the pull-down menus. If you pull-down the Edit menu, for example, you can see that Ctrl-Z is used to access the Undo function.
Alt	The Alt key (short for Alternate) is used for three things:
	• Modifying the action of function keys (Ctrl-F1, etc.)
	• Accessing pull-down menus (Alt-F for the File menu, for example)
	• Assignment of single key macros

continues

Table 0.3
continued

The Key	Its Responsibilities in WordPerfect
Backspace	Nothing special here. Backspace moves your cursor back one space, deleting whatever was immediately to the left of the cursor.
Enter	Moves your cursor to the next line, inserting a hard return code into the document.
Tab	Very useful for getting around in WordPerfect, particularly if you decide not to use a mouse. Aside from its traditional use for creating tabs, the Tab key can be used to highlight and select text and can be used to move across a dialog box quickly.

TRICK

WordPerfect provides a default tab setting every five spaces. If you want to move over five spaces before you start typing, press the tab key once instead of the space bar five times.

The tab key is very important if you want to line up your work properly.

Jump Start WordPerfect and Create a Document

You're probably anxious to get going and play, er, work with the WordPerfect program, so let's get to it. The setup and customization of WordPerfect is not covered here. Instead, just open WordPerfect and take a shot at writing a few lines, saving them, and then reopening the lines of text.

FOOD FOR THOUGHT

These steps use WordPerfect's default installation. If, for some reason, you cannot follow along with this quick-success lesson, don't panic! Each step is covered in detail starting with Chapter 2.

Start Your Engines

First, you need to tell the computer that you want to start the WordPerfect program:

1. Turn on your computer and monitor (details, details).

2. Change to the directory where WordPerfect was installed. Type **CD \WP60** and press Enter.

3. Type **WP** and press Enter.

And here comes the WordPerfect opening screen, followed closely by the document screen.

Creating a Great Work of Non-Fiction

You will see the cursor at the upper left-hand corner of your screen, waiting patiently for you to type something in. Promptness counts, so type something now.

4. How about if you type:

   It was a dark and stormy night. I was flying along in my Sopwith Doghouse, scouting the front for the evil Red Baron. Suddenly, my flight was interrupted as Charlie brought me my dog dish. Blech. It's always the same old stuff. Curse you, Red Baron!

Figure 0.7 shows the same thing.

Don't worry if you make mistakes; Chapter 5, "Whoops! (the Basics of Editing)" shows you how to delete, move text, and much more.

Figure 0.7:

The beginnings of the great novel.

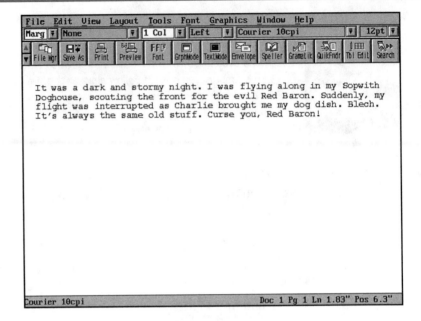

Saving Your Masterpiece

Now it's time to save your important document.

5. Press the Alt-F keys. Press and hold down the Alt key and press the letter F on your keyboard. Hey, look at that! One of the pull-down menus appears on your screen.

6. Choose the command **C**lose. You can do so in one of three ways: click on **C**lose with the mouse, use the down arrow key to highlight the word and then press Enter, or press the letter C on your keyboard (notice how the letter C is underlined or highlighted on that word in the menu).

A dialog box appears. Across the top it says **Document 1**, and should look just like the one shown in figure 0.8.

Notice that the word Cancel is the default. Rather than cancel and return to the document:

7. Select the word **Y**es by either clicking on the **Y**es button, pressing the Tab key two times and then pressing Enter, or pressing the letter Y on the keyboard.

Figure 0.8:

Working within a dialog box.

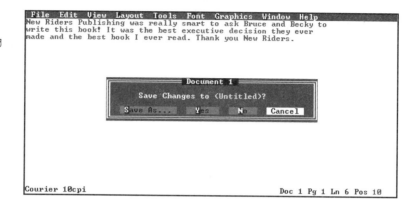

Another dialog box appears that says Save Document 1. Your cursor is positioned in the Filename entry field, ready to save your document with any name that you type:

8.   Type **book.doc**. If you make a mistake, press the Backspace key to erase letters and then retype the correct name.

Your screen should look like the one in figure 0.9.

Figure 0.9:

Saving your first Document.

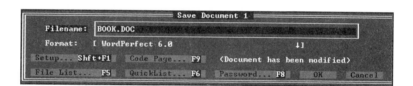

9.   Now tell WordPerfect to finalize your entry by doing one of three things: click on the OK button, press the Enter key, or press the Tab key five times until the OK button is highlighted and then press Enter.

And zip! There goes your document to your hard disk, and the screen is cleared!

SAVE THE DAY

Make frequent backups of your work. Neither computers nor humans are perfect and they can and will fail. Frequent backups will help ease some of life's little disappointments.

Recalling Your Masterpiece

You of course want to make sure your masterpiece is really on the hard disk, just in case you need to edit or print it. To check, follow these steps:

10.   Press Alt-F to activate the **F**ile menu.

11.   Select the item marked **R**etrieve (Highlight the word and press Enter, click on the word, or press the letter R on your keyboard).

You see a Retrieve Document dialog box with its Filename entry field waiting for you to type something. Let's oblige it:

12.   Type **book.doc**. Once again, use your backspace key if you make a mistabe, er, mistake.

Your screen will look like the one shown in figure 0.10.

Figure 0.10:

Retrieving your
first Document.

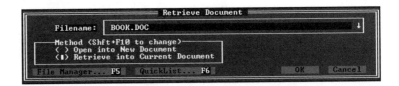

13.   Make your selection final by either: pressing Enter, clicking on OK, or pressing Tab two times and then pressing Enter.

Look at that! There's your document, just as you saved it. Enough of this foolishness, however; let's get down to serious business and the rest of the book.

Exit This Way...

To exit the WordPerfect program, follow these steps:

14.   Press Alt-F. The **F**ile menu appears.

15.   Select E**x**it WP from the **F**ile pull-down menu.

FOOD FOR THOUGHT

Don't panic. There is really very little you can do wrong with your computer. Even if you accidentally erase a file, the worst thing that can happen is you have to retype it. So? Is it really that important in the cosmic scheme of things?

Now you will see the Exit WordPerfect dialog box, shown in figure 0.11. There is your file name, book.doc. Notice that the little checkbox under the word Save isn't checked. This is because WordPerfect knows that you haven't changed the file since you loaded it from the hard disk. You don't need to save the document again, so just choose Exit by pressing Enter or by clicking on Exit with the mouse.

Figure 0.11:

Exiting your first Document and the WordPerfect program.

WordPerfect will now quit and you'll be back at your PC's DOS prompt or whatever operating environment you use.

STOP!

If you are using Microsoft Windows, make sure to exit Windows before turning the computer off.

If you are using OS/2, make sure you perform a Shutdown before turning off the computer.

Windows and OS/2 sometimes hold data in memory until they are exited or shut down. Fully exiting those operating systems ensures that the data is completely written to disk.

Well done!

The Next-to-Last Word

Well, this isn't precisely the last word, but you should keep in mind the following whenever you need to use this book or the WordPerfect Help files and lessons.

 You are in control of your work, not the computer or the WordPerfect program. Don't get frustrated, and don't panic.

 Programmers are people (well, sort of) and they make mistakes. If you try to do something and WordPerfect doesn't seem to be working the way it should, maybe the program is actually making the mistake. Double check to see if you are following the instructions properly, but don't discount the possibility that the program isn't working properly.

If you're not sure who or what is at fault, either check with a nerdy friend or call the WordPerfect Corporation.

 Never hesitate to ask for help. Remember: The only dumb question is the one that isn't asked.

Rambling Thoughts for Newbies

If you are new to working with computers, these are some thoughts you should keep in mind. These apply to using any program, not only WordPerfect.

 Take frequent breaks. Get up, walk around, pet your kids or give your dog a hug. Frequent breaks ease your back, eyes, and wrists from any strain; they also help to keep you refreshed.

 Know when to quit. Don't let yourself get frustrated over a stupid computer or a stupid word processor. If something isn't working correctly, get up, walk away, and come back to it later. You would be amazed and surprised what this will do for you. After a break the instructions tend to make more sense and you can follow them easily. All will be well in your world.

 Don't hesitate to ask. The only dumb question is the one that isn't asked. Yes, this does bear repeating.

 Avoid thirty-day old pizza for snacks. Remember, pizza doesn't have enough preservatives to last thirty days in your refrigerator. Hint: If there are green things on the top, they are not necessarily green peppers.

Word Perfect

CHAPTER 1

Installing WordPerfect 6.0 (No Bananas Necessary)

Sitting down for a pleasant day of installing WordPerfect? Sorry to disappoint you, but you'll have to find other things to do because installing WordPerfect doesn't take a whole day. As much as some nerdy authors like to install software, we could only make the installation last about 15 to 20 minutes at the most.

Preparing for the Big Day

Before you do actually sit down and install WordPerfect, you need to do a few things in preparation. You will need to:

 Make backup copies of your original WordPerfect disks

 Know the name and type of your monitor

 Know the name and type of your printer

 Know how much disk space you have

WordPerfect will do the rest of the work for you. A checklist appears later in this chapter to aid in your installation.

Backup Copies

The very first thing to do when you buy any software is to make backup copies of the original disks. This does not mean making photocopies; you need to make disk copies of the disks that came with WordPerfect. DO NOT PROCEED until after you make backup copies of your original disks. All sorts of nasty things can happen to original disks that will ruin them. If backups are ruined, it won't ruin your day because you can always make more backups. Before you proceed, you need to make sure you have one box (ten disks per box) of high-density floppy disks by your side.

FOOD FOR THOUGHT

WordPerfect ships version 6.0 on high-density floppy disks. If your disk drive can read only low-density floppy disks, call WordPerfect at 1-800-321-5906 and the friendly folks there will be happy to help you out. These same people can help if you bought 3.5" floppy disks but need 5.25" floppy disks and vice versa.

At the DOS prompt, type **DISKCOPY A: A:** and press Enter. (If you are using Drive B, then type **DISKCOPY B: B:**.) You will be prompted to insert the source disk—the one WordPerfect sent you. After it churns away, you will be prompted to insert the target disk—the new blank disk from the box you just bought.

STOP!

During this process, be careful that you don't confuse the SOURCE (the original) and TARGET (the backup) disks.

TRICK

Before you begin to make backup copies of the original floppy disks, sit down and write out all the labels first so that you can label your copied floppy disks as they are finished. This helps avoid confusion later.

Be sure to label your disks. Put them in a safe place when you're finished. Hopefully you won't need them again.

FOOD FOR THOUGHT

You may have the type of drive where you need to flip a "gate" down to secure the disk in place. Some drives need a little button pressed before the floppy disk is secured.

How Much Disk Space?

If you want to install all the bits and pieces of WordPerfect, you will need about 16M of free space on your hard disk drive. If you want to install the very minimum, you will need about 7M of free space. If these terms don't make any sense, Appendix A, "(Im)Perfect Computers," defines these nerdy measurements.

Naturally, this megabyte (M) requirement does not include the space you'll need for actually saving the documents you'll create with WordPerfect. No one could even begin to guess how much room you will need for that—everyone has different requirements. After all, some people consider a nice letter, "Hello. How are you? I am fine." Others like to expand the "I am fine" part to 50 detailed pages.

You don't really have to understand nerdy measurements such as megabytes to know if your WordPerfect will fit. The WordPerfect install program measures and calculates storage space for you. Just follow along in the install process, and you'll be alerted when you get to that part. And don't worry, WordPerfect gives you plenty of opportunities to quit the install process if you change your mind.

If you do understand nerd measurements such as megabytes and think the space on your computer might be a little tight, no problem. Just follow along as you go through the "Custom Installation" section later in this chapter. There, you'll have a chance to tell WordPerfect that you don't want certain parts of the program installed (so they won't take up disk space). If, for instance, you don't want to install the fax portion of WordPerfect because you don't have a fax modem, simply say so during the install process. You can always add it later.

How Much Memory?

WordPerfect needs less than 640K of memory to run. WordPerfect states the program can run in 520K of space, and even 480K in a pinch. It won't run well in 480K; you certainly won't be able to use some of the nifty features because every feature takes up memory. These days most computers come with 1M-4M of memory; memory problems probably won't be of too much concern to you.

If you have questions about how memory is measured, refer to Appendix A, "(Im)Perfect Computers." You may also want to check with your favorite nerd.

Making a Checklist and Checking It Twice

You will need to know what type of monitor and printer you have when you install WordPerfect, but for now you'll mostly need to know the manufacturer name and model number.

Specifying Your Type of Monitor

The important thing about monitors isn't the name of the monitor itself, but the *interface board* the computer uses to talk to the monitor. You'll need to know, at the very least, if you are using an EGA- or VGA-type video system. If you have an SVGA (Super VGA) system, then you need to know who made the interface board and what the model name of the interface board is.

TRICK

If you cannot find out what sort of video system you have, then follow this little tip: If your computer is less than three years old, it probably uses a VGA system. If it's older than that by one or two years, it probably uses an EGA system; if it's even older than that, then it probably uses a CGA system.

Fortunately, WordPerfect will make a guess during installation, and it's usually right, so don't worry too much about this.

Installing Printer Drivers

To get the manufacturer and model information about your printer, check the front, sides, back, and bottom. If you have a laser printer, be VERY CAREFUL in moving it around, especially if you have to check the bottom. You don't want to spill any of the toner from the print cartridge. If you do, you will end up with a mess inside the printer and lousy printouts outside. If you handle it like a delicate vase filled with water you should be okay. If you must check the bottom of the printer, just lift the edge and look underneath with a mirror. (Actually, very few laser printers hide their name on the bottom; the label/logo is usually displayed prominently on the outside.)

TRICK

If you cannot find any manufacturing tags on your laser printer, it's a good bet that it's HP (Hewlett-Packard) compatible. When you get to the printer installation part of WordPerfect, select the HP LaserJet Series II. Most laser printers are compatible with this model. If you have a dot-matrix printer, then try installing a few of the Epson printer drivers (LQ and FX series) and an IBM ProPrinter driver or two. Most dot-matrix printers are compatible with Epsons or ProPrinters.

If you do not see your printer listed during the installation process, and none of these suggestions help, call WordPerfect's Orders Department at 1-800-321-4566, or write to them at WordPerfect Corporation, Orders Dept., MS SC-30, 1555 N. Technology Way, Orem, UT 84057. They have over 1200 printer drivers on hand and will send you the one for your printer at no charge.

Installing WordPerfect's Fax Modem Capabilities

WordPerfect 6.0 has the capability to fax your beautiful WordPerfect documents directly through your fax modem. Not every modem has faxing capability; check your modem documentation to see if it can fax. If you install WordPerfect's faxing capabilities, you will need to know what class your modem is (I, II, and so on), where on your computer it is hooked up (what port), as well as a number of parameters about dialing.

If you're not sure whether you have this information on hand, don't let it hold up the rest of the WordPerfect installation. You always can install the fax capabilities at a later date when you have all the answers. Check both the WordPerfect and your modem documentation before you install.

Installing Sound Capabilities

During installation, you also have the option of installing some nifty sound files. These files are useless unless you have a special sound board in your computer. These files do not work with the PC's standard speaker.

TRICK

You can create your own sound clips or use the ones that come with WordPerfect to create a multimedia presentation. With the proper equipment (microphone, sound board, speakers) you can also add voice dictation to a document.

The Installation Checklist

To help make sure you have all the information you need before you install WordPerfect, here is a handy checklist:

WordPerfect Pre-Installation Checklist

 Disk drive where WordPerfect will be installed FROM:

Drive A

Drive B

 Disk drive where WordPerfect will be installed TO:

Drive C

Drive D

Drive E

Video type (circle ONE):

CGA   EGA

VGA   SVGA

Manufacturer: _____

Model #: _____

Printer type (circle ONE):

Laser   Dot Matrix   Ink Jet

Printer port (circle ONE):

LPT1   LPT2   COM1   COM2

Manufacturer: _____

Model #: _____

I have a fax modem (circle ONE):   YES   NO

I know the CLASS: _____

I know the COMM PORT: _____

I know about dialing parameters: _____

I have a sound board: _____

Manufacturer: _____

Model #: _____

Remember: You can always go back and install parts of WordPerfect without having to reinstall the whole program again. See the section "Returning to WordPerfect's Installation Program" later in this chapter.

TRICK

During the installation process, you shouldn't change the default directory names. Why? To make it easier on you. Throughout this book (and the WordPerfect documentation and Help files) you'll find references to the default directory names. By using the default installation directories recommended by WordPerfect, you avoid having to make the mental correction regarding critical system information.

Actually Doing It: Installing the Program

If you know your computer really well, or if you filled out the handy checklist in the preceding section, you're ready to install WordPerfect. By now you should have backup copies of WordPerfect to use for your installation.

TRICK

During the installation process, you may see a prompt at the bottom of the screen that says `Press any key to continue....` There is no key on your keyboard that is marked "any." When you see this message, you should press the Spacebar or Enter key.

To install WordPerfect 6.0:

1. Turn on your computer and monitor after you have checked to make sure everything is plugged in.

Please do not think this was thrown in to insult your intelligence. Many people fail to hook up all their hardware properly and then make the mistake of hitting the switch, not getting any power, and crying, "What's wrong?" It happens to everyone at some time or another (yes, including us). If you have the type of computer that locks, be sure to check that it's unlocked, too!

After the computer flashes a bunch of numbers, you'll see the *DOS prompt* (also called the *command line*), a rather bland looking collection of characters that looks like this: `C:>` (or this: `C:\>`).

2.   Insert the WordPerfect disk marked "Install 1" into the disk drive.

3.   If you have only one disk drive, it is designated drive "A." At the DOS command line type **A:INSTALL** and press Enter. If the drive you are installing from is the B drive, then type **B:INSTALL** and press Enter.

If you type **A:INSTALL** and the disk is actually in the B: drive, you'll see the error message:

```
Not ready reading drive A
Abort, Retry, Fail?
```

Type **F** for fail and press Enter, then type **B:INSTALL** after you have checked to be sure the correct disk is inserted properly.

If the error message `Bad command or filename` appears, you accidentally put in the wrong disk or designated a drive with another disk that is not the WordPerfect Install 1 disk. You also may have mistyped the command. Double-check your typing and also that you do have the disk marked "Install 1" in the drive that you are specifying (A or B).

4.   The first screen you'll see is shown in figure 1.1. WordPerfect asks you if you see little blocks of color on the screen. If you do, type **Y**; if you don't, type **N**. This is the WordPerfect color test. If you fail it, then WordPerfect will know that you were drinking last night and won't install until you sober up. Don't install with a hangover!

5.   The next question WordPerfect asks is what type of installation you want. Your choices include:

 Standard Installation. If you select this type of installation, all the WordPerfect programs install. You will be asked to verify the drive that WordPerfect is installing from and the drive and directory name that WordPerfect is installing to. If you have a lot of free disk space and you want the "whole enchilada," select this option.

Figure 1.1:

The Installation opening screen.

Welcome to the WordPerfect 6.0β Installation Program.
Install needs to know whether your monitor can display color.

Do you see red, green, and blue colored boxes? Yes (No)

(From the screen: WordPerfect 6.0 Installation. (C) Copyright 1993 All Rights Reserved WordPerfect Corporation Orem, Utah USA)

 Custom Installation. If you select this type of installation, you can pick and choose which of the WordPerfect options you want to install. If you do not want to install certain portions of WordPerfect, such as the Fax Services, select this option. WordPerfect will make two other directories besides the one where the base programs go. You also can change the names of these directories, but it's not recommended.

 Network Installation. If you are going to run WordPerfect on a network, let the network administrator install it. In fact, you probably won't be able to install it unless you are the network administrator.

Highlight your preference and press Enter. You also can exit the installation here by pressing 9.

STOP!

If you decide to perform a Custom Installation, skip the next section.

If you are running on a network, the network administrator should be the person to install on the network. The authors both work with networks, and they know what they're talking about here. Really!

Specifying Standard Installation

The first screen you'll see in Standard Installation asks you what drive WordPerfect will be installed from and where WordPerfect will be installed to. Make any corrections that you need concerning drive designators, but it's not recommended that you change the directory name (see figure 1.2).

Figure 1.2:

The Standard Installation first question.

```
WordPerfect will be installed from:
    A:\

WordPerfect will be installed to:
    C:\WP60

Do you want to change these directories? No (Yes)
```

The next screen shows how much free space you have on your drive and how much space the WordPerfect installation will take. If you don't have enough space, this screen will tell you so. You can respond with an **N** (no) to the question of "Continue with installation?" If you have enough space, respond **Y** (yes).

The next screen asks you about replacing existing files. This means if the installation program finds any files on your disk that have the same name as the one it is about to install, you need to specify whether you want to replace the existing files. You should probably select **S**mart Prompting, which is the default. You can either press the number 3 or press Enter.

WordPerfect next prompts you about your AUTOEXEC.BAT file. This file contains certain commands that are executed when you turn on your PC or reset it. Go ahead and let WordPerfect add itself to the path. Respond by selecting **Y**es here.

If you have a standard EGA/VGA display, the correct driver is automatically installed with the WordPerfect files. If you do not have a standard EGA/VGA display, the next screen that appears presents a list of video drivers. Press the **Y** or **N** key as appropriate here.

You will then be asked about installing a printer driver. Press **Y** here if you have a printer hooked up to your computer. If you do have a printer and you select **Y**es, a screen full of a bizillion different types of printers that looks like figure 1.3 appears. Select your printer's driver; use the arrow keys to scroll through the selections.

Figure 1.3:

The printer driver selection set screen.

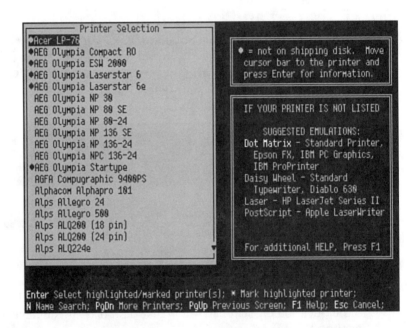

Now the installation begins. Pretty soon you will see a screen that looks just like the one in figure 1.4, prompting you to take out the Install 1 disk and insert the Install 2 disk. Proceed as instructed.

When you are finished feeding your computer all the disks, and it has emitted a satisfied burp, skip to the "Installation Complete" section in this chapter.

Figure 1.4:

The floppy disk shuffle.

Specifying Custom Installation

If you're feeling a little sure of yourself and know which parts of WordPerfect you can live without, you probably chose the Custom Installation option. The first screen you will see after selecting the Custom Installation is shown in figure 1.5:

Figure 1.5:

The Custom Installation opening screen.

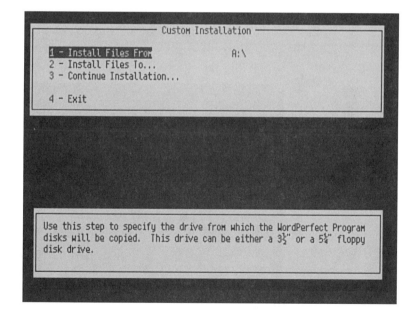

The first item—**Install Files From**—should be accurate. You may need to change the disk drive designator for **Install Files To**, however. Once again, you shouldn't change directory names unless you know what you're doing.

6. Press the down arrow key to highlight the **Continue Installation** line and press Enter, or press 3.

The next screen shows you how much free space you have on your drive and how much space the WordPerfect installation will take. If you don't have enough space, this screen will tell you.

7. At this point you can respond with an **N** (no) to the question of "Continue with installation?" If you have enough space, respond with **Y** (yes).

The next screen, as shown in figure 1.6, is the reason you chose Custom Installation. This screen is used to indicate which options you do not want to install.

8. Use the arrow keys to highlight an undesired option, then press Enter. If you accidentally clear a checkbox of an option you want to install, simply highlight the item again and press Enter.

Figure 1.6:

The Custom Installation program files selections.

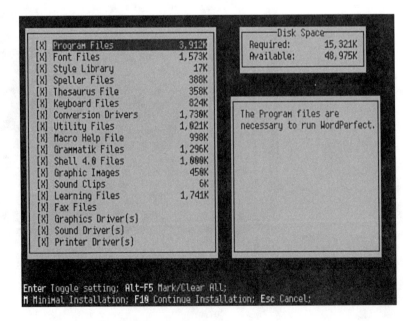

A few parts of WordPerfect you might want to leave out include:

 Sound Clips and Sound Drivers. If you do not have a special sound board installed, clear the Sound Clips and Sound Drivers checkboxes.

 Fax Files. If you do not need (or want) the fax capabilities, clear the Fax Files checkbox.

 Conversion Drivers. If you do not have a previous version of Word-Perfect, or do not need to convert your WordPerfect files to or from other word processing program formats, clear the Conversion Drivers checkbox.

 Grammatik Files. If you don't want or need the Grammar Checker, clear the Grammatik Files checkbox.

FOOD FOR THOUGHT

The authors strongly recommend that you install all Help and Learning files. You should also install the speller and thesaurus files just to try them.

If you chose the Custom Installation because you are worried about disk space, keep an eye on the Disk Space window in the upper right corner of your screen. Whenever you clear the checkbox of an option you don't want to install, the number after `Required:` decreases.

9. If you have any questions about whether you need certain files installed, highlight the file and read the description that is in the window on the right side of your screen.

10. After you make your selections, press F10.

The next screen that appears asks about replacing existing files. This means if the installation program finds any files on your disk that have the same names as the one it is about to install, you need to specify whether you want to replace the existing files.

11.   Select **S**mart Prompting by pressing Enter or the number 3.

WordPerfect next prompts you about your PC's AUTOEXEC.BAT file. This file contains commands that are executed when you turn on or reset your computer.

12.   Let WordPerfect add itself to your AUTOEXEC.BAT file's path line by pressing **Y** (yes).

If you have a standard EGA/VGA display, the correct driver is automatically installed with the WordPerfect files. If you do not have a standard display, the next screen enables you to tell WordPerfect the standard driver won't do and you'll need to make a custom selection.

13.   Press **Y** if you need to change the display driver; press **N** if the driver chosen by WordPerfect is appropriate.

14.   The next question is if you want to install a printer driver. If you have a printer hooked up to your computer, press **Y** here.

      If you press Y, you'll see a screen with a bizillion different types of printers. Select the drivers you need by using the arrow keys and pressing Enter.

Now the installation will begin. Pretty soon you will see a screen that looks just like the one in figure 1.4, prompting you to take out the Install 1 disk and insert the Install 2 disk.

15.   Proceed with the installation by replacing each disk with the disk requested by WordPerfect.

Installation Complete

After you have followed all the instructions on the installation screens and inserted the necessary disks, a screen similar to figure 1.7 appears.

Follow the instructions by turning your computer off, waiting ten seconds, and then turning it on again. Then turn to Chapter 0 for instant success with WordPerfect 6.0!

Figure 1.7:

You did it!

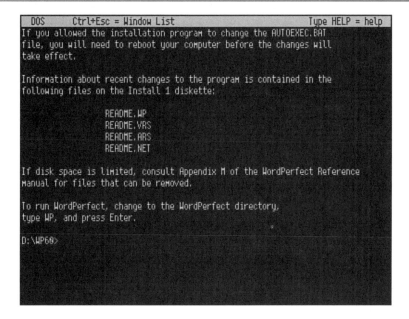

```
  DOS      Ctrl+Esc = Window List                    Type HELP = help
If you allowed the installation program to change the AUTOEXEC.BAT
file, you will need to reboot your computer before the changes will
take effect.

Information about recent changes to the program is contained in the
following files on the Install 1 diskette:

              README.WP
              README.VRS
              README.ARS
              README.NET

If disk space is limited, consult Appendix M of the WordPerfect Reference
Manual for files that can be removed.

To run WordPerfect, change to the WordPerfect directory,
type WP, and press Enter.

D:\WP60>
```

Returning to WordPerfect's Installation Program

If you did not install all the options (the fax, Grammatik modules, and other stuff) or you need to add a printer driver, it's easy to do. Just follow along:

1. Insert the floppy disk marked Install 1 in your floppy disk drive and at the DOS prompt, type **A:INSTALL** and press Enter. (If you are installing from Drive B, type **B:INSTALL** and press Enter.)

2. Press **Y**es if you have a color screen; press **N**o if you have a monochrome screen.

3. If you are installing one of the features such as Grammatik or Spell Checker, highlight the **C**ustom Installation option and press Enter. Skip the next section and proceed with the "Returning to Custom Installation" section.

Device Installation

4. If you are installing an additional printer, video, or fax driver, highlight **D**evice Files and press Enter.

5. At the Install:Device screen, select **S**ound Board Files, **G**raphics Card Files, **F**ax Files, or **P**rinter Files. You may also elect to **E**xit at this screen.

If you select the Sound Board Files, you will need to follow the prompts to insert the correct floppy disks and finish the installation.

If you select the Fax Files, you will need to answer the appropriate questions about the type and class. Follow the prompts and read the explanations shown on the screen.

If you select Graphics or Printer files, you will need to select the driver desired. Make your selection by moving the down and up arrow keys to highlight the driver. Press F10 when your selection is made.

You will be asked to confirm your selection. Follow the prompts on your screen.

In all cases of Device Installation, answer the appropriate questions or insert the requested floppy disks.

Returning to Custom Installation

6. If you installed to the default directory names and drives, press the down arrow key to highlight the **Continue Installation** line and press Enter, or press 3. If you need to make adjustments to the default directory name and drive, select Item 2, and make the adjustment now.

7. If you have enough disk space to add some more WordPerfect goodies, press **Y**. If you don't have enough disk space, you can't add any more goodies.

8. Use the arrow keys to highlight an undesired option, then press Enter. If you accidentally clear a checkbox of an option you want to install, simply highlight the item again and press Enter (or press the Spacebar).

9. After you make your selections, press F10.

10. Select **S**mart Prompting by pressing Enter or the number 3. If WordPerfect finds a file with a duplicate file name and is unsure about whether it needs to be replaced, you will be prompted to overwrite it.

11. WordPerfect should already be in your AUTOEXEC.BAT file's PATH line, so press the Spacebar or Enter to continue.

12. WordPerfect will ask for the appropriate floppy disk to be inserted in the drive and for you to press Enter when ready. The appropriate programs will be installed.

13. When the installation of the requested item(s) is complete, the Custom Installation screen offers you the opportunity to **E**xit the installation. Press the number 4 to do so.

14. At the WordPerfect 6.0 Installation main screen, select 9, **E**xit again, and confirm.

That's it!

Upgrading from an Older Version of WordPerfect

If you are upgrading from a previous version of WordPerfect, don't worry about the installation process overwriting any of your existing files. All the WordPerfect 6.0 program files are installed in completely different directory names from the ones you have now. In addition, if you follow instructions you will always be prompted before any existing files are overwritten.

Your documents should not need any conversion. Any macros that you have customized will need to be run through the macro converter because WordPerfect 6.0 uses a new format for macro files and isn't compatible with old files. To convert your existing macros, follow these steps:

1. Copy your existing macro files from their current location to the directory x:\WP60\MACROS. The funny-looking *x* thing represents the drive letter on which WordPerfect is installed (usually C:\). If you need help with this, see Chapter 8, "A Word about Files."

2. Exit WordPerfect, and move to the *x*:\WP60\MACROS directory with the command `CD \WP60\MACROS`. If your prompt indicates that you are currently on a drive different from the drive where you installed WordPerfect, you'll need to change to the drive on which Word-Perfect is installed by typing `x:`. Again, the *x* parameter represents the drive letter that contains the WordPerfect files.

3. Type `MVC [old macro name] [new macro name]` and press Enter. For example, if your old macro was called ALTA.WPM, and you want the new one to be called ALTN.WPM, you would type:

   `MCV ALTA.WPM ALTN.WPM.`

CHAPTER 2

Setting Up for Success: Changing WordPerfect's Default Settings

B efore you do anything else in WordPerfect, take a few minutes to set up your working environment and change a few of the WordPerfect system defaults. Some settings are the key to unlocking WordPerfect's best features (such as the File Manager). Other settings may not seem very flashy, but are important in setting up WordPerfect to meet your every need (such as automatic backups). This chapter also shows you how to make WordPerfect's already friendly user interface even friendlier. You learn how to:

 Change modes to suit your work style

 Back up your documents time after time

 Change screen colors

 Customize your mouse settings

 Customize the WordPerfect environment

 Set up the QuickList

 Accessorize your WordPerfect Screen with all the latest buttons and ribbons

Most of these changes are made using the Setup menu window, a multipurpose menu that you'll find under the <u>F</u>ile pull-down menu. The Setup menu is the place to go to change the colors on-screen, retrain your mouse, change cryptic formatting measurements, and set your backup options.

You can't change WordPerfect too much if it isn't running. If you're staring at a blank screen and the computer is off, and you know WordPerfect is in there somewhere, follow these steps:

1. Find the PC's switch and turn it on. Turn on the monitor too.

A bunch of text should fly by and then the beautiful c:\> appears.

2. At the c:\> prompt, type **CD \WP60** (or the directory in which WordPerfect was installed) and press Enter.

3. If the message Invalid directory appears, find whoever owns the computer and demand an explanation. If it's your PC, go dig up a nerd.

4. At the c:\WP60> prompt, type **WP**.

SAVE THE DAY

WordPerfect 6.0 should start after you type **WP** at the C:\>prompt. If it doesn't you will see one of the following two messages on-screen:

Bad command or filename.

This means the WordPerfect program is not installed in this directory or may not even be on your computer. Double check your typing or check with the nerd (usually found at computer clubs) who owns the computer.

LC: Insufficient file handles. MINIMUM of FILES=25 required.

WordPerfect is installed, but you (or someone you trust) needs to change your CONFIG.SYS file to modify or include the line: FILES=25 (but don't be TOO cheap, make it FILES=30).

Getting in the Mood, er Mode: Changing WordPerfect's Display Mode

One of the first decisions you have to make when you begin to use WordPerfect is which display mode to use. *Mode* refers to the manner in which WordPerfect and your documents display on-screen.

Three display modes are available in WordPerfect. Each has its advantages and disadvantages.

FOOD FOR THOUGHT

Don't panic! Changing display modes is not setting anything in stone; you can change display modes at any time.

What's Text Mode?

If you're starting WordPerfect for the first time, Text mode is the default mode that appears. Text mode displays only simple letters and numbers; no fancy-shmancy little pictures or carefully sculpted screen images appear in this mode. Text mode operates much faster than Graphics or Page modes (which are both graphically oriented). The downside to using Text mode is that different types of text attributes, such as *italicized* or BOLD text, are all represented using the same screen font. Different colors designate different font attributes, which can make it confusing to figure out just what you will end up with when you print your document.

FOOD FOR THOUGHT

Any type of graphics display on your computer runs much slower than text-only modes because the computer has to work much harder filling in all the little pixels (display dots). These little pixels aren't necessary when working in plain text mode.

Text mode is great for power typists and slower computers. If you're a fast typist you probably can't stand computers that can't keep up with your fast pace; leave WordPerfect in this mode. Text mode still excels for other uses, such as general memo and letter writing, but it isn't of much use when it comes to fancy stuff with pretty pictures or fancy fonts.

Choosy Mothers Choose Text Mode

Use Text mode for all your writing and editing, unless you have a very fast computer. When you are ready to polish up your work, switch to Graphics or Page mode to add the final sparkle to your prose. This method—Text mode when writing, Graphics or Page mode for the polish—is the most productive overall.

FOOD FOR THOUGHT

A "very fast computer" is a PC that uses an 80386 processor running at 25MHz or faster. If these numbers have your eyes glazing over, check with your computer supplier or local nerd to find out if your computer is faster or slower than this.

What's Graphics Mode?

This mode is entirely new to WordPerfect for DOS. Before version 6.0, your only choice was Text mode, which looked pretty lame next to the sexy Windows version of WordPerfect. Just so all of WordPerfect's DOS users could keep up with the Joneses, they added this nifty new Graphics mode.

Graphics mode accurately represents all the text on-screen. If you make some text italic, it shows up that way on-screen; change to a different typeface, and there it is in living color. Change the size of the text and, presto!, your screen accurately shows the change. Aside from its pleasing display, Graphics mode is great for documents with drawings and pretty fonts. If you want to add figures to a letter or create some funky invitation with lots of typefaces and line art, Graphics mode is the best choice.

Even though it has power, Graphics mode is slower than Text mode. Just how much slower depends on the speed of your computer.

How is Page Mode Different?

Page mode is almost exactly like Graphics mode, except it accurately shows everything that will appear on the printed page. Text and Graphics modes don't show headers and footers or the amount of blank space at the bottom and top of each page. Page mode, on the other hand, displays these items.

Page mode is like Print Preview mode because it shows headers, footers, margins, and other sections that you don't type in the body of your document. In Page mode, you can scroll through your document and make changes to the text in the body of the document, which is something you can't do in Print Preview mode. Page mode is useful for double-checking the formatting of headers, footers, and page number placement.

Page mode is just a touch slower than Graphics mode, but can be very useful when you are putting the finishing touches on your Very Important Document.

FOOD FOR THOUGHT

One important thing to remember about all these different modes: Although dialog boxes (boxes that pop up when you choose a command) in each mode look different, they are all laid out the same and do the same things. The same keys on your keyboard do exactly the same things in the different modes, and where and how you click your mouse is also the same.

Changing to Graphics Mode

As soon as you start WordPerfect you will see a lovely blue screen. This is the standard Text mode screen. This book primarily uses Graphics mode, which offers a number of features discussed in this book. To follow along, it would be a good idea for you to switch your computer into Graphics mode. To do so, follow these steps:

1. Press Ctrl-F3.
2. Press the numeric 3 key.

As an alternative, press Alt-V and select **G**raphics mode. Your screen should look like the one in figure 2.1.

Figure 2.1:

The opening screen in Graphics mode.

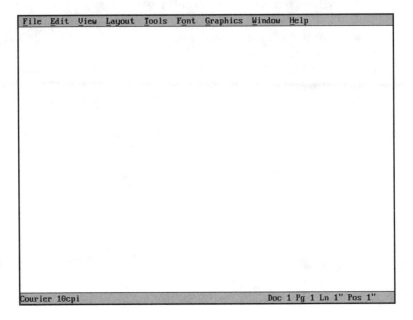

| File | Edit | View | Layout | Tools | Font | Graphics | Window | Help |

Courier 10cpi   Doc 1 Pg 1 Ln 1" Pos 1"

FOOD FOR THOUGHT

WordPerfect makes extensive use of Ctrl (Control), Alt (Alternate), and Shift in conjunction with the special function keys (the ones marked F1 through F10). Using these key combinations is faster than taking your hands off the keyboard to maneuver a mouse. Don't worry about memorizing them; all actions can be made through the menus, which can be accessed with or without a mouse.

Your screen is now transformed into Graphics mode—you're all set to go! You don't have to change to this mode again because WordPerfect remembers what mode you were using when you later start the program.

Accessing the Menu Bar

At the very top of your screen you'll see a bar with some words on it and one letter in each word underlined. This bar contains pull-down menus. You can activate the pull-down menus in one of two ways:

Press and hold down the Alt key and press the underlined letter in the menu item. To access File, for example, use Alt-F.

 If you're using a mouse, move your pointer so that it is somewhere on the word that you want to select and click once with the left mouse button.

Unleashing WordPerfect's Power: Changing System Defaults

The Setup menu window is the key to changing many of the WordPerfect system defaults, including everything from screen colors to mouse tracking to backup options and much more. These settings remain until you change them, even if it's two years down the road.

Changing Colors

The first thing you'll notice after you change to Graphics or Page mode are the dull colors on the screen. Let's change those and spruce things up a bit.

Creating a Color Scheme

WordPerfect comes with a few color schemes, but they aren't very exciting, so you might want to create your own. After all, you may end up staring at your WordPerfect screen for several hours at a time, so you might as well make it pleasant to stare at. You can change nearly all of the colors or just the ones that bug you.

To change the colors, follow these steps:

1. Select the File menu by pressing Alt-F or by clicking on the word with your mouse.

2. Select Setup from the menu by moving the highlighted bar with your arrow keys and pressing Enter, pressing T on your keyboard, or clicking on it.

3. Select Display by pressing D or by clicking on it.

4. Select Graphics by pressing G or by clicking on it.

5. Press the number 2 on your keyboard or click on the word **C**olor Schemes.

6. Select **C**reate by pressing C or by clicking on it.

FOOD FOR THOUGHT

If you just want to modify one or two colors in an existing color scheme, select **E**dit instead of **C**reate.

You are now staring deeply into a little box that is waiting patiently for you to type something. Go ahead. Make it wait. It's important for you to assert yourself with your computer once in a while just so it knows who's the boss.

OK, now type in your name because this will be your own color scheme, then click on the button marked OK or press the Enter key. Wow! Now look at your screen! It should look just like the one shown in figure 2.2:

Figure 2.2:

Wow! What choices!

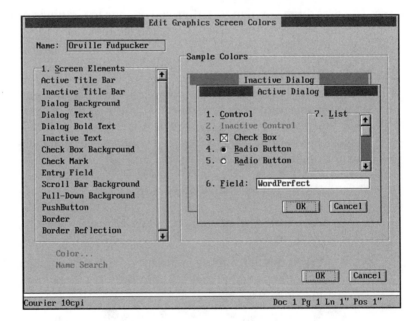

Selecting Colors for Items

Here's where you have a chance to be the Vincent Van Gogh of WordPerfect. The steps that follow walk you through changing the first color; you can finish the rest of them by yourself.

1. Select **S**creen Elements (press S or click on it).

Notice that the first item in the list, Active Title Bar, is highlighted. Now look down below that box and you'll see that **C**olor also has a dotted box around it. The dotted box around **C**olor means that the action taken on the selected highlighted item in the list affects that color.

From now on, follow this procedure for changing the color of each item in the list:

2. Double-click on Active Title Bar (or any other item on the list) or simply highlight the desired item with your up- and down-arrow keys and press Enter.

A color palette appears on-screen.

3. If you have a mouse, choose a color by clicking on the color you like. You can also use the arrow keys to move the box around on-screen, which frames the color you have selected. To choose from even more colors, move the color palette's scroll bar down (the scroll bar is just to the right of the palette). You can also use the page up and page down keys to access additional colors.

4. If you like the color inside the frame, either click on **S**elect or press Enter.

Get back! Look how the color on the side of the window labeled Sample Colors changed. Now you can go through the entire list on the left side of the window by double-clicking on it or by using your arrow keys.

FOOD FOR THOUGHT

As you work with changing the colors of screen elements you are unknowingly familiarizing yourself with the proper names of each element. This is a good thing because these proper names are used throughout the book, the WordPerfect manual, and all the help functions.

Exiting Your Latest Color Scheme

When you finish your interior decorating of the screen colors, follow these steps:

1. In the Edit Graphics Screen Colors window, click on OK or press your tab key once and then press Enter.

As that window fades into the sunset you will see the Graphics Mode Screen Type/Colors window. The color scheme with your name should be the one marked with the highlighted selection bar.

2. Click on **S**elect or press S on the keyboard to make your color scheme active.

Now you are left alone with the Display window.

3. Click on Close or press Enter.

Your beautiful new color scheme is now on-screen. Enjoy your masterpiece or follow the steps in the section "Selecting Colors for Items" to change the colors again.

Catch That Mouse! Changing Your Mouse's Characteristics

The heading for this section sort of let the cat out of the bag, but you may not know that WordPerfect has options for setting your mouse's speed and a few other mouse-related things. People who use laptop or notebook computers may be particularly interested in this section. The default mouse speed on notebook or laptop computers is often too fast to comfortably follow with the eye, so you may need to retrain the little beast. Changing the mouse settings is done in pretty much the same way as changing colors. Read the following Save the Day note before you operate on your mouse.

SAVE THE DAY

Don't worry if you don't have a mouse. You can still use all the exercises in this book and can access all the humdrum and fancy features of WordPerfect.

The more you use WordPerfect, the less you'll use the mouse. It takes longer to take your hands off the keyboard, move the mouse, and click on something than it does to use the function keys or the Alt-key combinations.

Accessing the Mouse Dialog Box

1. Activate the **F**ile menu (press Alt-F or click on it).

2. Choose Se**t**up by clicking on it or pressing the T key.

TRICK

To get to the Setup window faster, press Shift-F1.

3. Click on **M**ouse or type M.

Changing the Double-Click Interval

The Double-Click Interval sets the amount of time WordPerfect waits in between mouse clicks to determine if you meant to double-click or just make two single clicks. This value can be from 0 to 200. If you specify a low number, a lot of time can pass between two clicks and WordPerfect will count the clicks as a double-click. If you set double-click interval at 200, you'd better click quick for WordPerfect to recognize your clicks as a double-click. To change these settings:

1. Press Shift-F1 to access the Setup window.

2. Click on **M**ouse or type M.

3. Change the Double-Click Interval setting by clicking on the arrows just to the right of the value or by typing a number. Experiment to determine the value that meets your athletic abilities.

4. Click on OK and then click on Close or press Enter twice.

Changing Mouse Acceleration: Vroom!

The fourth item on the Mouse dialog box, Acceleration Factor, uses 0 as no acceleration and 100 as fast acceleration. The 0 setting doesn't mean your pointer won't move at all, only that it will move as slowly as it can. 100 is very, very fast; you need excellent hand-eye coordination to use the mouse at this value. To change this setting:

1. Press Shift-F1 to access the Setup window.

2. Click on **M**ouse or type M.

3. Change the Acceleration interval setting by clicking on the arrows just to the right of the value or by typing a number. Experiment to determine the value that meets your visual abilities.

4. Click on OK and then click on Close or press Enter twice.

TRICK

For you lefties, notice item number five in the Mouse dialog box in case you need to make your mouse left-handed. Simply click in the checkbox. Click on OK and then Close and you're in business! The mouse now uses the opposite buttons; in other words, whenever you see "click on the left button," you have to click on the right button and vice versa.

Accessing WordPerfect's Environment Settings

There are several items in the Environment menu window that help you customize the way WordPerfect handles everything from backups to hyphenation. You also have the chance to tell WordPerfect how you want certain things displayed on the screen. You don't have to let WordPerfect bully you with settings you don't want; change your preferences to suit yourself. When you take control, WordPerfect must cater to your every whim.

The Environment dialog box contains a number of helpful options. To access this dialog box:

1. Press Shift-F1 to access the Setup dialog box.

2. Double-click on **E**nvironment or press the number 3 or the letter E.

Wow! There are more things to play with on this screen than there are peanuts in peanut butter! Your screen should look something like figure 2.3.

Figure 2.3:

Wow! What a lotta options!

```
╔══════════════════ Environment ══════════════════╗
║                                                  ║
║  1. Backup Options...                            ║
║  2. Beep Options...                              ║
║                                                  ║
║  3. Cursor Speed            │ 50 CPS  ♦ │        ║
║                                                  ║
║  4. ☐ Allow Undo                                 ║
║                                                  ║
║  5. ☒ Format Document for Default Printer on Open║
║                                                  ║
║  6. Prompt for Hyphenation  │ Never      ♦ │     ║
║                                                  ║
║  7. Units of Measure...                          ║
║                                                  ║
║  L. Language...                English           ║
║                                                  ║
║  K. ☐ WordPerfect 5.1 Keyboard (F1 = Cancel)     ║
║  T. ☒ Auto Code Placement                        ║
║  W. ☐ WordPerfect 5.1 Cursor Movement            ║
║                                                  ║
║  D. Delimited Text Options...      │ OK │ │Cancel│║
╚══════════════════════════════════════════════════╝
```

Backing Up Your Work

WordPerfect's Timed Document Backup feature automatically backs up your work to disk at preset intervals. This feature has saved people more time than you can possibly imagine! We can't count the number of times people accidentally turned off their computer or lost electricity while working on some important document, only to have it lost for all eternity because they weren't saving their work. With the Timed Document Backup, WordPerfect saves your work for you.

SAVE THE DAY

Do yourself a favor and make sure the **T**imed Document Backup option is checked. Timed backup will undoubtedly save your work some day, usually when you can least afford to waste time. If you've ever had the Fed Ex person knocking at your door just as you lost power and lost your 100 page report due yesterday, you can understand the benefits of timed backup.

Accessing the Backup Options Dialog Box

1. Press Shift-F1 to access the Setup dialog box.

2. Double-click on **E**nvironment or press the number 3 or the letter E.

3. Select **B**ackup Options in the Environment window by clicking on it or pressing B or 1 on your keyboard.

The best dialog box WordPerfect has appears, as shown in figure 2.4. The Backup dialog box contains options for saving your work automatically, which is extremely important, considering how easy it is to delete work. Pay very close attention to the **T**imed Document Backup and Back Up **O**riginal Document (.BK!) on Save or Exit checkboxes. These little options are the most beneficial features included with WordPerfect.

Figure 2.4:

Don't back yourself into a corner—use the backup options!

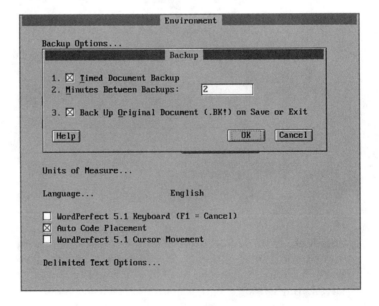

4. Make sure the checkbox next to **T**imed Document Backup is checked!!! The WordPerfect folks ship WordPerfect to you with the box already checked, but someone may have slipped in and changed it on you.

5. Also make sure the Back Up **O**riginal Document (.BK!) on Save and Exit checkbox is checked. Read the section "Automatically Backing Up When You Save or Exit a Document" on the next page for more information.

Selecting Intervals between Each Backup

It's time for an executive decision. You need to decide how many minutes pass between backups. As you are working on your document, WordPerfect automatically makes a backup copy to the hard disk every ten minutes (the default setting is ten minutes).

If the electrical power in your area is "iffy," select a number below 10. If you are fairly confident of your capabilities and your electricity, select a number between 10 and 20. Don't go over 20 minutes, though. The default of 10 is just fine for most work. To change this option:

1. Press Shift-F1 to access the Setup dialog box.

2. Double-click on **E**nvironment or press the number 3 or the letter E.

3. Select **B**ackup Options by clicking on it or pressing B or 1 on your keyboard.

4. Make sure the **T**imed Document Backup option is checked.

5. To change the number, select the item and type a value.

FOOD FOR THOUGHT

If you (or your local utility company) cause WordPerfect to exit the program without gracefully saving your document, the next time you start WordPerfect the opening screen will ask you if you want to Delete, Rename, or Open the backup copy of the document that was saved with the timed backup option.

If you KNOW that you saved your document after the last timed backup but before the ill-timed exit from the program, just select <u>D</u>elete and open your document in the usual manner. If you're not sure you saved it after the last timed backup, select Rename, so that you can look at both copies and decide which one you want to keep.

Automatically Backing Up When You Save or Exit a Document

Sometimes you want to recall the last version of a document because you just made some big changes that turned out to be a big mistake. WordPerfect can help you out by using the Back Up <u>O</u>riginal Document (.BK!) on Save or Exit option. Here's how it works:

 If you leave the Back Up <u>O</u>riginal Document (.BK!) on Save or Exit checkbox unchecked and then save or exit from the document, your work is saved to the original file name you selected when you save or exit the document. Any changes you made are now permanent, so if you goofed up and deleted or reformatted portions that you wished you hadn't, that's too bad; there's no way for you to say "I didn't mean it!"

 If you check this box when you save or exit the document, the original document (the one before you started working) is named with a .BK! extension and the edited version is saved with the document name. What a great idea! You can go back to the unedited version (the one with the .BK! extension) in case you screw up and save an edited version you really didn't want!

SAVE THE DAY

There's no such thing as too many backups! Save your work to disk frequently, and let WordPerfect help you "roll back" to the previous version of your document by checking this box. If the discussion about file names and extensions seems confusing, turn to Appendix A.

To access this tireless lifesaver, just press a few buttons:

1. Press Shift-F1 to access the Setup dialog box.

2. Click on **E**nvironment or press the number 3 or the letter E.

3. Select **B**ackup Options by clicking on it or pressing B or 1 on your keyboard.

4. Check the checkbox on Back Up **O**riginal Document (.BK!) on Save or Exit. You can select it by typing the number 3, pressing the letter O, or clicking on the checkbox.

5. Press the Enter key or click on OK.

SAVE THE DAY

We highly recommend you save your work to a floppy disk at least once a day in case something goes wrong with your computer. You cannot rely solely on the WordPerfect Backup options to save your work in all emergencies. Check out Chapter 8, "A Word about Files" for details on using WordPerfect to copy your files.

This is the type of thing that may only pay off once a year, but you will be so glad you did it you'll dance around the room cheering yourself—and no doubt get some very strange looks from your co-workers.

Timed backup lets you know when it's working. Every 10 minutes (or whatever interval you set) a little square appears in the middle of the screen with the words **Timed Backup**. This message does not disturb what you are typing or what you are doing in any way, and usually only takes a second.

Measuring Up: Changing WordPerfect Measurements

If you take a peek at the bottom line of your display screen, you'll see what those in the know call a status line. (Now you're in the know, too.) The status line has some helpful information, like the type of font you're using, or the file name that you're working on. On to the right-hand side is Word-Perfect's attempt to communicate the position of your cursor to you. This is useful information because you can determine just where you are in your document—the page, the line on that page, and the position on that line.

Right now, your measurement line might look something like:

```
Doc 1 Pg 7 Ln 3.17" Pos 4.3"
```

What is this? Does your ruler have a 3.17" mark on it? How about a 4.3" mark? No? Turn this into plain English with a few simple changes:

1. Press Shift-F1 to access the Setup dialog box.

2. Double-click on **E**nvironment or press the number 3 or the letter E.

3. Select **U**nits of Measure.

4. Select Display/Entry of Numbers. This indicates how WordPerfect displays measurements for everything from paper size to font size.

5. Select the last item, **u** = WP 4.2 units (Lines/Columns).

As long as you're here, change the second item, the **S**tatus Line Display, which controls how the measurements on your status line are displayed:

6. Select 2, **S**tatus Line Display.

7. Select the last item, **u** = WP 4.2 units (Lines/Columns).

8. Click on OK twice and then click on Close.

Ahhh! That's more like it. Now the numbers in the lower right corner specify how many lines the cursor is from the top edge of the page and the number of character positions from the left edge of the page. This is a lot easier for most users to understand and relate to than 3.17". Using the lines/columns measurements, it is easier for most people to understand line 19 of a 54 line page than line 3.17".

Allowing for Mistakes: Allow Undo

Everyone makes mistakes; WordPerfect allows us to undo whatever it is we last did—everything from erasing half the document to making awful changes to a previously well-formatted document. But everything has its price: It takes a certain amount of time for WordPerfect to save the last command and its effects on the document. With some fairly large operations, like sorting, letting WordPerfect keep the unsorted stuff in memory can take a long time. That's why you may want to uncheck the **A**llow Undo checkbox in the Environment menu window before hand.

If you uncheck the **A**llow Undo checkbox, go into your Environment and recheck it when you are finished. Don't forget: When this checkbox is not checked, you don't have the chance to say "I didn't mean it! I take it back!"

To check and uncheck the box:

1. Press Shift-F1 to access the Setup window.

2. Select **E**nvironment.

3. Check or Uncheck **A**llow Undo by pressing the number 4, pressing the letter A, or using your mouse to click in the checkbox.

4. To exit the Environment menu window, click on OK and click on Close, or press enter twice.

STOP!

Leave the **A**llow Undo checkbox checked—don't mess with it. The undo capabilities of WordPerfect are life savers, especially if you block a large piece of text and accidentally delete it. This happens all the time!

Automatically Formatting for Selected Printer

The way a document prints on paper and the way it looks on-screen are often quite different. Most people use the same printer for all their printing, and want to see their document on the screen the same way the printer sees it, or at least as closely as possible. Different printers also print the same document in two different ways, depending on their capabilities. That's why the **F**ormat Document for Default Printer on Open checkbox is the default setting. If you want to see the document formatted with the printer settings that were the default when it was created, you may want to uncheck this option. To uncheck or check this option:

1. Press Shift-F1 to access the Setup window.

2. Select **E**nvironment.

3. Check or uncheck **F**ormat Document for Default Printer on Open by pressing the number 5, pressing the letter F, or using your mouse to click in the checkbox.

4. To exit the Environment menu window, click on OK and click on Close, or press Enter twice.

WordPerfect 5.1 Keyboard

WordPerfect 6.0 changed some of the keyboard keys to do different things than in WordPerfect 5.1. If you know WordPerfect 5.1 so well you can run it in the dark with one hand tied behind your back, you might want to check the box labelled K. WordPerfect 5.1 **K**eyboard. Or, you may be new to WordPerfect but the old settings make more sense to you. The differences are shown in table 2.1.

Table 2.1
WordPerfect 6.0 and 5.1 Key Functions

Key	WordPerfect 6.0 Function	WordPerfect 5.1 Function
Esc	Cancel	Repeat
F1	Help	Cancel
F3	Repeat	Help

To change them, do the following:

1. Press Shift-F1 to access the Setup window.

2. Select **E**nvironment.

3. Check or Uncheck WordPerfect 5.1 **K**eyboard (F1 = Cancel) by pressing the letter K, or using your mouse to click in the checkbox.

4. To exit the Environment menu window, click on OK and click on Close, or press Enter twice.

Auto Code Placement

If you are in the middle of a page or a paragraph and decide to make a formatting change that might really belong at the beginning, WordPerfect can correctly place the code for you. The default in this box is already checked. If you turn this option off by unchecking the box, your formatting codes will stay where you place them.

FOOD FOR THOUGHT

If you are unfamiliar with codes and their proper placement, see Chapter 5, "Whoops! (The Basics of Editing)."

1. Press Shift-F1 to access the Setup window.

2. Select **E**nvironment.

3. Check or Uncheck Au**t**o Code Placement by pressing the letter T, or use the mouse to click in the checkbox.

4. To exit the Environment menu window, click on OK and click on Close or press Enter twice.

WordPerfect 5.1 Cursor Movement

The cursor movements to navigate your documents aren't different in WordPerfect versions 6.0 and 5.1. The way the cursor moves over or past formatting codes is what is different. In WordPerfect 6.0, the cursor doesn't land on any codes unless you have Reveal Codes on (Alt-F3). In WordPerfect 5.1, you can manipulate the codes without having to reveal them. The default setting in WordPerfect 6.0 is to have the codes turned off. To change it:

1. Press Shift-F1 to access the Setup window.

2. Select **E**nvironment.

3. Check or uncheck **W**ordPerfect 5.1 Cursor Movement by pressing W or by using the mouse to click in the checkbox.

4. To exit the Environment menu window, click on OK and then click on Close, or press Enter twice.

FOOD FOR THOUGHT

We didn't delve into other Environment dialog box items like Cursor Speed or Language because they aren't really necessary to mess with at this point. Check your WordPerfect reference manual for info about the rest of these options.

Quick—List My Files! Fast (Easy) and Slow (Tiresome) File Management

WordPerfect allows you to save and retrieve files using the WordPerfect file manager in two different ways: The long way and the short way.

With the long way, you need to know a lot of really annoying details about where you might have stored a file. You need to know the disk drive designation, directory name, file name, and the phase of the moon when you stored it. Okay, just kidding; you don't need to know the phase of the moon, but it sure seems like it.

The short way is the best way. WordPerfect created a *QuickList* to store and retrieve files. QuickList does most of the work for you. All you have to know—or be able to guess—is the type of file and what you might have named it. Remembering where you put all your files puts a strain on anyone's memory, no matter what their age.

Chapter 8, "A Word about Files" discusses the full use and advantages of using QuickLists, but you set the stage for using QuickLists in the Environment settings right here.

Using QuickLists

To set yourself up to take full advantage of QuickLists, use the following steps:

1. Press Shift-F1 to access Setup.

2. Select **L**ocation of Files.

3.   Select **B**ackup Files.

4.   The cursor is now in the entry field for Backup Files. Type the exact same thing that appears in your **D**ocuments box and press Enter. If you leave the location of your backup files entry empty, all the backup files are written to the \WP60 directory. Because many files exist in the \WP60 directory already, it can be confusing to sift through all of them trying to find your backups.

5.   Check the box labelled **U**pdate QuickList.

6.   Choose OK, then Close.

Now you're ready to use QuickLists. To find out more about drive designators, directories, and file names, you might want to skip ahead to Chapter 8, "A Word about Files," or peek at the glossary.

Adding Mousey Gadgets to Your Screen

If you're worried your dog might eat this book (like he used to eat your homework) or the WordPerfect documentation, set up your screen to display the Ribbon and/or Button Bar. Both of these are accessed only with a mouse, but can be used in all three modes: Text, Graphic, or Page. The Graphic and Page modes really show off the icons on these bars to full advantage, because you can see little pictures in addition to word abbreviations on each button.

If you really like using the mouse, you'll find that the buttons and ribbons provide faster access to some functions than going through the menus. If you don't use the mouse much, there is no particular advantage to having them available on-screen.

 The Button Bar. This contains frequently used menu items, features, macros, and even other button bars. WordPerfect comes with seven button bars, but you can only display one at a time. However, you can customize your button bar with a mix and match of the options you most frequently use. The prepackaged bars cover Fonts, Layout, Macros, Outline, Tables, Tools, and one called WPMain, which is a combination of the others.

The Ribbon. Unlike the Button Bar, this is not customizable. It only deals with the appearance of text—features and sizes. It can be useful if you often have a need to change the appearance of your text within the same document.

The WordPerfect Button Bar? Do They Serve Drinks Too?

Add the Button Bar to your screen. Get this up on-screen first:

1. Select the **V**iew pull-down menu.

2. Choose **B**utton Bar.

You'll notice that a whole row of buttons, or *icons*, appeared near the top of your screen. See those two arrows? By clicking on the right arrow, you'll see even more options. Although you won't need to use the Button Bar for anything that's not already on a menu, it sure is a help when you can't find a #!@$%& command.

Moving the Button Bar

Part of the fun of working with WordPerfect is arranging everything to your personal tastes. You can arrange the Button Bar on any side of the screen. Experiment with the Button Bar to find the most satisfying side:

1. Select the **V**iew pull-down menu.

2. Choose Button Bar Se**t**up.

3. Select **O**ptions.

4. You can choose among **T**op, **B**ottom, **L**eft side, or **R**ight side to position the button bar at any of those locations. Nifty!

5. Choose OK to close the button bar options.

Tie a Yellow Ribbon: Adding the Ribbon

Another helpful aid in working with WordPerfect is the Ribbon. Put it on-screen by doing the following:

1. Select the **V**iew pull-down menu.

2. Choose **R**ibbon.

Look at that! Now that you have buttons and ribbons, you'd think bows would be next. Thank goodness the WordPerfect folks didn't add those too. At any rate, your screen should now look something like the one shown in figure 2.5.

Figure 2.5:

Your screen after adding buttons and ribbons, but before bows.

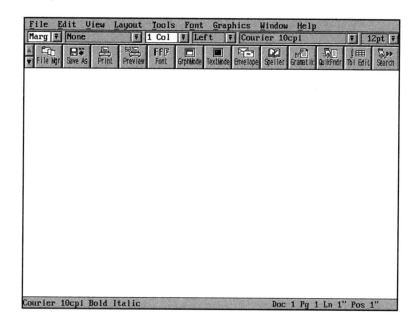

The ribbon appears just below the pull-down menus and in some ways replaces menus. The ribbon enables you to get to some of the more frequently-used functions in the pull-down menus with a lot less effort.

TRICK

Another way to make changes to your screen is to select **V**iew,Scree**n** Setup. If you look at the box under **S**creen Options you will see checkboxes for the Button Bar and Ribbon.

Help! My Menus are Gone!

If you accidently uncheck the Pull-Down menus checkbox (which turns off all the pull-down menus) while you're mousing around with screen options, here's how to get the Screen Setup window on-screen to correct this major error:

1. Press Ctrl-F3 to access the Screen window.

2. Press Shift-F1 to get back to the Screen Setup window.

Now you can recheck the pull-down menus box (or any of the other boxes).

Word Perfect

CHAPTER 3

Setting Up a Document

Now you're almost ready to type something: Maybe the poem you wrote in third grade (or not). Or how about a letter to the President? Or your collection of award winning egg salad recipes from around the world? It doesn't matter, because setting up a document in WordPerfect—no matter what kind of document—requires some basic information.

The original intent of this chapter was to unearth the secrets of the universe, reveal the mystery of man's origins, and answer the age-old question, "Why does bread always fall buttered-side down?" But the editors didn't allow it, on the grounds that *WordPerfect for Wimps* was supposed to be a computer book. Imagine that... Instead, you learn how to do the following:

 Understand WordPerfect's formatting codes

 Navigate WordPerfect's formatting menus

 Modify codes to format a letter

 Set up margins

 Set up a header with a name, date, and page number

Cracking the Code

Like every other word processor, WordPerfect formats documents by using codes. *Codes* tell the word processor how to display a document on the screen and how each page should appear when it prints. For example, when you set up a document to skip the first eight lines of the paper before it begins to print, WordPerfect records the setup as **[Top Mar:8]**. Translated, this code means that the top margin should be eight lines (nearly two inches) wide.

Before you begin working with formatting codes, you can do yourself a favor by setting up WordPerfect to show the full code name. The default is to show an abbreviated name when you are looking at the formatting codes in the Reveal Codes window (Alt-F3). To set up WordPerfect to show the full code names, follow these steps:

1.   Pull down the **V**iew menu and choose Scree**n** Setup.

2.   Select **R**eveal Codes. Check to see if the checkbox for **D**isplay Details has an 'x' in it. If it does not, select **D**isplay Details to add the checkmark.

3.   Choose OK.

You will now see full details about any formatting codes in your documents. This change will apply to all of your documents.

WordPerfect features a variety of built-in codes for many different formatting jobs. Such built-in codes are called *default* codes because if you don't tell WordPerfect to do something different, the program uses the built-in codes automatically—or "by default."

You don't have to use the built-in codes, however; you can set up your documents any way you like by creating your own kinds of formats. When you create a setting or format that is different from a default setting, WordPerfect records your new setting in the document to display and print properly. You can peek at the codes and change them as you set up the document and as you type it in.

Laying Out a Page

One of the advantages of a word processor over a typewriter (or a pen) is that a word processor lets you change your mind and rearrange things without having to retype everything. Even so, it's usually a good idea to begin by formatting the page settings, tabs, and other settings the way you want them. By setting up your document before you type the text, you gain a better idea of how the final document will appear.

You have to decide on many settings for your document. Begin by doing the following:

1. Select the **L**ayout pull-down menu.

2. Select **D**ocument. The Document Format window appears, as shown in figure 3.1.

Figure 3.1:

The Document
Format window.

```
┌─────────────────── Document Format ───────────────────┐
│                                                        │
│  1. Document Initial Codes...                          │
│  2. Initial Codes Setup...                             │
│  3. Initial Font...                                    │
│     ┌────────────────────────────────────────────┐    │
│     │ Courier 10cpi                                │    │
│     └────────────────────────────────────────────┘    │
│                                                        │
│  4. Summary...                                         │
│                                                        │
│  5. Redline Method        ┌──────────────────────┐    │
│  6. Redline Character:     │ Printer Dependent ▼ │    │
│                            ┌─┐                         │
│                            │¦│                         │
│                            └─┘                         │
│  7. Display Pitch:        ┌────────┐                   │
│       ● Automatic          │ 0.1"   │                   │
│       ○ Manual            └────────┘                   │
│                                                        │
│  8. Character Map...      ┌──────────────────────┐    │
│                           │ WordPerfect Default Map│    │
│                           └──────────────────────┘    │
│  9. ☐ Baseline Placement for Typesetters              │
│       (First Baseline at Top Margin)                   │
│                                     ┌──────┐ ┌────────┐│
│                                     │  OK  │ │ Cancel ││
│                                     └──────┘ └────────┘│
└────────────────────────────────────────────────────────┘
```

TRICK

If you prefer to use the keyboard, press Shift-F8, then D to bring up the Document Format window.

The window's first two options, Document Initial **C**odes and Initial Codes Se**t**up, are similar. You need only Document Initial **C**odes for your letter. The settings in Document Initial **C**odes affect only the active document (that is, the document you are currently working on). If you change the settings in Initial Codes Se**t**up, the new settings will affect every document you create.

TRICK

Later, if you want to change the settings in Initial Codes Se**t**up for the kind of document you create most often, that's fine. You can always change codes back to their original settings, or you can override them in any one document by setting Document Initial **C**odes to suit your current needs.

3. Select Document Initial **C**odes. The Document Initial Codes window opens, where you can enter the codes you want to apply to the document.

4. Notice that this new window is empty; that's not very helpful if you've never formatted a document before. You need to decide what part of the document you want to format, whether it's just a line, a page, the whole thing, or whatever. Press Shift-F8 and the Format window appears, giving you a menu of choices (see fig. 3.2).

Figure 3.2:

Windows, windows, windows....

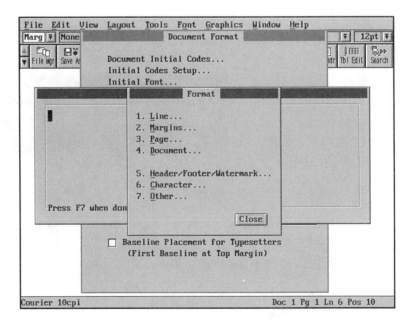

Formatting Lines

To format lines in your document:

1. Select **L**ine from the Format window; the Line Format dialog box appears, as shown in figure 3.3

2. Select **J**ustification

3. Select **F**ull

4. Select OK

5. Choose Close

Figure 3.3:

Lining up the options.

```
╔════════════════════ Line Format ════════════════════╗
║                                                       ║
║  1. Tab Set...  │Rel; -10,-5,+0,+5,+10,+15,+20,+25,+30,...│ ║
║                                                       ║
║ ┌─2. Justification──────────┐ ┌─Hyphenation─────────┐ ║
║ │    ○ Left                 │ │ 6. ☐ Hyphenation    │ ║
║ │    ○ Center               │ │                     │ ║
║ │    ○ Right                │ │ 7. Hyphenation Zone │ ║
║ │    ● Full                 │ │      Left:  │10│ %  │ ║
║ │    ○ Full, All Lines      │ │      Right: │4 │ %  │ ║
║ └───────────────────────────┘ └─────────────────────┘ ║
║  3. Line Spacing: │1.0  │⇕    ┌─8. Line Height──────┐ ║
║                                │    ● Auto           │ ║
║  4. Line Numbering... │Off│    │    ○ Fixed:         │ ║
║                                └─────────────────────┘ ║
║  5. Paragraph Borders...                              ║
║                                      │ OK │ │Cancel│  ║
╚═══════════════════════════════════════════════════════╝
```

The code [Just:Full] appears in the Document Initial Codes window, with the cursor positioned immediately after the code.

Justification is the only item you're going to change for your letter, but you might want to spend a moment looking at the other settings in the Line Format window. To bring the Line Format window back up, press Shift-F8 again, and then select **L**ine.

The Line Format window offers these options:

 Tab Set. You can see the WordPerfect default is to set a tab every five spaces. You usually don't bother changing the default unless you set up a cute little table or something, but if you want to change tab settings, you do it in the Line Format window.

Justification. Many ways exist to justify text. *WordPerfect for Wimps* is written (and printed) using Left Justification. The text lines up on the left side of the page and is ragged on the right. Right justification is the opposite (ragged on the left, lined up on the right), and if you choose full justification, both margins line up straight. Full justification gives your letter a polished, professional look (to *some* people, anyway).

 Line Spacing. The Line Spacing option is used to control the amount of space between the bottom of one line and the top of the next line. Here you indicate the amount of space you want between the lines. Sometimes you want 1 1/2 or 2 lines to make it easier to edit or read on the printed page. If you send a letter to Aunt Edna, you might want to make it three lines. Her eyesight ain't what it used to be.

 Line Numbering. If you want to number each line, turn on line numbering (lawyers *love* this feature). It has no effect on the document. You can also turn off line numbering as easily without affecting the document. Line numbers don't appear on-screen; they only show up when you print your document. WordPerfect enables you to print the document with or without line numbers. A good use for the feature is during the editing process.

 Paragraph Borders. You can use paragraph borders to emphasize a particular paragraph or pithy saying. For example:

> *"I claim this land for Texas."*
>
> —What Neil Armstrong was dissuaded from saying when he stepped onto the moon.

Because you're setting initial document codes, now isn't the best time to play with borders. Don't worry; Chapter 12 shows you how to add borders, lines, and other graphics to your documents.

 Hyphenation. WordPerfect doesn't normally hyphenate words (by default, the automatic hyphenation feature is turned off). As a result, you can end up with a very large hole on a line if you happen to have a veryveryveryveryveryveryverylong word and you don't turn Hyphenation on. To turn on hyphenation, just click on the check box by the Hyphenation option.

Hyphenation Zone. This is not where your hyphens go when you aren't looking at them. Rather, this controls how wide your words must be before WordPerfect decides that they need to be hyphenated. The values are given in terms of percentage of page width. Under almost all circumstances you'll want to leave these settings alone.

 Line Height. *Line height* refers to the amount of vertical space from the bottom of one line to the bottom of the next line. Normally, WordPerfect adjusts line height automatically if you use a bigger point size or a larger font.

FOOD FOR THOUGHT

The bottom of a printed line is called the *baseline.*

If you want the line height to remain the same no matter what font you select, turn on the Line **H**eight option by selecting Fixed. Otherwise, WordPerfect automatically adjusts the line height to the size of the font. You don't use Line **H**eight often; WordPerfect's automatic line height is almost always the best choice.

Setting Up Margins

If word processing is new to you, a *margin* is the space between the text and the edge of the page. Every document has a margin on all four edges of the page, and you can control the size of each margin.

SAVE THE DAY

Most laser printers simply cannot print with margins smaller than 1/4 inch on any edge. Printers vary, though.

If the Line Format window is still on your screen, you should close it and return to the Format window by pressing Esc or selecting Cancel. You use Esc or Cancel in case you changed an option and don't want to record it.

Now, open the Margin Format window by selecting **M**argins from the Format window. You can see the Margin Format window in figure 3.4.

Figure 3.4:

The Margin Format window.

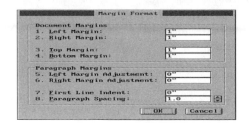

Changing the Top Margin

The only option you want to change for your letter is the top margin. You want to set it so the first page begins to print ten lines from the top edge of the paper. To set the top margin, do the following:

1. Select **T**op Margin

2. Type in the number 2 for two inches

3. Press Enter

4. Select OK or press Enter again to make this change effective

5. Select Close to close the Format window

The Document Initial Codes window appears, updated to disclose your modification (see fig. 3.5).

If you want to return to the Margin Format window to explore some other options, press Shift-F8 to return to the Format window, and then press **M** or number **2**.

Figure 3.5:

The perfect code.

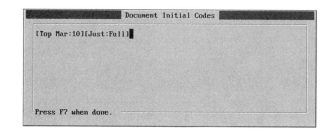

```
                        Document Initial Codes
 [Top Mar:10][Just:Full]█




 Press F7 when done.
```

Document Margins

The Margin Format window is divided into two sections, Document Margins and Paragraph Margins.

The settings in Document Margins are pretty self-explanatory, so a quick summary should be enough. If you need to change a setting, you can. Sometimes you print on paper that has a border, or you have to leave plenty of space for extensive editing comments. For example, the editors insisted on 3-inch margins on both sides of the paper for their corrections. *(And a good thing we did, too. —Ed.)* Use Document Margins to change such settings.

Paragraph Margins

The Paragraph Margins are for use in the body of a document. For example, to narrow both margins for a paragraph, position the cursor right before the paragraph you want to change, press Shift-F8 and select **M**argins. (You also can select **M**argins from the **L**ayout pull-down menu.)

The Margin Format window appears, and you make the appropriate changes to the settings, then type the paragraph. When you finish typing the paragraph, place the cursor *after* the paragraph you're working on, return to Paragraph Margins, and change the settings back. And if you need to change the margins for an existing paragraph, block the paragraph with Alt-F4 before changing the margins; your settings will automatically apply to that paragraph and no others.

TRICK

If you want to temporarily change any settings in the Format window for your document, don't do it in the Initial Codes Setup window. Do it by putting the cursor at the point in the document where you want the settings to change. Then call up the Format window by pressing Shift-F8. Make your selection, type what you want, and then change the setting back to normal by putting the cursor at the end of the area you change. Call up the Format window again to change the setting back to its original value.

Now, exit from the Margin window by pressing Esc. It's time to move on.

Formatting Pages

Select the Page Format window (see fig. 3.6) by selecting **P**age from the Format window.

Figure 3.6:

The Page Format window.

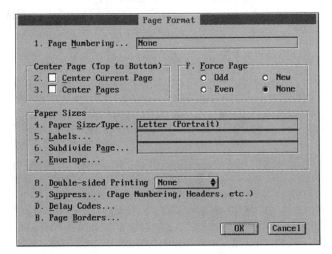

A Quick Cruise

If you want each page to have a page number, select Page **N**umbering. But you probably don't want to paginate your letter, so skip it for now. (Numbering pages is covered later when you work with multipage documents.)

The other item of interest for the letter is Paper **S**ize/Type. Regular 8 1/2" x 11" letter size is the WordPerfect default, and the default orientation is portrait. *Portrait* orientation has the short edge of the paper at the top, and *Landscape* orientation has the long edge of the paper at the top. The WordPerfect defaults are fine for your letter.

Delay Codes

Okay, now for the good part: The **D**elay Codes setting! Delay codes are the niftiest thing since sliced bread.

Delay Codes enable you to set up formatting codes at the top of your document that take effect after a certain number of pages. For many letters, you'll set up delay codes to format every page except the first. Succeeding pages often have different formatting requirements from the very first page.

When you type a document or letter longer than one page, the second and subsequent pages often need to be slightly different from the first page. Perhaps you need different margins, or a header or footer. A *header* is one or more lines at the top of every page and a *footer* is one or more lines at the bottom of every page.

In your letters, the first page needs a lower top margin than the following pages to compensate for your preprinted letterhead. The following pages need to have a header that contains the following information:

 Date

 Page number

You know you need different settings for the second and subsequent pages from the outset. You can create settings right from the beginning by using the delay codes feature. Then you can just concentrate on writing.

Using Delay Codes to Change Subsequent Pages

Select **D**elay Codes from the Page Format window. A new window appears and prompts you for the Number of Pages to Delay Codes. The default is one. In other words, by default, WordPerfect waits one page before activating the codes. One is good, so select OK. The Delay Codes window opens. You want to enter two items:

A new top margin

 A header

Changing the Top Margin

To enter a new top margin, take the following steps:

1. Press Shift-F8 to call up a new Format window

2. Select **M**argins; The Margin Format window appears

3. Select **T**op Margin

4. Type in the number **6**

5. Select OK or press Enter to make the change effective

6. Again, select OK or press Enter

Setting Up a Header

With the first page's margin taken care of, continue with the following steps to add a header to the second and subsequent pages:

1. Select **H**eader/Footer/Watermark from the Format window

2. Select **H**eaders

3. Select Header A...

4. Make sure that the **A**ll Pages button is selected

5. Select **C**reate

6. Press Enter for a new line

Adding a Date to a Header

It's time to put the date in, but the date you write the letter and the date you print it may be two different dates. You can avoid having to go back and change it by using a code that automatically fills in the date from the computer's internal calendar. (Bet you didn't know your computer had a calendar built into it!) See the following steps:

1. Press Shift-F5 to select the Date window

2. Select Insert Date **C**ode

3. Press Enter for a new line

Violins! The current date appears on the screen. Each time you look at the screen, or print your document, the current date is automatically used.

Adding Page Numbers to a Header

To finish off the header by preparing the page number line, take the following steps:

1. Type **Page**. (Don't forget the space at the end!)

2. Press Shift-F8 to bring up the Format window.

3. Select **P**age.

4. Select Page **N**umbering.

5. Choose **I**nsert Formatted Page Number.

"But," you may say, "the number 1 is inserted!" That is precisely what you want! Even though you want the header to begin on page 2 with number 2, it prints properly because you are using the Delay Codes feature. Keep going:

6. Press Enter twice.

7. Press F7.

The updated Delay Code window appears (see fig. 3.7).

Figure 3.7:

The perfect delay!

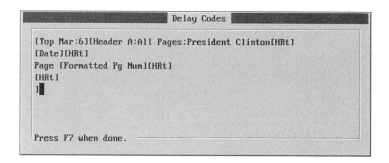

```
████████████████ Delay Codes ████████████████
┌────────────────────────────────────────────┐
│[Top Mar:6][Header A:All Pages;President Clinton[HRt]│
│[Date][HRt]                                   │
│Page [Formatted Pg Num][HRt]                  │
│[HRt]                                         │
│]█                                            │
│                                              │
│                                              │
│                                              │
└Press F7 when done.───────────────────────────┘
```

Closing the Format Windows

Good job! You are finished with the header and have initialized your document the way you want. You just need to get out of the morass of windows (really quite simple) and then you're set to begin typing your letter/poem/recipe in the next chapter. To exit, follow the yellow brick road:

1.   Press F7 to exit the Delay Codes window

2.   Select OK to exit the Page Format window

3.   Select Close to exit the Format window

Before you exit all the way, look at the Document Initial Codes window (see fig 3.8).

Figure 3.8:

The Document Initial Codes window with the codes you've set in this session.

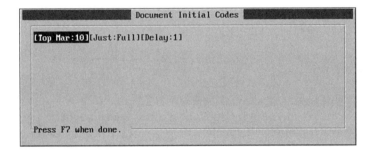

To get back to the WordPerfect document screen:

1.   Press F7 to exit from the Document Initial Codes window.

2.   Select OK at the last remaining Document Format window.

CHAPTER 4

The Basics of Entering and Formatting Text

Entering text in your WordPerfect document is easy. It only seems difficult at first because you have so many executive decisions to make—choices about fonts and styles, attributes, and formats.

In this chapter, you learn that:

 WordPerfect provides and is compatible with a great deal of type-faces and fonts

 The Status Line is your friend

 Word wrap is not the latest music craze (thank goodness)

 Justifying your document is no excuse, it's a formatting command

 WordPerfect has different types of tabs for different types of text

 How to save your document for a rainy day (or at least until tomorrow)

Font First

One of the nicest advances in WordPerfect 6.0 for DOS is in the area of fonts. WordPerfect now supports more fonts than you can shake a graphic artist at. While WordPerfect itself does not come with an enormous number of fonts, it is quite easy to add additional fonts to WordPerfect. These additional fonts can either be purchased separately, or often come with other software packages. For example, Windows 3.1 comes with a number of fonts that you can use in WordPerfect, as do many graphics programs like Micrografx Designer and CorelDRAW!. This section will teach you:

 How to look at the different fonts installed in WordPerfect

 How to make WordPerfect print out a list of all of the fonts it has installed

 How to work with the fonts installed in WordPerfect

 What types of fonts WordPerfect supports

 How to install the extra fonts that come with WordPerfect

 How to use the fonts from other programs and install them into WordPerfect

 How to delete fonts you have added

FOOD FOR THOUGHT

A font is a typeface with a particular style and size. You can also select the point size for some fonts. An inch has 72 points, but most printing is done with 10- or 12-point fonts. Usually the smaller the point size, the smaller the print, but this varies with the style of the font.

Checking Out Your Fonts

The font choices available depend on the capabilities of your printer. When WordPerfect was installed on your machine and the printer was selected, all the fonts available on your printer were installed. To see what is available:

1. Select the F**o**nt pull-down menu.

2. Select F**o**nt again, and refer to figure 4.1.

Figure 4.1:

The Font dialog box.

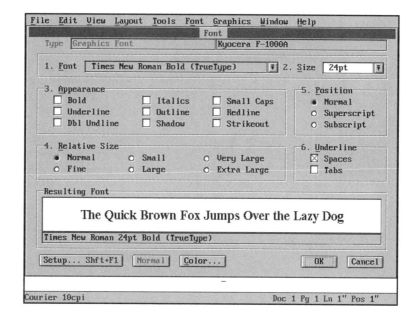

The Font dialog box appears.

3. Choose **F**ont.

Go ahead and select some of the different fonts here by using the arrow keys or the mouse. You'll notice two things on the screen change. The most obvious thing that changes is the Resulting Font dialog box immediately under the list of fonts. It shows a sample phrase followed by the font style and additional information, such as the *cpi* (characters per inch) and the point size (if applicable). If it's bold or italic, it tells you.

Printing Your Font Inventory

Sometimes what you see on your screen isn't quite what you see when you print. This can be caused by limitations in your printer or difficulties that WordPerfect has in working with your printer. For this reason, it's a really good idea to tell WordPerfect to print out all of the fonts you have installed and then to take a look at the results. By doing this, you can decide which fonts you want to use. Fortunately, WordPerfect makes doing this printout extremely easy by including a macro that will automatically generate a document containing all of your installed fonts. Follow these steps:

1. Start with a blank document.

2. Press Alt-F10 to play a macro.

3. In the field that is asking for the name of the macro, type **ALLFONTS** and press Enter.

Once you press Enter, WordPerfect will generate a document listing and demonstrating all of the installed fonts. Once it is finished generating it (it takes a while), just press Shift-F7 and then press Enter to print the list.

Changing Text to a Different Font

If you're in the middle of your letter to the IRS and you need to emphasize a few words, you'll probably want to change their font. In other words, you may want to make some words larger, bolder, underlined, or even different. Changing text is easy! Here are the steps:

1. Block (highlight) the text you want to change. For mouse lovers, click and hold down the left mouse button while you drag over the word. If you're too poor to buy a mouse, press Alt-F4, then use the arrow keys.

2. Select F**o**nt,F**o**nt, press Alt-O, then Alt-O.

TRICK
Press Ctrl-F8 for quick access to the Font dialog box.

The largest, most complicated dialog box ever—the Font dialog box—appears. Actually, all the features in this dialog box are easy to use. Your options include:

 Font. Select the typeface and font you want to use. The type of font you have is listed next to the font's name. The words Type 1, TrueType, Speedo, *xx.x*cpi, and others indicate whether the font is scalable, if it requires a printer compatible with the PostScript language, or if the PC does all the work interpreting the font before it prints.

FOOD FOR THOUGHT

You may not have many fonts in this dialog box. If you have only the fonts that came with WordPerfect, you may want to add extra fonts. Fortunately, finding fonts is easier than ever. One family of fonts that is widely available is the TrueType font family. Go to a computer software store and ask if they sell TrueType fonts. The dealer will show you several software packages chock full of TrueType fonts.

If you have a nerdy computer friend, ask him or her for some fonts. Many public-domain fonts (they're free to the public) and shareware fonts (play before you pay) are available on on-line services. Your nerdy friend probably can get these fonts for you.

If you already have more fonts, but can't figure out how to add them to WordPerfect, see the section "Adding Fonts to WordPerfect" for a few clues.

 Size. Select point size.

 Appearance. Mix and match bold, underline, double underline, italics, outline, shadow, small caps, redline, and strikeout.

FOOD FOR THOUGHT

All the options in the **A**ppearance box are called attributes. If you highlight the phrase "Get off my back!" and make it bold and italic—***Get off my back!***—the text has bold and italic attributes.

Position. Normal, superscript, subscript.

Relative Size. Normal, fine, small, large, very large, extra large. This controls how large the font should be, relative to your base font. The base font is the default font for wherever you are in the document. For example, let's say your base font is set to Times Roman, 18 points. If you then select some text and tell WordPerfect to make it large, the size will be increased to 120 percent of the base font size, or 21.6 points. To see what these relative size adjustments are, press Shift-F1 while you are on the Font dialog box. There will be a box at the bottom of the resulting dialog box that shows the percentage changes for each relative size change.

Underline. Spaces, tabs.

3. Select the font you want and check all the appropriate check boxes in the **A**ppearance box, then see a sample of it in the Resulting Font box.

4. If you've found the font you need, click on OK.

FOOD FOR THOUGHT

Be careful when using many different fonts and attributes in a document. Many beginning users go completely overboard in their use of these nifty features, and, as a result, their work ends up looking amateurish. Selecting the appropriate font and attribute is very much an art, and elegance and simplicity are important watchwords. Pay attention to good-looking documents as you learn to use these features.

Understanding Font Support

One of the most confusing areas in modern computing is the use of fonts. Many different ways exist to get different fonts onto your printed page, and these different methods have limitations you should be aware of.

Basically, all fonts can be divided into two different families: fixed and scalable. Fixed fonts come in a number of sizes that you cannot change. Many printers include a certain number of fonts at these fixed sizes. If you want a size that is not built into your printer or computer, then you're out of luck.

The other main branch of the font family is made up of scalable fonts. These fonts can be scaled (sized up and down) to virtually any size. Either your computer or your printer automatically draws the font each time you use it. Since they have the description of how each letter should appear stored in them, they can simply draw the appropriate font size on demand.

Keep this in mind, though: Fixed fonts usually come out looking better than scalable fonts. This is because the fixed font was carefully crafted to look as good as possible at the size it was drawn for. Scalable fonts, on the other hand, are more general, and come out looking a little fuzzier. This difference is more or less noticeable depending on your particular printer.

Fortunately, WordPerfect supports both font technologies, so you can choose just the right font for the job. Aside from supporting the fonts built into your printer, WordPerfect also includes the capability to generate a wide variety of scalable fonts.

Several different technologies exist for generating scalable fonts. WordPerfect supports the most popular types of scalable fonts:

 Autofont

Bitstream Speedo

 CG Intellifont

 Adobe Type 1 PostScript

TrueType

 HP Printer Fonts (fixed)

If you own fonts created for any of these programs, you can install those fonts into WordPerfect. If you are going to purchase additional fonts for WordPerfect, you should make sure to get fonts that will be compatible with one of the listed font families.

Adding Fonts to WordPerfect

WordPerfect includes some supplemental fonts on disks labeled "Additional Fonts." Depending on the size of disks you have purchased, there may be two or three of these disks. To install these additional fonts, follow these steps:

1. Exit WordPerfect and return to the DOS prompt.

2. Change to the directory in which you have WordPerfect installed by typing **CD \WP60** and press Enter.

3. Start the installation program by typing **INSTALL** and press Enter.

4. Insert the disk labeled "Additional Fonts 1."

5. From the menu that appears, choose Install Disk(s).

6. You will see a dialog box asking where to install from. If you are installing from your A drive, type **A:** in this box. If installing from your B drive, type **B:** in the box and press Enter.

7. Follow the prompts. WordPerfect will install the fonts contained on the disk, and will prompt you for the remaining disks.

8. When the installation is complete and you have returned to the main installation menu, choose Exit.

Adding Fonts Already on Your PC

One of the nicest tricks you can make WordPerfect do is to use the fonts that other programs have included. For instance, you can use the TrueType fonts that you use with Windows 3.1. Or you might have a different word processing program that includes some additional fonts you can now incorporate into WordPerfect. To install these fonts into WordPerfect, follow these steps:

1. Start from WordPerfect. If you are not already running WordPerfect, type **WP** and press Enter to start it.

2. Press Ctrl-F8 to bring up the Font dialog box.

3. Press Shift-F1 to bring up the Font Setup dialog box.

4. Select Install Fonts. You will see the WordPerfect Font Installer program begin.

5. From the menu that appears, choose the type of font you wish to install. For example, if you are using the fonts included with Windows 3.1, you would choose TrueType.

6. You will now see a dialog box that will ask for the location of the font files. Fill in the directory name where you have the fonts on your hard disk. For example, if you are installing the fonts built into Windows 3.1, you would indicate that the .TTF (TrueType Font) files are located in the directory C:\WINDOWS\SYSTEM.

7. After specifying the correct directory, you will see a list of the fonts contained in that directory. Use the asterisk key to mark all of the fonts you wish to install. If you want to mark all of the fonts listed, press Home,* to select them all.

8. When you have finished indicating the fonts you want to install, choose Install Marked Fonts.

WordPerfect will now process the fonts in that directory, and will add them to its own font definition files. When the process is complete, you will be able to use the fonts in WordPerfect. Just press the Escape key until you return to the WordPerfect Font dialog box.

Adding New Fonts from Floppy Disks

You are not able to install fonts directly into WordPerfect from floppy disks. You must first use the installation program or procedure contained on the disk and install the fonts onto your hard disk. With some fonts, all you will have to do is to copy the font files from the floppy disk to a directory on your hard disk. Instructions for doing this should be found with the font disks.

Working with Formatting

As you would expect, WordPerfect includes a veritable smorgasbord of features that let you control how your text is placed on the page. This section will show you:

How to set up and change the tabs on your page.

 Justifying your text. No, not justifying your work, but justifying your text.

 Working with different alignments, such as indents, hanging indents, double indents, and other tricks with which to impress your co-workers.

 Working with wordwrap and understanding hard and soft returns in your document.

 Understanding hard and soft page breaks.

Working with Tabs

WordPerfect has an amazing selection in the Tab Set dialog box for tab settings, as shown in figure 4.2. You'll be able to present your ideas in such nicely aligned columns that you'll impress everyone with your great-looking lists. If your keyboard has 12 function keys, you press Ctrl-F11 to call up the Tab Set dialog box. Alternately, select Ta**b** Set from the **L**ayout menu.

Notice that a "ruler" appears across the top of a dialog box with the current tab settings noted. The options are:

 Ab**solute and Re**l**ative.** Select whether your tabs should be set at an absolute setting from the edge of the page or relative to the margins. The absolute setting might be handy if you are going to print on a preprinted form. You can easily measure the distances you need from the edge of the paper with your ruler. Relative tabs are the most common setting used in letters and documents. Tab stops set every five spaces relative to the margin is the default setting, so you don't even need to call up the Tab Set dialog box if that's what you want to use. (See figure 4.2.)

Figure 4.2:

The Tab stops here.

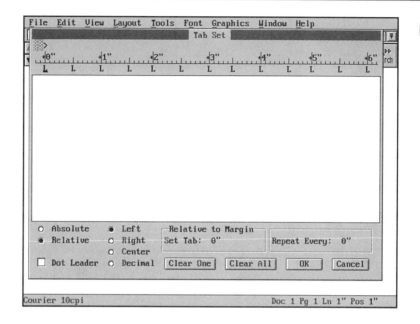

FOOD FOR THOUGHT

The advantage to using relative tab settings is that when you change your page margins it won't mess up your tab settings. The tabs will automatically adjust so that they are still correct.

Left, Right, Center, Decimal. The setting you select here decides how the text will be typed relative to the tab. The Left tab is the most common and is the default setting. When you use a Left tab, the left side of the text will align on the tab stop. For the Right tab, the right edge of the text entered will be aligned. If you decide on the Center setting, the text is centered on the tab stop. Decimal tabs are used for typing in columns of numbers. All the digits typed in before a decimal go to the left of the stop and digits typed in after the decimal go to the right of the stop. (See figure 4.2.)

STOP!

Don't forget to use decimal tab stops when typing columns of numbers. If you try to align columns of numbers using left, right, or centered tab stops, or—heaven forbid—by using the space bar, your alignment will go all screwy if you change fonts or change your page layout. Using decimal tab stops prevents this from happening.

TRICK

WordPerfect's default settings for the Decimal tab are a comma (,) as the thousands separator and a period (.) as the decimal separator. You can change those settings in the Character Format dialog box. To get there, either press the Shift-F8 keys or select the Layout pull-down menu. Select Character and then Decimal/Align Character or Thousands Separator. Click on the OK button when finished, or press your Tab key until the OK button is selected and then press Enter.

 Relative to Margin. Use this option to type in one tab setting relative to the margin. To use this, enter the distance from the left margin where you want a single tab to be placed. You can use this option in place of setting tabs with your cursor on the desired position on the "ruler." But don't stop there. Use this setting in conjunction with the Repeat Every setting described below to set regularly spaced tabs across the page. (See figure 4.2.)

 Repeat Every. This option helps the lazy typist set tabs evenly spaced according to the number typed in. This is used in conjunction with the Relative to Margin setting explained above. If the number in the Relative to Margin setting is 10, for example, and you want tabs every 5 spaces after that, you would enter a 5 in the Repeat Every entry field. (See figure 4.2.)

Dot Leader. This is a great option to check for some tab stops. It causes dots (periods) to be inserted from the place the cursor was at to the tab stop when Tab is pressed. It really helps the reader follow the spaces between columns. For example, if you have two columns of information, you would check this checkbox for the second tab stop. That way, when you finished your entry in the first column, a press of Tab will cause dots to fill in the space between your last entry and the tab stop. (See figure 4.2.)

TRICK

To change the dot leader character from a dot (period) to an asterisk (*) or any other symbol that strikes your fancy, press the Shift-F8 keys or select the Layout pull-down menu. Select Character and then Dot Leader Character. Notice that you also can change the Spaces Between Dots in the same place by tabbing or clicking on that selection. Click on the OK button when finished, or press your Tab key until the OK button is selected and then press Enter.

 Clear One and Clear All. To clear one tab stop, position your cursor (with the arrow keys or mouse) on the tab and select the Clear One button (by tabbing or with the mouse). If you want to clear all the tab stops, just tab to the key or use your mouse to select it. (See figure 4.2.)

TRICK

Clear all tabs from the position of your cursor to the end of the page by pressing the Ctrl-End keys. Clear one tab stop by using the Del key.

Creating New Tabs

A new tab stop is created by either double-clicking with the mouse on the desired position using the Relative to Margin box, or using your arrow keys to position the cursor. By using the Repeat Every box you can save time and keystrokes (or mouse movements). Don't forget to indicate what type of tab you want with the Left, Right, Center, and Decimal settings.

The following example shows how you would clear the default tab settings and create two new tab stops appropriate for one text entry and one dollar-value entry, separated by dot leaders:

1. Select the **L**ayout pull-down menu and then select Ta**b** Set. (All selections can be made by double-clicking on the word with the mouse button, or pressing the letter that is shown here as underlined.)

2. Clear all tabs by pressing Ctrl-End or clicking on the Clear **A**ll button.

3. Select **S**et tab and then type in the number **30** and press Enter. This will place a Left tab 30 spaces to the right, relative to the left margin.

4. Select **S**et tab and then type in the number **50** and press Enter.

5. Select **D**ecimal.

6. Select Do**t** Leader.

7. Select OK with a click of the mouse or press Tab until it is selected and then press Enter.

Deleting Existing Tabs

Use the Clear One or Clear All buttons to delete tabs. You can use the arrow keys or the mouse to position your cursor at the proper place to perform the task.

TRICK

Use Reveal Codes (Alt-F3) to take a quick peek at your current tab settings. You cannot change the settings in Reveal Codes, but you can see them at a glance.

Justification

WordPerfect provides five different methods of justification that you can use in your documents:

 Left. The text aligns on the left margin and leaves the right margin ragged. Letters and memos are often left-justified.

 Right. The text is aligned on the right margin, while the left margin is ragged. Use right justification for your name and address on a title page or for an advertisement. This can be a real eye-catcher.

 Center. The text is aligned in the center of the page, the left and right margins are ragged. Headings and title pages are a good place to use center justification.

 Full. Both the left and right margins are even. Spacing within a line is adjusted proportionally. Most documents, agreements, and reports use full justification. Only lines that end with a soft return will be aligned on both sides. Partial lines will be left-justified.

 All. The text is aligned between the left and right margins evenly. This would be a good justification mode to use in newsletter headlines. All lines typed with this justification—even very short ones—will be "stretched" to take up the full width of the line.

To access and change your justification, select **J**ustification from the **L**ayout menu. Highlight the type of justification you want and press Enter, or double-click on your choice. Alternately:

1. Press the Shift-F8 keys.

2. Select **L**ines.

3. Select **J**ustification.

4. Select the number that corresponds to the desired justification mode or click on the button next to the mode.

5. Press Enter three times to return to your document, or click on the OK button and then the Close button.

Alignment

Alignment is different from justification because you are working with tab stops as a point of reference, rather than the margins. One other key difference is that pressing Enter ends the alignment setting and returns the cursor to the justification mode in effect. Alignment settings are used for paragraphs or short lines on a page.

To access the alignment settings, select the **L**ayout pull-down menu, and then **A**lignment. Highlight the desired setting and press Enter or click twice with your mouse. Better yet, use the shortcut keys that are shown right after the option. Here are your options, and an explanation of what they do:

 Indent. (F4) The complete paragraph is indented by one tab stop.

 Indent. (Shift-F4) This is a double indent. The paragraph is indented one tab stop from both the left and right margins.

 Hanging Indent. (F4,Shift-Tab) All lines in the paragraph except the first one are indented by one tab stop.

 Back Tab. (Shift-Tab) Move the cursor, not the text, to the previous tab setting.

 Center. (Shift-F6) If you press Tab just before you select this item, the text is centered within the tab stop. If you don't press Tab, the text is centered within the margins. This is a good choice for a one- or two-line heading, because pressing Enter ends the centering.

 Flush Right. (Alt-F6) Any text entered after selecting this item is flush with the right margin. Use this option when you want one or two lines, or part of a line, flush with the right margin. If you use right justification, the entire line is flush with the right margin. Pressing Enter returns the cursor to the justification mode selected.

 Decimal Tab. (Ctrl-F6) Using this option turns a regular tab stop into a decimal tab stop. This is great when you have a column of entries consisting of both text and numbers, or you want to type in text and align it flush right to the tab stop.

Wordwrap: Soft Returns vs. Hard Returns

As you type your document in WordPerfect, you will notice that any words that would extend beyond the right margin automatically wrap around and become a new line. This is called *wordwrap*. Every time WordPerfect wraps a word to the next line, a *soft return* is inserted in the document. As you edit your document by adding and deleting words, changing margins, and so on, WordPerfect automatically adjusts your text to compensate for the changes. It does that by adjusting where the soft returns are located in your text.

When you press Enter, you create a *hard return*. A new line always begins right after a hard return.

Of course you want to use a hard return on certain things like headings and address lines. In the body of your text you want to let WordPerfect do the work of putting in the returns where they belong. If you don't, you would have to manually adjust your text to compensate for adding and deleting words, changing margins, and other changes. What a pain that would be!

FOOD FOR THOUGHT

Wordwrap, soft returns, and hard returns all work the same way in all the justification modes.

Hard and Soft Page Breaks

As you type your document, WordPerfect keeps track of where one page ends and the next page begins. You can see where WordPerfect inserts a page break by the single solid line across your screen. This is called a *soft page break*. If you change any of the margin settings, or add/delete text, you will see that the page break adjusts automatically to compensate for the changes.

If you want to force the page to break at any place in your document, you can insert a *hard page break* by pressing Ctrl-Enter. WordPerfect tells you there is a hard page break by displaying two solid lines across your screen.

Using the Status Line

While you work in WordPerfect, you may notice the status line at the bottom of the screen. It is the last display line on your screen. Toward the left side of the screen you see the name of the font that you have selected. On the right side of the status line is a rather cryptic series of letters and numbers. After you decipher them, they are very helpful in telling you the position your cursor is at in your document. You may want to know this for any number of reasons, but one of the most common is to help you determine where your text will appear on the printed page. You will see the following:

 Document number

 Page number

 Line number

 Position number

What's Up, Doc? Checking out the Document Number

The first item on the status line is the Document number for the document you are working on. It probably reads **Doc 1** unless you are working on more than one document. You can work on as many as nine documents in different document windows; the Document number is useful for keeping track of all the documents you have open at any one time. To find out how to work with multiple documents, read on to the next section, "Working with Multiple Documents."

The Status Line's Page and Line

The two items next to the document number are page number and line number. "Pg 1," for example, indicates that you are on page 1 of the document you're writing.

The page number has no literal relationship to the screen, but to the actual printout of the document. The page number shown on the status line indicates the printed page on which the cursor is currently located.

The line number also refers to the line number of the actual printed page, not the line number of the screen you are currently viewing.

What's Your Position? The Status Line's Position Number

The last item on the status line is the position of the cursor, relative to the left edge of the page. Like the other numbers in the status line, the position number indicates the relation of the cursor to the printed page, not to the screen.

FOOD FOR THOUGHT

The Line and Position places are displayed in inches. If you want to change it to lines from the top of the page and columns from the edge of the page measurements, refer to Chapter 2, "Setting Up for Success."

Working with Multiple Documents

WordPerfect enables you to work with more than one document at a time. You can work with—and view—up to nine documents at the same time! This is very helpful if you:

 Want to cut and paste from one (or more) documents to another.

 Want to have easy access to one or more documents throughout the day, such as a schedule or "to do" list.

Having the option of being able to switch from one document to another with the Window feature is a great time-saver. Without this option you would have to save your document to disk, find the other document you want to look at or work on, open the new document, and wait for it to load and format on your screen. While these are easy tasks to accomplish, it's a time-saver if a document is already loaded and formatted and can appear on your screen with a few clicks of your mouse button or with a few easy keystrokes.

Opening a Document into a Window

To open a document into a "fresh" window, you simply follow the normal steps of opening (recalling) any document:

1. Select the **F**ile pull-down menu.

2. Choose **O**pen.

3. At the Open Document dialog box, make sure the Method selection is Open into New Document. If Retrieve into Current Document is marked, use Shift-F10 to change the selection.

4. Type the file name in the Filename entry field or use the File Manager or QuickList Option. Refer to Chapter 8, "A Word about Files," for details on these options. Press Enter or click on the OK button to finalize your selection of the file name.

You can have up to nine documents open at any given time. If you run out of windows, you will need to **C**lose a document (from the **F**ile pull-down menu) before you can open another document.

Viewing and Working in Multiple Documents

To view all the documents that you have open at one time, select the **W**indow pull-down menu and then choose **T**ile. The *active window* is the one that has the blinking cursor showing. To switch between windows:

1. Select the **W**indow pull-down menu.

2. Choose S**w**itch.

3. Type in the document number from the list shown. This lists the document file name as well as the window number it is in.

TRICK

If you already know the document number of the window you want to switch to, simply press the Home key and then type the document number.

To resize a document window so that it takes up the whole screen again, simply select **W**indow and then **M**aximize.

STOP!

If you are editing two similar-looking documents at the same time, be sure to use the status line to help you track which one you are working on at any given time. Check the "Doc" number on the status line. If you get mixed up, use the "Save as..." option that appears on the dialog box when you exit or close the document and save it to a different file name. See Chapter 8, "A Word about Files," for details on file names.

Closing or Exiting a Document

In order to close a document or exit from it, it must be in the active window. If you don't want a document in a window anymore, you can close the document by selecting **C**lose from the **F**ile pull-down window. An alternative method would be to press the F7 key.

If you have made any changes to the document, you will see a dialog box asking if you want to save your changes or cancel the request to exit. Select whatever action is appropriate.

Saving Your Work

No matter how hard you try, you cannot exit the WordPerfect program without WordPerfect reminding you to save changes that you make to a document. But why wait to exit the file or the WordPerfect program before you save your work? Get in the habit of saving your file frequently as you work. If you do, you don't lose time trying to reconstruct your work or having to retype something if you suddenly lose power or make a drastic change to your document that you didn't mean to make.

You can save your document in several ways, but many of the save dialog boxes have several options and questions in common. Those include:

Filename entry field. Click on this field or use Tab to select the entry field. When you see the cursor blinking in this field you can type the name of the file. If this is the first time you are saving your document, this field is blank. You will need to type the full path name here. If this is not the first time you have saved the document, the last name that you used to save the file is shown in the entry field. If you want to keep it the same, press Enter.

FOOD FOR THOUGHT

For a complete discussion on file names, full path names, directories, and proper use of the File Manager and QuickList, refer to Chapter 8, "A Word about Files."

TRICK

If you want to save your document to a floppy disk, one of the ways to do it is to edit the Filename entry field. First, use your right arrow and move two places over, just past the colon (:) in the file name. Delete the directory name(s) with your Delete key (leaving the file name intact), then use your left arrow to position your cursor at the beginning of the entry field. Type in the "A" or "B" and delete the other drive designator. Press Enter when you're finished editing the file name field.

File Manager. To access the button marked File Manager, either press the F5 key or use your mouse and click once on the button. Using the File Manager can help you to find the correct drive and directory where your file should go. See Chapter 8, "A Word about Files," for a complete discussion about the File Manager.

QuickList. To access the button marked QuickList, either press the F6 key or use your mouse and click once on the button. If you have set up your QuickList according to the suggestions in Chapter 8, you will be able to quickly check where you have put other files similar to the document you want to save now. Using QuickList is faster than using the File Manager because you have already told QuickList the directories where you keep your document files.

 Setup. Either click on this button with your mouse or press the Shift-F1 keys. There will be a two-item dialog box on your screen. The first item is 1, **F**ast Save. If the Fast Save option is checked, then WordPerfect will not format the document for the default printer as it is saved. This makes the save faster, but printing slightly slower because the document will need to be formatted before it is printed. The other option is Default Save Format. Leave this option at the default, WordPerfect 6.0 format, unless you really do need to save all your documents formatted for a different word processor for some reason.

 Password. Even if you are not a double-triple secret agent, you may want to use a password. If you select this option, you will need to type a password before the file is saved. WordPerfect will then jumble up the file (encrypt it) so that the only way to read it again is by entering the same password when you open the file. If you feel compelled to use this option, write down the password and keep it in your wallet.

STOP!

We recommend that you do NOT use the Password feature when you save a file.

The Password feature requires you to enter a password to save the file and then to enter the same password to read the file. A password may sound pretty neato, but if you forget it, get hit by a truck, or leave the job where you are using WordPerfect, no one, not even the fine folks at WordPerfect, can help you or anyone else read, edit, or print the file without the password.

TRICK

If you are a secret quadruple agent and don't want other people to read your files, don't save them on your hard disk. Save them to a floppy disk and carry it around in your pocket. Be sure to erase the backup copy that is on your hard disk (made with the Backup **O**riginal Document on Save or Exit feature in the Environment Setup; See Chapter 2, "Setting Up for Success"). The file name on your hard disk will be the same, but the extension will be ".BK!".

Be sure to take the floppy out of your pocket before you put your shirt in the washing machine or take it to the cleaners. Also, avoid wearing your magnetic underwear.

FOOD FOR THOUGHT

Don't rely solely on the WordPerfect Timed Backup feature to save your files as you work. Save your document to both your hard disk and a floppy disk throughout your workday. If either one should get mangled for any reason you haven't lost all your hard work!

Saving Your WorkSaving Options

WordPerfect offers two basic options for saving your documents. You may:

1. Save your file and continue working on it. Those options are **S**ave and Save **A**s. The only time you need to use Save **A**s is if you either want to save your document to a different drive, directory, or file name; or if you want to save the document in a word processing format other than WordPerfect 6.0.

2. End your editing session on the file. Those options are **C**lose, **E**xit, and E**x**it WordPerfect. Close will not prompt you to save the file if you have not made any changes. Exit and Exit WordPerfect will prompt you to save your file whether or not you have made changes to it.

SAVE THE DAY

Be sure to set the Save as .BK! on Save or Exit option in the Environment Backup Options described in Chapter 2, "Setting Up for Success." After you turn that option on, each time you save, the last version of your document is renamed to [document].BK!. This feature will definitely save your day if you accidentally mangle your original file!

Saving without Exiting WordPerfect

One of the best ways to prevent disaster and guarantee a good day is to save your work often. Fortunately, you can save your work and remain in WordPerfect to continue your work. Frequent saves are a good idea, even if you have the Timed Backup option set. Especially after you've made major changes and want to make sure your changes are preserved in case you experience a power outage before the next timed backup.

SAVE THE DAY

You cannot save your document too often, especially if you aren't sure about the electricity in your home. Save as often as you want. (Actually, saving every 10 to 15 minutes works well.)

To save without exiting WordPerfect:

1.   Select **F**ile,**S**ave.

TRICK

To do the preceding two steps even faster, just press F10.

The Save Document window appears on-screen and displays several options. Your cursor sits in the Filename entry field waiting for a file name:

2.   Type the name of your document (it doesn't matter what case the name is in).

FOOD FOR THOUGHT

Mix and match uppercase and lowercase all you want with file names; DOS and WordPerfect are not case-sensitive. In other words, they can't tell which case you use.

3.   Press Enter or click on OK.

If a document has been saved before, the Filename field always defaults to the most recently selected file name. You can change it or leave it the same.

Saving and Exiting WordPerfect

You can save your document and exit WordPerfect in six easy keystrokes:

1.   Select the **F**ile pull-down menu.

2.   Select the last item, E**x**it WP. Don't panic. You are asked about saving your document. WordPerfect includes a built-in safeguard so that you can't wipe out all your hard work. You can't exit without WordPerfect reminding you about saving.

3. In the Exit WordPerfect dialog box are a Save checkbox, a Filename entry field, and three buttons: Un**m**ark All, Save and Exit, and Cancel.

STOP!

Do NOT select the Unmark All button. This innocent-looking choice erases all your hard work and you will exit the WordPerfect program. Your Timed Backups are erased every time you exit the WordPerfect program, so even those can't save you if you don't save your files.

If you've made it to this dialog box and you aren't sure what you want to do, take a deep breath and select Cancel. Your work is preserved for the moment and you can use WordPerfect's **H**elp system to look up whatever you need to know.

4. Select the Filename entry field.

5. Give your document a name, then click on Save and Exit or press Enter twice.

TRICK

Check out Chapter 8, "A Word about Files," for more on file names.

You're saved! Well, at least your document is, and WordPerfect exits.

6. If you're turning in for the night, wait until all disk activity on your system abates, then shut off the computer. Your data is safe and saved and now you can sleep well. Good night.

One WordPerfect feature is Document Summary, which enables you to provide a summary that contains the date of original document, date of revision, author, typist, abstract, and all sorts of information for every document you save.

Document Summary is great for busy office environments in which no one person works on the same document. Document Summary provides information that can help someone who needs to find out who "owns" the document and who typed it. Another benefit is you can perform searches on information contained in the Document Summary to help locate an errant document.

To access Document Summary:

1. Select the **F**ile pull-down menu.

2. Choose S**u**mmary.

The Document Summary is saved with the document, but not printed.

TRICK

If you want a summary to be created for every document you create, click on the Setup button in the Document Summary dialog box, then click on **C**reate Summary on Exit/Save.

FOOD FOR THOUGHT

There is a downside to using the Document Summary feature: the Document Summary dialog box will demand attention every time you save your document. This can be a real annoyance if you save your document frequently.

Customizing Document Summary

You can also customize Document Summary to include anything from whom to bill to an abstract:

1. Select **F**ile,S**u**mmary.

2. Click on Select Fields (press F4 if you're still saving for that mouse).

A strange-looking Select Summary Fields dialog box appears with more buttons and options than the Space Shuttle. Two boxes appear side by side. One box, Summary Fields, contains the fields currently in use by the Document Summary box.

The other box, Available Fields, contains dozens of choices. The buttons **M**ove, **R**emove, and **A**dd are used to shuffle around these options. The currently selected options that appear in the Summary Fields box have an asterisk next to them in the Available Fields box. These options can only be removed.

3. In the Available fields box, click on the fields you want to add, then click on << **A**dd. If you only want to remove fields, click on the field in the Summary Fields box, then click on **R**emove.

4. When you finish shuffling these options, click on OK.

CHAPTER 5

Whoops!
(The Basics of Editing)

In this chapter you're going to cover the good stuff: changing your mind, changing your document, and changing your clothes (you should do that at least once a day). Enough about fashion; learn how to:

 Retrieve your document

 Move around in your document: word-to-word and top to bottom

 Highlight text

 Look between the lines: the secrets to editing your document unveiled

 Search and replace

 Work with keyboard shortcuts

Retrieving Your Document

Before you can edit anything, you need to start WordPerfect and have a document on-screen. If you're not already in WordPerfect, type **WP** and press Enter to start it. To retrieve a letter:

1.   Select **F**ile from the pull-down menu.

2.   Choose **R**etrieve.

3.   Type the name of your document in the Filename entry field in the Retrieve Document window.

4.   Choose OK or press Enter.

There it is—the masterpiece that you just wrote.

Moving around the Document and around the World

To revise your document efficiently, you need to be able to access any part of that document in the shortest amount of time. There are many options for moving around in your document; don't worry about memorizing them all at once. Table 5.1 is a neat summary of the "movement" commands.

FOOD FOR THOUGHT

Whenever you see two keys with a hyphen in between, as in Alt-F3, you need to press and hold down the first key (the Alt key in this example), press the second key (F3), then release both keys.

Keys separated by commas, such as the Alt,F combination, are pressed one after the other. Press and release the first key (the Alt key), then press and release the second key (F), and so on if you have a string of three or more of these keys.

Table 5.1
Cursor Movement Shortcuts

Keystrokes	Description
Ctrl-Right arrow	Move one word forward
Ctrl-Left arrow	Move one word backward
Home,Right arrow	Move to right edge of screen
End	Move to right end of line
Home,Left arrow	Move to left edge of screen
Home,Home,Right arrow	Move to right end of line
Home,Home,Left arrow	Move to left end of line
Ctrl-Up arrow	Move up one paragraph*
Ctrl-Down arrow	Move down one paragraph*
Home,Up arrow	Move to top of screen, then up screen by screen
Home,Down arrow	Move to bottom of screen, then down screen by screen
PgUp	Move to top of previous page
PgDn	Move to top of next page
Home,Home,Up arrow	Move to top of document
Home,Home,Down arrow	Move to bottom of document
Home,Home,Home,Up arrow	Move to top of document, before most formatting codes
Home,Home,Home,Left arrow	Move to left end of line, in front of all formatting codes
Home,Home,Home,Right arrow	Move to right end of line, in front of all formatting codes

*If your keyboard has the required chip. Most computers do.

Oh, My Word! Moving the Cursor

You can always move anywhere in your document by using the arrow keys: up, down, left, and right. If you are using a mouse, you can move anywhere by moving the pointer to where you would like the cursor to appear, and clicking once on the left mouse button. Either way can be tedious, however; fortunately, nice little keyboard shortcuts are everywhere in this program.

Moving the Cursor Word by Word

To advance the cursor a word at a time:

1. Hold down the Ctrl key and press the right arrow key once. Be sure to let up on the arrow key quickly, or the cursor will advance quickly as your keyboard starts repeating the keystroke.

2. To move back by one complete word, use Ctrl-Left arrow.

TRICK

Control-Right arrow and Control-Left arrow are really handy when you use the right-hand control key because you can work this key combination with only one hand.

Moving to the Right or Left Edge of the Screen

To move quickly to the right edge of the screen:

1. Press Home,Right arrow.

Simple!

TRICK

A really zippy way to move to the end of the line on the far right is to press the End key. Shazam! You're there in a flash.

To move to the beginning of a line:

1.   Press Home,Left arrow.

Super simple!

When the line goes beyond the edge of your screen, you need to add an extra Home; in other words, press Home,Home,Left arrow and Home,Home,Right arrow to move to the edge of text that is off-screen.

TRICK

Think of the Home key as a sort of "wind up" key. When using Home with the arrow keys, pressing Home winds up WordPerfect for when you press the following direction key. For example, pressing Up arrow moves up a line, Home,Up arrow moves up a screen, while Home,Home,Up arrow moves all the way to the top of the document.

Moving Down or Up One Paragraph

WordPerfect includes shortcuts to move between paragraphs. Not all keyboards have the keyboard controller that enables you to do this, however, so you'll need to see if your PC can handle it. If it works, great; if it doesn't, don't worry about it. No one will point at your keyboard and snicker.

To move down a paragraph:

1.   Press Ctrl-Down arrow.

To move up a paragraph:

1.   Press Ctrl-Up arrow.

Remember that WordPerfect defines a paragraph ending as a hard return.

FOOD FOR THOUGHT

When you press Enter at the end of a sentence, you create a hard return, which appears as **[HRt]** in the WordPerfect Reveal Codes window (press Alt-F3). A hard return is one you actually enter into the document, as opposed to a soft return, which WordPerfect automatically inserts when it reformats a paragraph. Hard returns will never get moved around by WordPerfect, while the soft returns will change position automatically as you reformat a paragraph.

Moving Up and Down a Screen at a Time

To move your document a screen at a time:

1. Press Home,Home,Up arrow to get to the top of the document.

2. Advance a screen at a time with Home,Down arrow. When you are at the top of the screen, this key combination positions your cursor at the bottom of that screen.

3. Continue to press Home,Down arrow to move down a screen at a time.

Using Home,Up arrow works the same way, only backward! (Or is that upward?)

TRICK

Another way to advance a screen at a time is to use the plus key (+) on your keyboard's numeric keypad. Use the minus key (-) to go back a screen at a time.

This works only when the NumLock key is off (unlit); you cannot use the plus and minus keys on the keyboard.

Moving between Pages

Rather than move a screenful at a time, you can move between the virtual physical pages that will be printed. To get to the top of the next page:

1. Press the Page Down (PgDn) key

To get to the top of the preceding page:

1. Press the Page Up (PgUp) key.

Moving to the Top and Bottom of Your Document

To pop up to the top of your document (no matter how many pages it is):

1. Press Home,Home,Up arrow.

Yes, you can even move the cursor to the end of the document:

1. Press Home,Home,Down arrow.

TRICK

WordPerfect provides other ways for you to navigate within your document, but they can't all be covered here. Click on <u>H</u>elp in WordPerfect's menu bar or use your WordPerfect manual (although that's not nearly as much fun) and look at the help provided for the Go To, Repeat, and Bookmark functions.

Hey, Blockhead! Highlight that Text!

Since you know how to motor around inside our document, you need to be able to "block" text before you can actually edit it. *Blocking* is the process of selecting text for moving or copying, or for deleting.

You can use either the keyboard or the mouse to select and block text.

Mouse Blocks and Rodent Cul-de-Sacs

You can block any amount of text with your mouse—from one character to the whole document:

1. Just press and hold down the left mouse button (right button if you've set it up differently) where you want to start your block and then move the mouse (without releasing the button) to the end of the text you want to block.

FOOD FOR THOUGHT

In some programs, the process of blocking text is also called "highlighting," or "selecting." WordPerfect just loves to be different.

2. If you accidentally block more text than you want, you don't have to unblock it and start over. While you are still pressing down on the mouse button, drag the mouse backward until just the appropriate text is highlighted.

3. To unblock text that you have blocked, release the mouse button and click once. The text is now unselected.

TRICK

If you are a mouse connoisseur (and who isn't these days?), you'll enjoy this nifty trick: to block one word, double-click on the word. To block a sentence, triple-click, and to block a whole paragraph, quadruple-click!

Blocking Text with the Keyboard

To block with the keyboard:

1. Position the cursor in front of the text you want to block.

2. Press Alt-F4, then move the cursor. If you have a newer keyboard, you can also use F12.

3. To eliminate the block, simply press Alt-F4 again or choose **E**dit,**B**lock.

TRICK

You can quickly block a sentence, paragraph, or page, by using **E**dit,**S**elect. A submenu appears with options to block a **S**entence, **P**aragraph, or P**a**ge.

Notice that while you block text the status line changes. When you activate blocking, **Block on** appears in the lower left corner of your screen; when you're finished, the file name or font you're using reappears.

Slick Editing Moves

One quick note before you edit your document: don't worry about spelling now. After all, WordPerfect includes a spelling checker that you can read about in "Avoidng Stoopid Misakes" in Chapter 6. Don't do any work for yourself that the computer can do for you. Now if the computer could only vacuum...

Deleting a Word

One of the most frequent tasks in editing is removing words (why do you think they call it editing?). To delete a word:

1. Move your cursor to the beginning of the word you want to delete. Use either the mouse or the arrow keys.

2. Now block (highlight) the troubling word. With the mouse, press and hold down the mouse button and move the mouse pointer over the word. With the keyboard, press Alt-F4, then press Ctrl-Right arrow or Ctrl-Left arrow to move the cursor over the word.

3. Now that the word is highlighted, you can delete (remove) the word in one of four ways:

    Choose **E**dit,Cu**t**.

    Press the Backspace key.

    Press the Delete (Del) key.

    Press Ctrl-X.

SAVE THE DAY

"Oh no! I screwed up!" If you delete something you really didn't want to, you can get it back. Either select the **E**dit pull-down menu and then choose **U**ndelete or press the Esc key. You can restore up to the three previous deletions this way.

Deleting a Sentence

Need to delete an entire sentence? Try this method:

1. Move to the paragraph with the ornery sentence.

2. Position your cursor at the beginning of the sentence.

3. Highlight the sentence, including the period at the end.

FOOD FOR THOUGHT

See the section on blocking text earlier in this chapter to learn how to highlight text.

4. You can delete the sentence in one of four ways:

    Choose **E**dit,Cu**t**.

    Press the Backspace key.

    Press the Delete (Del) key.

    Press Ctrl-X.

TRICK

To delete from the cursor position to the end of the line, press the Ctrl-End keys. It doesn't matter if the line is blocked to make this deletion.

Quick Simple Changes to Blocked Text

Once you block text, you can do a lot with it. Experiment on your own to find other uses besides the ones shown here.

Changing Lower Case to Upper Case and Vice Versa

You can convert upper case to lower, or lower to upper, or convert all the words to initial capitals in one step:

1. Block your text and press Shift-F3. Then toggle among the three options.

Changing Fonts

Change the font or font attribute of the blocked text. To do so in one easy step:

1. Block your text and press Ctrl-F8 to select a new one.

Changing Formatting of Highlighted Text

Perhaps you'd like to change the justification of only the text you block (highlight):

1. Select the **L**ayout pull-down menu and choose **J**ustification.

FOOD FOR THOUGHT

If you block a word in the middle of a sentence or paragraph, the **J**ustification command will affect the entire paragraph or sentence.

Moving Text

Whenever you need to juggle some text (a lot less scary than juggling knives), WordPerfect provides a few ways to rearrange your masterpiece. The most common method is to use the **E**dit pull-down menu's Cu**t**, **C**opy, and **P**aste commands.

Moving Text by Cutting and Pasting

You need to cut and paste; that is, *cut* a phrase from one location and *paste* it somewhere else. To do this, you first need to highlight the text you want to cut:

1. Position your cursor at the beginning of the sentence or paragraph you need to move.

2. Block the ornery text. Use the mouse, or press Alt-F4 and the arrow keys.

3. Select the **E**dit pull-down menu and then choose the command Cut and Past**e**, or press Ctrl-Del.

Poof! The text disappeared into a holding area. It's safe there until you cut something else. Before you do that, however, paste it somewhere:

4. Reposition the cursor to wherever you want the text to reappear.

5. Press Enter.

Isn't that great? The line and the whole paragraph adjust to whatever you do!

SAVE THE DAY

If you ever move text or change something you wish you hadn't, don't retrace your steps to correct it. Select **E**dit from the pull-down menu and then choose **U**ndo, or press Ctrl-Z. This command restores whatever you had before you screwed up.

Copying and Pasting

Copying and pasting works just like cutting and pasting. The same basic steps are involved:

1. Block the text you want to copy. Use the mouse (see the earlier section "Mouse Blocks...") or press Alt-F4 and the arrow keys.

2. Select **E**dit,Cop**y** and Paste, or press Ctrl-Insert.

3. Reposition your cursor to the place you want the text copied.

4. Press Enter.

The Cop**y** and Paste command in the **E**dit menu is a faster alternative to the separate **C**opy and **P**aste commands. You can also use the **E**dit,**C**opy command to copy text, but you then have to choose **E**dit,**P**aste when you want to add the copied text.

TRICK

Although the **E**dit,Cop**y** and Paste command functions about the same way as the **E**dit,**C**opy and **E**dit,**P**aste commands, the **C**opy only command is the optimal choice for repeated copying. Whatever text you blocked and then copied is kept in the copy buffer until you copy another block; you can paste it as many times as you want until you copy or cut something else. The Cop**y** and Paste command is optimal for immediate action.

Cutting and Pasting between Documents

Do you need to move or copy some text from one document into another document? A few clicks and you're on your way:

1. Block the text you want to move or copy.

2. Select the Edit menu and choose Cop**y** and Paste.

3. Switch to the second document by choosing **W**indow,S**w**itch.

4. Position the cursor where you want the new text to appear, then press Enter.

Reading Between the Lines: Using Formatting Codes

With WordPerfect you can read between the lines. To be more precise, you can read between the words. You aren't looking for hidden messages, however; you're looking for the codes that WordPerfect uses to keep track of the settings you want and the attributes you've selected.

WordPerfect embeds formatting codes into your document that control how and where text appears. When you center text, WordPerfect inserts a centering code before and after the centered text. When you make text bold, WordPerfect inserts a code for that at the beginning and end of the bold area.

Some codes are automatically placed at the beginning of your document. For instance, if you change your page size from standard to envelope, a code gets inserted at the top of the page for that.

Other codes are inserted right where your cursor is, and the change flows downward from that point on. For example, if you are in the middle of your document and you change the position of the tab stops, WordPerfect inserts a code right at your current cursor position which affects the rest of the document, until it encounters another set of codes changing the tabs to something else.

Being able to look at and change these codes is extremely important if you want to master and fully understand WordPerfect.

By pressing the right buttons, you can peek at the codes in your document.

Accessing Reveal Codes

To reveal the hidden codes that indicate every formatting specification in your document, follow these steps:

1.   Either select <u>V</u>iew,Reveal <u>C</u>odes, press Alt-F3, or press F11.

What you see on-screen should look something like figure 5.1.

TRICK

The fastest way to call up the Reveal <u>C</u>odes window is to press F11.

Figure 5.1:

The code is cracked.

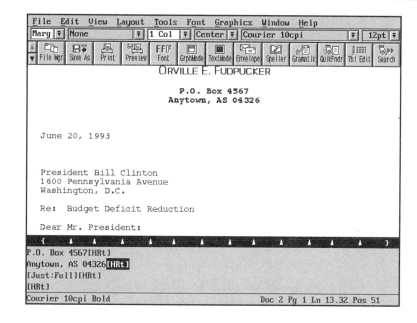

The first thing to notice is that your screen is now divided into two viewing areas: the larger part is your regular screen, while the bottom part shows the codes and text. The second thing to notice is that as you move your cursor around (move it to the left a few places with your left arrow key), the cursors on both halves of the screen move at the same time.

Editing in the Reveal Codes Window

In this section you'll type some text along with some formatting codes while the Reveal Codes window is open. Along the way, you'll learn how to maneuver around the codes and move the codes around.

Follow these steps. While you are following them, watch what happens in the Reveal Codes window at the bottom of the screen.

1. If the Reveal Codes window isn't visible, press Alt-F3 or F11 to activate it.

2. Press Shift-F6 to center what you'll be typing.

You'll see the code **[Cntr on Mar]** (Center on Margin) appear.

3. Press F6 to turn bold on.

You'll see two codes appear, **[Bold On]** and **[Bold Off]**. These are the codes that turn bold text on and off (OK, you probably guessed that). Notice that the **[Bold Off]** code is highlighted by your cursor. At this point, when you type, you'll see that the **[Bold Off]** code gets "pushed" by your text.

4.   Type your name.

5.   Press Enter.

Note the **[HRt]** code that is inserted, but also notice that you're still "pushing" the **[Bold Off]** code. If you continue to type, the text will continue to be bold.

6.   Press Backspace.

The **[HRt]** code is deleted, and you're back at the end of the line you just typed.

With a knowledge about codes, there are several ways to edit the document that you wouldn't be able to use otherwise:

1.   You could press the right-arrow key to move your cursor past the **[Bold Off]** code. This is a quick way to get past the bold area and start typing normal text.

2.   If you didn't want the text to be centered, instead of selecting the text and then changing the justification, you could just position your cursor on the **[Cntr on Mar]** code and press the Delete key.

3.   If you didn't want the text to be bold, you could just highlight either the **[Bold On]** or the **[Bold Off]** code and press the Delete key. Since these are matching codes, both will be deleted.

Editing Matching Codes in the Reveal Codes Window

In some documents, you may see some codes that are a matched set. Things like font attributes always come in pairs. With every **[Bold On]**, for example, there will always be a **[Bold Off]** somewhere.

This is helpful to know because you can change something like bold type back to normal type simply by removing either the **[Bold On]** or the **[Bold Off]** code. With matched codes, the deletion of one deletes the other. That's a lot easier than blocking and then reselecting the font.

Editing codes in WordPerfect is also valuable if you are working in your document and something doesn't look right. When that happens, it's a good time to use Reveal **C**odes so that you can see your document the same way WordPerfect sees your document.

Searching and Replacing

WordPerfect has given you really powerful tools by including the Sear**ch** and Rep**l**ace commands. With Search and Replace, you can search for every occurrence of a word or code and replace it with something else or nothing at all.

With Sear**ch** only, you can quickly find any occurrence of a code or a word in the document, which is helpful if you want to find the last reference you made to a specific word, or the first reference, and so on.

Searching for a Word

1. Press Home,Home,Up arrow to reposition the cursor to move to the top of the document.

2. Select the **E**dit pull-down menu and then choose Sear**ch**, or press F2.

3. The cursor is waiting for an input in the Search For entry field; type the word or phrase you want to find and press Enter.

TRICK

You can select (click on) the Backward Search checkbox if you want to search from your current position backward.

4. Press Enter again or click on Search.

FOOD FOR THOUGHT

Those strange buttons at the bottom of the dialog box are concerned with searching for codes and formatting codes that appear in the Reveal Codes window. If you accidentally made something bold (**I QUIT!**) or added too many tabs to a table, you can use these buttons to search for specific codes in the document.

Pressing F5 will bring up a list that lets you choose one of the document codes for which you want to search. Shift-F5 brings up a list of specific codes. The specific codes button lets you search for a specific code option. For example, if you wanted to search for a particular font selection, like Courier 12 pt., you would use this to do that specific search.

Searching For and Replacing a Word

WordPerfect always searches by default from the position of your cursor forward in the document. If you are at the end of your document, select (click on) the Backward Search checkbox. To start searching from the beginning:

1. Press Home,Home,Up arrow to reposition the cursor.

2. Select the **E**dit pull-down menu and then choose Rep**l**ace, or press Alt-F2.

3. The cursor is waiting for an input in the Search For entry field; type the word or phrase you want to replace and press Enter.

4. The cursor is now waiting for an input in the Replace With entry field; type the new text and press Enter.

5. Click on the Replace button or press Enter to start the search and replace.

The Search and Replace dialog box that appears after you choose **E**dit,Rep**l**ace also includes several important checkboxes (see fig. 5.2). Pay attention to these options; if you don't use them properly, your boss or teacher may find some interesting words sprinkled throughout your document.

Searching for Whole Words Only

One of the more important checkboxes in the Search and Replace window is Find Whole Words Only. You need to remember that you are working with computers and they do everything you tell them. If you are trying to find all occurrences of the word **he** and replace them with **she**, and you don't check Find Whole Words Only, you could end up with some very interesting results.

Figure 5.2:

Search and Replace options.

```
╔══════════════ Search and Replace ══════════════╗

  Search For:   [                                    ]

  Replace With: [<Nothing>                           ]

    ☐ Confirm Replacement      ☐ Find Whole Words Only
    ☐ Backward Search          ☐ Extended Search (Hdrs, Ftrs, etc.)
    ☐ Case Sensitive Search    ☐ Limit Number of Matches:

  [ Codes... F5 ] [ Specific Codes... Shft+F5 ]      [ Replace F2 ] [ Cancel ]
```

Why? Because the letters 'he' are in the words "the," "there," and "where," for instance. If you forget to check the Find Whole Words Only checkbox, some new words will appear. People will either think you are really smart, using a foreign language and all, or that you really don't know how to use Search and Replace. They would then probably take your computer away from you.

Are You Sure You Want To Do That?

Another option you might want to consider is the Confirm Replacement checkbox. If you want to replace the instances of some words but not others, click here. When the box is checked, WordPerfect stops every time it finds the word you're looking for and asks if you want to replace it. It never hurts to check this box, just to be sure.

Extended Searches

Another important checkbox is Extended Search (Hdrs, Ftrs, etc.). A normal search and replace operation does not look in headers, footers, footnotes, or endnotes, which means no replacements are made to the text within them. A normal search and replace searches only the current document you have on-screen. If your document has any fancy academic stuff like these items, be sure to check Extended Search (Hdrs, Ftrs, etc.).

CHAPTER 6

Nagging Details

E ven great masterpieces need a bit of polishing and a few finishing
touches. Your document is no exception. And it's fun when you have
some really neat writing tools at your fingertips. In this chapter, you will
explore some of those options and learn that:

- Everyone can misspell a word now and then, but with WordPerfect's Speller, you can correct such errors automatically.

- The thesaurus did not walk the earth 40 million years ago. (It was really only 37 million years ago.)

- Your English teacher would have approved of the WordPerfect grammar checker, if not the spelling of the name.

Avoidng Stoopid Misakes

As you work with the spelling checker in WordPerfect, you'll wonder how
you ever did without such a thing. There are a number of really nice features
in WordPerfect's Speller:

It allows you to add your own words to its built-in dictionary.

 You can check for Incorrect Capitalization and double words words (heh heh).

 It lets you chain together two dictionaries. Twice the dictionaries, twice the fun!

 If you consistently misspell a particular word, it can automatically correct every occurrence in your document.

 It keeps a special document dictionary of the words you told it to skip. Within just that document, it won't bug you about those words again if you run the spell check function again.

Accessing the WordPerfect Speller

You'll need to retrieve your document if it's not already on-screen.

1. Make sure you are at the top of your document (Home,Home,Up Arrow).
2. Select the **T**ools pull-down menu.
3. Select **W**riting Tools.
4. Choose **S**peller.

TRICK

You can quickly call up the Speller with Ctrl-F2.

You'll see the Speller menu window, as shown in figure 6.1.

Figure 6.1:

How do you spell relief?

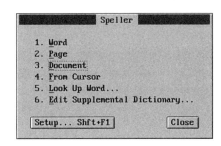

Spell Checking an Entire Document

To check your entire document for misspelled words:

1. Make sure you are at the top of your document (Home,Home,Up Arrow).

2. Select the **T**ools,**W**riting Tools,**S**peller.

As you can see, the third option in the menu window—**D**ocument—is high-lighted; this is the default option.

3. Click on **D**ocument or press 3 or D.

The first word the spell checker will probably ponder is your name or something else you know you spelled correctly, yet isn't in a dictionary.

4. When you encounter a word that you know is spelled correctly, but the spell checker doesn't seem to agree, press Add to Dic**t**ionary.

5. When the spell check is completed, select OK to return to your document.

Manually Editing Misspelled Words

Sometimes the spell checker will encounter a word that simply isn't in its list, which means that, yes, you occasionally have to consult an actual dictionary. If you encounter a misspelled word that WordPerfect can't fix, change it yourself:

1. Select Edit **W**ord, correct it manually, then press F7.

Skipping Words that Speller Wants to Fix

Sometimes the spell checker encounters a word that you probably don't want or need to add to the supplemental dictionary :

1. To bypass every occurrence of the word in your document, select **S**kip in this Document.

Accessing Speller Setup

The WordPerfect Speller includes more options that you can shake an English teacher at. To examine the default setup for Speller, open its Setup dialog box:

1. Select the **T**ools pull-down menu.

2. Select **W**riting Tools.

3. Select **S**peller.

4. Select Setup...Shift+F1.

The Setup dialog box is shown in figure 6.2. Each option is discussed as follows.

Figure 6.2:

The Speller dialog box.

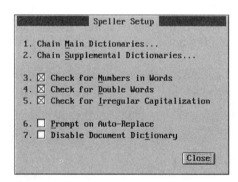

A Tale of Two Dictionaries

The Chain **M**ain Dictionaries command in the Speller dialog box is handy if you want to link two dictionaries, such as another language module from WordPerfect or a software program with a WordPerfect-compatible dictionary. Also, some companies sell specialized dictionaries, such as medical dictionaries, engineering dictionaries, and so on. This command lets you use both the WordPerfect dictionary and the additional dictionary.

To link two dictionaries:

1. Select **T**ools,**W**riting Tools.

2. Select **S**peller.

3. Choose Setup...Shift+F1.

4. Click on Chain **M**ain Dictionaries.

TRICK

Many companies sell supplemental dictionaries for WordPerfect, such as Steadman's Medical Dictionary. Legal dictionaries and other specialized dictionaries are available. Check with your software supplier for more information.

Creating Your Own Private Dictionary

In WordPerfect you can create your own supplemental dictionary to store words that you use, but which aren't part of the standard WordPerfect dictionary. In fact, when you choose the Speller dialog box's Add to **D**ictionary in the middle of a spell check, WordPerfect adds the word to your own supplemental dictionary automatically.

WordPerfect also enables you to keep several personal dictionaries. If you want to string together several personal dictionaries so that they are one big dictionary when you run the spell check, select the Chain **S**upplemental Dictionaries option.

Tales From the Spelling Crypt: Checking for Irregular Mistakes

A few options in the Speller Setup dialog box are pretty self-explanatory, and are already checked as the default. You probably want to leave these settings alone, unless you are working on some strange document. To examine these settings:

1. Select **T**ools,**W**riting Tools.

2. Select **S**peller.

3. Choose Setup...Shift+F1.

The **N**umbers in Words setting checks for funky words like L1011, tacky3, QE2, and UB40. If you think you're seeing double, **D**ouble Words can check your document to ensure the same word isn't typed twice in a row. And don't FoRgEt to Check for **I**rregular Capitalization.

Auto-Replace Option

The last two options in the Speller Setup dialog box are a little cryptic. To view these options:

1.   Select **T**ools,**W**riting Tools.

2.   Select **S**peller.

3.   Choose Setup...Shift+F1.

Normally, when you use the Speller, it will automatically take care of spelling errors that you've corrected once. For instance, if you always misspell the word 'thorough,' and tell WordPerfect to correct it once, it will automatically correct it everywhere in your document.

By checking the **P**rompt on Auto-Replace checkbox, WordPerfect will confirm these changes before actually making them.

Disable Document Dictionary Option

You probably won't use the Disable Document Dic**t**ionary option in the Speller Setup dialog box very often. If you spell check a document and tell WordPerfect to skip a particular word, WordPerfect adds the word to a *document dictionary*, a dictionary available only to that particular document. To see the Disable Document Dic**t**ionary option, open the Setup dialog box:

1.   Select **T**ools,**W**riting Tools.

2.   Select **S**peller.

3.   Choose Setup...Shift+F1.

When you click on the **S**kip in this Document option while spell checking, WordPerfect adds the word to the document dictionary automatically. If you check this box to disable the dictionary, Speller will find the word in error when you check it again.

4.   To return to the Speller window, Close the Speller Setup dialog box.

Editing a Dictionary Manually

Take a quick peek at the Edit Supplemental Dictionary dialog box. To get there:

1. Select **T**ools,**W**riting Tools.

2. Select **S**peller.

3. Click on **E**dit Supplemental Dictionary.

You should see a supplemental dictionary with an extension of .SUP in the Edit Supplementary Dictionary dialog box. The default button, Edit, lets you edit a particular dictionary.

4. Click on Edit to access the new words you've added.

If you've just finished a spell check, the words you added during the spell check appear in the Type Word window. One of the options below this box is **A**dd a word:

5. Highlight the word you want to add to a dictionary and Click on **A**dd.

The Add to Supplemental dialog box will appear with three options. When you add a word, you can tell the Speller to do one of three things with it:

 Word/Phrase to **Skip.** When you tell Speller to **A**dd the word or phrase to the Supplemental Dictionary, it is skipped automatically. Thereafter, you will never be questioned about that word again.

 Word/Phrase with **Replacement.** This option is handy if you consistently fumble your fingers on certain words. For instance, if you always type 'the' as 'hte' you can add the word 'hte' to your Supplemental Dictionary with this option. Thereafter, when you run Speller, the word is automatically corrected for you.

 Word/Phrase with **Alternates.** There might be words that you use regularly but you want to avoid using in a final document. You can enter the word here, enter several alternatives, and even enter a comment about why you did this. The next time Speller encounters the word, it stops and lists the alternatives that you entered. We tried this by replacing the word "crash" with "boo-boo." A system boo-boo sounds a lot less harsh than a system crash, don't you think?

6. To exit the Speller windows, choose Close until you return to your letter.

Procuring Apt Utterances (Using the Thesaurus)

Ever have one of those days where you can't think of the right, um, ah… word? That's why WordPerfect included a thesaurus with plenty of synonyms to fit your needs. To illustrate this lifesaver, pretend you were dumb enough to type this shoddy sentence:

I thought that was thoughtful of the President when he came right out and said he *had* to raise taxes.

Two "thoughts" that close to each other in one sentence sounds thoughtless, so look up a replacement word for "thoughtful." To do this:

1.   Position your cursor somewhere on the word "thoughtful."

2.   Select the **T**ools pull-down menu.

3.   Select **W**riting Tools.

4.   Choose **T**hesaurus.

Isn't that great! Your screen should look something like the one shown in figure 6.3.

Even if you don't like any of those suggestions, you can keep going by choosing each suggestion, which will lead to more suggestions, which will lead to more suggestions, and so on. You can keep doing this to your heart's content, until you find just the right word.

TRICK

As an alternative, the thesaurus also lists antonyms. For 'thoughtful', it lists 'inconsiderate' as an opposite meaning. Depending on your point of view, you might want to choose this word for our sample sentence.

Figure 6.3:

Food for "thought!"

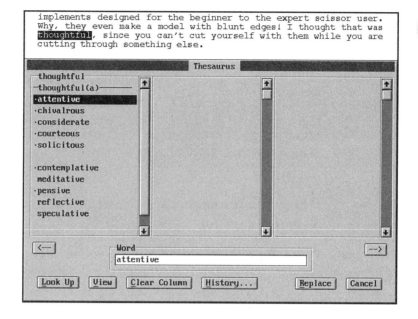

5. Notice that the word "attentive" is highlighted. Press Enter to display a whole new column of synonyms! Press Enter again to display a third column of words.

6. Now go back to the first column (use the left arrow or click on the first column) and highlight the word "considerate." That would sound right in this sentence.

7. Select **R**eplace. You're in business!

Finding Out about Your Document

WordPerfect contains statistics about every document, including even your worst letters. To see these statistics:

1. Select **T**ools,**W**riting Tools.

2. Choose **D**ocument Information.

Wait a few seconds while WordPerfect scans your letter. Suddenly the Document Information box appears with a whole bunch of information about your document, including:

Characters. The total number of characters in your Great American Masterpiece.

 Words. The total number of words in your Great American Masterpiece.

 Lines. The total number of lines in your Great American Masterpiece.

 Sentences. The total number of sentences in your Great American Masterpiece.

 Paragraphs. The total number of paragraphs in your Great American Masterpiece.

 Pages. The total number of pages in your Great American Masterpiece.

 Average Word Length. The average length of a word in your document.

 Average Words per Sentence. The average number of words in each sentence.

 Maximum Words per Sentence. The longest sentence in the document.

 Document Size. The file size of the document in bytes. If you're not sure what "bytes" are, check out Appendix A.

SAVE THE DAY

The Document Size figure is very important if you want to copy a file onto a floppy disk. If your document contains pictures or graphics, it might be too big. A graphic can easily be 200K, especially if it is a bitmap.

Before you exit your document, check this figure. If your document is over one megabyte, you probably will need to cut it in half and create two files. Highlight one half of it, select <u>E</u>dit,<u>C</u>ut and Past<u>e</u>, then create a new document by selecting <u>F</u>ile,<u>N</u>ew. Press Enter within the new document. You can always paste the two together later.

Who Needs Editors?
You Have a Grammar Checker!

The finishing touch you will use on your document is the grammar checker.

WordPerfect thoughtfully (there's that word again!) includes the Grammatik grammar checker. In fact, WordPerfect Corp. liked the Grammatik checker so much that they bought the company that makes it!

A grammar checker is a very useful writing tool, especially if English is your second language. With a grammar checker, you can have your document scanned for a variety of errors, such as:

 Mixed tense

 Improper subordination of clauses

 Dangling participles

 Passive voice

... and all sorts of other grammatical miscues they tried to drill into you in school. Never fear if you don't know what any of this stuff is, because Grammatik does and it'll show you!

1. Select the **T**ools pull-down menu (press Alt-T or click on **T**ools).

2. Select **W**riters Tools.

3. Choose **G**rammatik.

4. If you do not already have your document on-screen, press Alt-F or click on the **F**ile menu.

5. In the File selection menu dialog box, highlight the disk drive containing your document (drive C:, for example), then type the directory name in the Currently Selected File box. Press Enter.

6. Scroll down to your Great American Masterpiece (probably just a recipe list), and press Enter.

FOOD FOR THOUGHT

Grammatik can only examine WordPerfect-compatible files. If you want to check a document created in another program, you first need to open it in WordPerfect, then save it as a WordPerfect document.

WordPerfect can translate from a number of different word processors, but keep in mind that most formatting (tabs, bullets, tables, etc.) is lost during the translation. Make sure your document is cleaned up before you check it with Grammatik.

As you can see, this is an entirely separate program included with WordPerfect. Nevertheless, Grammatik functions in the same way as WordPerfect, with pull-down menus and such, and can be operated with a keyboard, mouse, or both.

A number of options can be changed in Grammatik. Default settings can be changed using the **P**references pull-down menu. Its options include:

Writing Style. Grammatik includes several *style templates* that look for specific grammatical problems common to different types of documents. If you're writing a paper on the laws of relativity, for example, select the Technical template. Grammatik will glance over several common grammatical errors, such as ending sentences with prepositions ("Where's the particle accelerator at?!") and passive sentences ("it was seen by the individual, it was conquered by the individual"). You can also create your own template by selecting different rules from over a hundred "rule" checkboxes.

Word Processor. Here you can set up Grammatik to work with various WordPerfect products, such as previous versions of WordPerfect, LetterPerfect, or straight ASCII files.

Options. This menu option brings up a dialog box that lets you control some of Grammatik's more esoteric features. Generally, you won't need to mess with this screen.

Screen Attributes. This menu selection brings up a list of different screen color schemes that let you change the colors Grammatik uses.

Grammatically Checking the Document

If you already have a document loaded into WordPerfect, or if you selected one using Grammatik's **F**ile,**O**pen command, you're ready to check the document:

1. Select **C**hecking (press Alt-C or click on **C**hecking).

Figure 6.4:

Grammatik having
problems with a
sophisticated name.

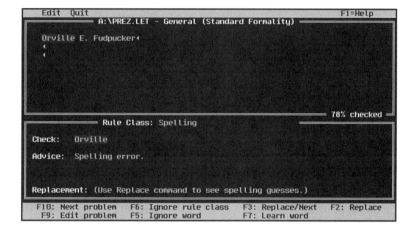

```
  Edit  Quit                                              F1=Help
┌──────────── A:\PREZ.LET - General (Standard Formality) ────────┐
│ Orville E. Fudpucker◄                                          │
│ ◄                                                              │
│ ◄                                                              │
│                                                                │
│                                                                │
│                                               78% checked ─────┤
├──────────────────── Rule Class: Spelling ──────────────────────┤
│ Check:    Orville                                              │
│ Advice:   Spelling error.                                      │
│                                                                │
│ Replacement: (Use Replace command to see spelling guesses.)    │
├────────────────────────────────────────────────────────────────┤
│ F10: Next problem    F6: Ignore rule class   F3: Replace/Next  F2: Replace │
│ F9: Edit problem     F5: Ignore word         F7: Learn word    │
└────────────────────────────────────────────────────────────────┘
```

2. Select **I**nteractive.

3. When Grammatik encounters a problem, such as a spelling error, it singles out the word and asks you to consider replacing it. Several options appear, as shown in figure 6.4.

4. The options you'll use the most are:

 F10: Next problem. This tells Grammatik to skip this problem and go on to the next one.

 F9: Edit problem. If you want to correct the problem manually, press F9. You can then make the change that corrects the problem that Grammatik is pointing out.

F5: Ignore word. If Grammatik is stuck on a word it thinks is misspelled, you can press F5 to tell it to continue past the word.

 F7: Learn word. This option is pretty much the same as WordPerfect's Add Word to Supplemental Dictionary option in the spell checker. Press F7 whenever Grammatik stops on such common words as names and addresses.

 F1: Help. The F1 key not only describes the steps you can take when Grammatik encounters an error, but also will display help about the error in question, how it can be recognized, and often why it is incorrect.

5.   When Grammatik finishes checking a document, you can pull down the **F**ile menu and choose **Q**uit to return to WordPerfect. WordPerfect will automatically have the corrected copy loaded.

Using Grammatik Advice for Grammatical Goofs

Whenever Grammatik encounters a common grammatical problem with the structure of a sentence, it alerts you and provides a number of options for fixing the sentence. To illustrate, suppose you wrote a letter to the president and you wanted to check for errors. You started the letter with this ground-breaking observation:

Dear Mr. President,

I have recently noticed that the U.S. Government has a large budget deficit. I thought someone should bring this to your attention.

To get Grammatik rolling:

1.   Select **C**hecking (press Alt-C or click on **C**hecking).

2.   Select **I**nteractive.

After you start the interactive checker, the first thing Grammatik chokes on is "deficit." With a 588 gazillion-dollar deficit, who wouldn't?

Look at the lower half of the screen. Grammatik gives you some advice on how the sentence should read, but there's just one problem: you slept through Ms. Bizby's English class and you're not quite sure what "article" or "modifier" are. That's okay, you can ask Grammatik for some help.

3. Press F1.

Helpful definitions for both "article" and "modifier" appear!

4. Use either the down arrow or your mouse to double-click on the term you didn't learn in seventh grade. Go ahead and select Define:article. Its definition is shown in figure 6.5.

Figure 6.5:

Ms. Bizby's English class—revisited.

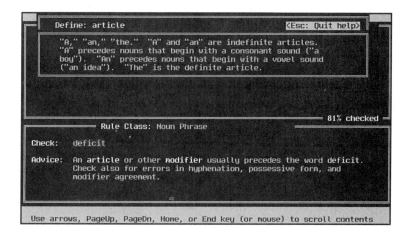

```
┌─────────────────────────────────────────────────────────────┐
│  Define: article                              <Esc: Quit help>│
│ ┌───────────────────────────────────────────────────────────┐│
│ │ "A," "an," "the."  "A" and "an" are indefinite articles.  ││
│ │ "A" precedes nouns that begin with a consonant sound ("a  ││
│ │ boy").  "An" precedes nouns that begin with a vowel sound ││
│ │ ("an idea").  "The" is the definite article.              ││
│ └───────────────────────────────────────────────────────────┘│
│                                              ═ 81% checked ═  │
│ ════════════════ Rule Class: Noun Phrase ══════════════════  │
│ Check:    deficit                                            │
│ Advice:   An article or other modifier usually precedes the word deficit.│
│           Check also for errors in hyphenation, possessive form, and│
│           modifier agreement.                                │
└─────────────────────────────────────────────────────────────┘
  Use arrows, PageUp, PageDn, Home, or End key (or mouse) to scroll contents
```

5. When you are finished using Help, press Esc to get back to the grammar checker.

Although you missed out on grammar class, you know this is the correct use of the word "deficit."

6. Continue your search by pressing F10: Next problem (press F10 or click on F10: Next problem). If you want to make the changes that Grammatik suggests along the way, you can use the F9: Edit problem key to edit.

7. When you're finished using Grammatik, select **F**ile,**Q**uit (press Alt-F, then Q or click on **F**ile,**Q**uit).

When you quit Grammatik, your work is saved and you are returned to the WordPerfect screen with the corrected file on your screen.

CHAPTER 7

Printing Your Letter

T he end result of all of your hard work with WordPerfect is your final printout. There you will be putting your image and reputation on the line for all to see. Fortunately, WordPerfect contains many features for getting the most out of your printer. In this chapter you will learn about:

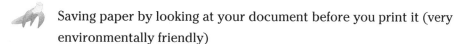

Saving paper by looking at your document before you print it (very environmentally friendly)

Printing your documents, in whole or in part

Adding new printers to WordPerfect, or choosing between multiple printers connected to your computer

How to print labels, but not dollar bills

Print envelopes with ease (even postal bar codes!)

Is Everything OK? Previewing Your Document

There is nothing more frustrating than printing out your 492-page document only to find that the font you used for the headings just doesn't look as good on paper as you thought it would. Then you are stuck with making the changes and printing the whole document again! That's just one of the reasons for using Print Preview. Some other reasons for using Print Preview include:

 To double check your formatting—indents, margins, and spacing

 To check the graphics images in relationship to your text

 To look at the overall visual presentation of your document

 To save a tree

Using Page Mode To Check Your Document

One of the ways to view your document before you print is to switch to Page Mode. To switch, select **V**iew, **Pa**ge Mode. Or, Ctrl-F3, and select **Pa**ge Mode.

In Page Mode you can edit your document while you are reviewing it, which is something you cannot do with Print Preview. Page Mode is similar to Graphics Mode, but unlike Graphics (or Text) Mode, it shows the headers and footers incorporated into your document.

TRICK

Pull down the **V**iew menu and choose **Z**oom, then **F**ull Page to look at and work with the entire page. While the letters will be extremely small in this viewing mode, it can be useful for moving blocks of text around and working with the overall layout of your document. To go back to normal view, pull down the **V**iew menu, choose **Z**oom, then Page **W**idth.

Using Print Preview

To use Print Preview, you must have the document on your editing screen; you cannot access your document from disk from the Print Preview function. You also need to have a printer selected. Check the section below on Changing Your Current Printer for more information on selecting a printer.

There are two ways to enter Print Preview:

 From the **F**ile pull-down menu and select Print Pre**v**iew; or

 From the Print/Fax dialog box (Shift-F7) select Print Pre**v**iew.

TRICK

If you have the Button Bar on your screen (and you don't have the Print/Fax window showing), select the Print Preview icon. It's the one with a pair of glasses beside a page that's coming out of a printer, and the word "Preview" on it.

Most of the options are available for use by clicking on the icons at the top of your screen with a mouse. But not everyone has a mouse, so we will use the pull-down menu commands which can be accessed with either the keyboard or a mouse.

Print Preview—File

In the **F**ile pull-down menu in Print Preview, you can:

Setup (Print Preview). The only option in this dialog box is to select or deselect **V**iew Text and Graphics in Black and White. When this box is checked, you won't see any colors on your Print Preview screen at all. The advantage to checking this box is that if you have incorporated color graphic images in your text they will draw faster in black and white. The disadvantage is that the Print Preview program uses a red line to frame the page that is "current" at any one time. (Current means that you can use the **V**iewing options on that page). Since all the pages are framed in a black border anyway, it is difficult for the eye to determine which page has a slightly darker frame around it than the one that is "current."

You can also Close. This does not exit the document completely, it merely closes Print Preview and returns you to your editing screen.

Print Preview—View

You can view your document a number of ways in Print Preview. Pulling down the **V**iew menu shows you many options.

100% View. View the current page at the actual printed size. How much of the page you see will depend on your monitor. Use the scroll bars on the sides and along the bottom of your screen to view more of the page.

200% View. View the current page at twice the actual printed size. This is helpful to zero in on one particular area, especially if you are a little hungover and your eyesight is blurry. Once again, you can use the scroll bars to view more of the page.

Zoom In. Increase the display size of the text and graphics by 25 percent. You can use this repeatedly to keep zooming in on a particular area. You can also use this feature in conjunction with Select Area. If you do not preselect an area (see following), the default is to zoom in on the beginning of the page.

Zoom Out. Decrease the display size of the text and graphics by 25 percent. Just like the Zoom In, you can repeatedly Zoom Out a particular area to keep decreasing the display size.

Select Area. This option helps you to focus on the particular area that you want to Zoom In on. Using a mouse is the easiest way to select an area. Just point at the edge of the area you wish to select, hold down the mouse button and drag until the area you want is in a dotted outline.

Reset. Print Preview remembers what viewing settings were selected when you first opened the Print Preview window and will return to those settings with this option.

Full Page. Display a complete view of the current page.

Facing Page. Display two consecutive pages on your screen at one time. The even numbered pages are on the left; odd numbered pages are on the right.

Thumbnails. If you select **T**humbnails, you can select how many pages you want to see on your screen at one time. The preselected options are 1, 2, 4, 8, 32, or **O**ther. If you select **O**ther, you can type in a number. Thumbnails are great to get a sense of the visual presentation of your document, but you cannot read any of the text (it's too small!).

Button Bar. If you have a mouse, you can use the button bar instead of the pull-down menus for making your selections in Print Preview. This option turns the Button Bar off and on.

Button Bar Setup. You can either use **E**dit or select **O**ptions from the Button Bar **S**etup. **E**dit will help you select which features you want displayed on your button bar; Options determines how your button bar is displayed on your screen and how it looks (you can set it up here to show or not show the pictures, and so on).

Print Preview—Pages

Print Preview allows you to quickly select the pages you want to see with the following options:

 Go To Page. Selecting this item will bring up a little dialog box in which you can type the number of the page that you want to view. On really long documents this is very helpful.

 Previous Page. View the page before the one that is current.

 Next Page. View the page after the one that is current.

If you get stuck in Print Preview, you can always holler for **H**elp. The complete WordPerfect **H**elp feature is available here.

Legitimate Hard Copy: Printing Your Document

One of the best parts of WordPerfect is its excellent printer management functions. With them, you can do all of these neat tricks:

Print in the background while you continue working

Reverse the order of your printouts

Choose which pages to print

Change the print quality of your printout

You can access the Print/Fax dialog box and its numerous features by either:

 Selecting File,Print/Fax, or

Clicking on the Print button in the button bar, or

Pressing Shift-F7

The Print/Fax dialog box appears as shown in figure 7.1.

Figure 7.1:

A slew of choices if you
need them.

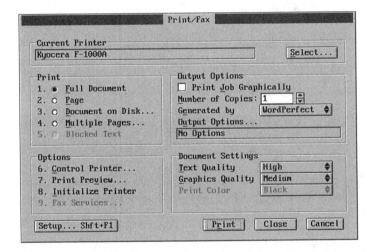

Checking Your Printer

Before you print, you might need to check out or change the information
WordPerfect has on your printer. Is the wrong printer listed for your print
job? If so, you can change to another printer—the setting stays set until you
change it. WordPerfect remembers your choice.

If the printer you want to use isn't installed, adding it is easy.

Changing Your Current Printer

Before you print, make sure the printer you want to use is selected. To change the current printer:

1. Choose **F**ile,**P**rint/Fax, or press Shift-F7

2. Click on **S**elect, or press S

3. Highlight the printer you need and press Enter

FOOD FOR THOUGHT

Some printers are PostScript-compatible, which means the printer can understand and print PostScript fonts. If you look in your Font dialog box (choose F**o**nt,F**o**nt or press Ctrl-F8), you might have some fonts installed with the words Type 1 or Type 2 next to them. These are PostScript fonts that only work on PostScript-compatible printers. If your document uses these fonts, make sure the printer you print to is PostScript-compatible.

If your printer can't read PostScript fonts, click on Print **J**ob Graphically to bypass the problem. Your document won't print as nicely, but at least you'll have something to show your friends.

Checking Your Printer's Capabilities

If you're having trouble with your printer and it doesn't seem to be working right, you might want to check the notes that WordPerfect Corporation has written about your printer. These notes often contain special setup instructions or other notes about your specific printer. To see these notes, follow these steps:

1. Choose **F**ile,**P**rint/Fax, or press Shift-F7

2. Click on **S**elect or press S

3. Select **I**nformation

4. Click on Close or press Enter to exit

When you return to the Printer/Fax dialog box, all the information for printing is updated, if necessary. With these settings, you cannot screw up your print job.

Changing the Current Printer's Configuration

Occasionally you might have need to change the configuration of your printer. For example, you might have connected your printer to a different printer port on the back of your computer, or you might be on a network and need to make sure the printer is set up correctly. To change the printer's configuration:

1. Choose **F**ile,**P**rint/Fax, or press Shift-F7

2. Click on **S**elect or press S

3. Click on **E**dit, or press E or 3

The Edit Printer Setup box is confusing at first. You don't need to mess with all of it, though. The most important parts of it are listed next.

Port. Here you can choose which connector on the back of your computer the printer is hooked to. Your choices will include all of your parallel printer ports (LPT1 through LPT3) and all of your communications ports (COM1 through COM4). Also, when you choose one of the COM port connections, WordPerfect will prompt you for the communications parameters for your printer. These include the baud rate, number of stop bits, parity bit, and a couple of other ugly techy settings. If you don't know what these settings are, get some help from your favorite computer nerd.

Network Port. If you are using WordPerfect on a network, this is where you tell WordPerfect how to find the correct printer on the network. You will need to get the correct names for this setting from your network administrator.

Sheet Feeder. If you have an additional sheet feeder or envelope feeder for your printer, this is where you define it. WordPerfect will already have a list of the possible options here, which vary from printer to printer. Just select **S**heet Feeder and then choose the attachments you have.

Printer Configured For Color. Some of the more popular printers these days, such as the Hewlett-Packard Deskjet 500C, have the ability to print color as well as black and white, depending on the ink module that is installed. If you have a printer like that, you use this setting to tell WordPerfect which ink module you have installed.

4.   Click on OK or press Enter when you finish

STOP!

Feeling environmentally unfriendly today? Would you like to see a dot matrix printer print a few characters a page while spinning hopelessly out of control? The best way to waste major amounts of paper is to set up a printer incorrectly in the Edit Printer Setup dialog box.

If you're about to use a printer you've never used before, make sure it is set to the correct port in the **P**ort field. If you're not sure what this is, find a computer nerd and ask if this setting is correct. If your letter is sent to a printer that differs from the one listed in Current Printer, the other printer will interpret the data incorrectly and may print only three or four characters a page—for hundreds of pages! On a dot matrix printer this can be a nightmare.

Adding a New Printer

1.   Choose **F**ile,**P**rint/Fax, or press Shift-F7

2.   Click on **S**elect or press S

3.   Click on **A**dd Printer, or press E or 3

4.   Scroll down to the printer you want to add, highlight it, then click on **S**elect

FOOD FOR THOUGHT

If your printer isn't on the list when you follow these steps, then you'll need to install it from the WordPerfect disks. See Chapter 1 for information on doing this.

Setting Print Options in the Print/Fax Dialog Box

Occasionally you may need to print only a few pages of your document or print a section of text you've highlighted. You may want to print a few copies of your document or print a quick draft of your letter for polishing later. All of these tasks are possible by using options in the Print/Fax dialog box.

1.   Choose **F**ile,**P**rint/Fax, or press Shift-F7

Deciphering the Print Box

In the Print portion of the Print/Fax dialog box are the options you will be using most. If you press Shift-F7, you will see the following five options:

1.   **Full Document.** This prints the entire document that is currently shown on-screen. You can have more than one document showing on-screen at one time; then only the document in the active window prints. This is usually the default unless you have some text blocked when you call up the Print/Fax menu. See **B**locked Text.

2.   **Page.** To print only the page that your cursor is on, select this option.

3.   **Document on Disk.** If the document you want to print is not the active one on-screen, you can always print one that you have stored on disk. If you select this item, you are presented with a window much like the one you see when you open or retrieve a file (use **O**pen or **R**etrieve). Just enter the file name for the file you want to print and click on OK. The file prints without even loading!

TRICK

Not only can you print a document stored on your hard disk, but you can also print one from a floppy disk. Just add either an A: or a B: before the file name to indicate which disk drive holds the file you want to print.

4.   **Multiple Pages.** With this option you can be very selective about the pages you want to print in your document. If you only need to print page 437, then select this item to avoid wasting 436 pieces of paper.

You can also print page ranges by separating the page numbers with a dash. To print only pages five through seven, type **5-7** in the **M**ultiple Pages window.

This option also enables you to print your Document Summary.

5. **Blocked Text.** Click on this option if you want to print some text you blocked (highlighted) on-screen. See Chapter 5 ("Whoops! (The Basics of Editing)") for information on how to block text. And see a football book on how to block William "The Refrigerator" Perry.

FOOD FOR THOUGHT

Remember that you don't have to change anything on the print dialog box if you just want to print—just click on **P**rint or press Enter.

Deciphering the Options Box

The Options box contains a few advanced settings that you probably will never need and a few settings of major importance—**C**ontrol Printer and Print Pre**v**iew. Take a look at these four options:

1. **Control Printer.** A really handy feature, especially if you forgot to select the **M**ultiple Pages option described previously. Just when you start printing page 1 of your 492-page document and realize you only want a printout of page 437, you can stop the print job after it has started. You can also send a rush job to the printer ahead of your other documents. You don't even have to pay extra for that service.

   To stop a print job, select **C**ontrol Printer, select **C**ancel Job, and then type the number of the job you want to cancel (it will be listed in the window).

2. **Print Pre**v**iew.** One of the more valuable options to select. So valuable that this option has an entire section devoted to it. See the section "Is Everything OK? Previewing Your Document" near the front of this chapter.

3. **Initialize Printer.** This option downloads fonts to a laser printer. Use this option only once when you first turn on your printer, and only if you need to. Fortunately, you don't have to worry about it most of the time. Usually, this only needs to be done when you have installed special "soft fonts" into WordPerfect. These fonts are in your computer rather than the printer, and WordPerfect needs to tell the printer about them.

4. **Fax Services.** If you installed the fax portion of WordPerfect and you feel comfortable with setting up and working with your modem, you use this option to send a fax. The Fax portion of WordPerfect is outside the scope of this book.

Understanding the Output Options Box

The Output Options box has one item of main interest, but the others are helpful also.

Print Job Graphically. Check this box if your job does not print what you saw in Print Preview. Any difference is typically caused by WordPerfect trying to use fonts that your printer doesn't contain. WordPerfect can print a page as a graphical image, which amounts to much the same thing on paper. Your job will print slower with this option checked.

FOOD FOR THOUGHT

Click on Print Job Graphically if your document uses Type 1 PostScript fonts and your printer is not PostScript-compatible. Printers must be purchased or updated to be PostScript-compatible before you can print Type 1 fonts.

Number of Copies. If you want to print 500 copies of your 492-page document, this is where you make that selection. Just make sure you bought plenty of stock in a paper company beforehand.

Generated by. If your printer is capable of printing multiple copies, make the printer do the work by selecting **P**rinter. Your printer will have to do all the work of making the multiple copies and will print more quickly. Note that when the printer does this, it will print all the copies of each page, one at a time. So, 10 copies of page one, 10 copies of page two, and so on. When WordPerfect generates all the copies, they come out collated properly.

Output Options. Click on Output Options to see several options for sorting your printout. These options are active only if your printer can support them. If your printer can sort, group, and send output to particular bins, you can select the options here.

Changing Print Quality in the Document Settings Box

The document settings are generated when you Update your printer selection. If you want to change them for a particular print job, this is where you do it. You can reduce or enhance the output quality of your document by selecting from three basic options:

Text Quality. Here you can choose how fine of a resolution to use for your text. Laser printers won't benefit from this setting; they always print at their highest quality. Dot-matrix and ink jet printers, on the other hand, can use this feature. When you just want a quick printout to review, set this to Draft. When you're ready for the final spiffy copy, set this to High. On some printers, draft mode may print as much as five times faster than High.

Graphics Quality. Graphics images often take the longest time to print. Depending on your printer and the complexity of the image, your printouts could get bogged down significantly when you have Graphics Quality set to High. By setting the graphics quality to a lower resolution (Draft) or even telling WordPerfect not to print graphics at all (Do Not Print), you can get that all-important quick printout quickly. When you're ready for the prettiest pictures possible, set it back to High.

Print Color. The choices here are entirely dependent on your printer. However, if you have a printer that can print using different colors, you can change this option to select between Full Color or just Black.

Working with Labels and Envelopes

WordPerfect 6.0 has some very nice features when it comes to printing envelopes and labels. You can:

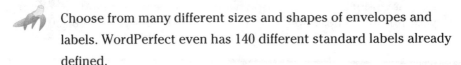

Choose from many different sizes and shapes of envelopes and labels. WordPerfect even has 140 different standard labels already defined.

Print anything WordPerfect can print on your labels and envelopes, even graphics!

Automatically extract the name and address of the person you're writing to from standard letters, and put that name and address on the envelope.

Have WordPerfect remember your name and address, and automatically insert that in the normal place at the upper-left corner of the envelope if you want.

Print PostNet bar codes on your envelopes for those really big mail jobs. A direct mail salesperson's dream!

Preparing Your Default Envelope

When you first set up an envelope, the information you enter becomes permanent; later when you need to print another envelope, the information is still there. WordPerfect uses your settings as the default for envelopes. To set up your first envelope (aren't you excited?) you need to access the Envelope dialog box:

1. Select the **L**ayout pull-down menu and choose En**v**elope, or press Alt-F12 if you have this key (some keyboards end at F10).

2. If for some reason you don't like the envelope size shown, you can change it here, or go into Setup (or press Shift-F1) to create your

own. To change the selected envelope, press Shift-F1, and then **E**nvelope Size. To create a new envelope size, press Shift-F1, and then choose **C**reate and then **C**reate again. Fill in the screen, making sure to set the **P**aper Type to envelope and the Paper **S**ize to the size of your envelope.

3. If you want to be secretive about your identity, you can check the checkbox marked **O**mit Return Address.

STOP!

An envelope without a return address is obviously not of much use if it has to be returned. If you forget to put a stamp on the envelope, the post office will not know who to return the letter to and your letter will go to the Post Office Black Hole where a gazillion other letters die. It will never be seen again.

4. The best checkbox to check is the one that says **S**ave Return Address as Default. As soon as you type in your return address, WordPerfect will remember it and you'll never have to type it again.

5. Now select **R**eturn Address, and type in your name and address. Press the F7 key when done.

The box POSTNET **B**ar Code is useless unless you are sending out presorted mail. That's the only time the post office uses it. If you plan to send out mass or bulk mail, find out your presorted code. You can go into Setup (Shift-F1) and click on the button marked Remove Bar Code Option to take this off if you like. It doesn't really matter.

Printing Your Envelope

With the Envelope dialog box on the screen, and the return and mailing addresses filled in, you have a couple of choices on how you deal with your envelope.

1. Select the Print button to immediately print the envelope.

2. Select the Insert button. This will cause a new page to be created at the end of your document. This new page will contain the envelope. When you print your normal document, the envelope will follow right along and print at the same time.

Labels

To work with labels, you start by saving and exiting any work you have on the screen so that you have a fresh screen staring at you. If you like, you can just switch to a clean screen by using the **W**indow pull-down menu and choosing the **S**witch option, or by pressing Shift-F3.

Label Measurements

The best way to work with labels is with measurements in inches rather than columns and lines. You may recall how you changed your measurements from the WordPerfect default in an earlier chapter. To change it back:

1. Select **F**ile and then Se**t**up or Shift-F1

2. Select **E**nvironment

3. Select **U**nits of Measure

4. Select "=inches

5. Now choose OK and Close the windows until you are out of Setup

TRICK

Even if you are using line/column measurements, WordPerfect lets you enter measurements using inches, which is translated automatically to lines/columns. Just be sure to enter a quotation mark after your measurement. So, if you wanted to enter 5 5/16 inches, you can type that into WordPerfect as 5 5/16".

Label Options

To set up your page for labels, you will need to:

1. Select **L**ayout pull-down menu or press Shift-F8.

2. Select **P**age.

3. Select **L**abels.

4. Browse through the many label types and sizes to find the one that matches the sheets you purchased. Notice that besides address and shipping labels, this is where you also can select Rolodex cards (you can buy them in punchout sheets to feed through your printer) and even file folder labels.

5. If the dimensions of the labels you are looking at don't match any of the ones that WordPerfect has provided, skip to the next section. If you have individual labels that you think are big enough to feed through your printer without jamming, skip to the following section, "Creating Your Own Labels."

STOP!

Check your printer documentation before trying to feed individual labels through your printer. Many printers will jam with paper sizes that are too small. Never use sheet labels when some of the labels have already been removed; it increases the chance that some of the remaining labels will come off inside the printer, which is bad.

Also, make sure that the labels you are using are specifically designed for your printer. Some people try to use labels in laser printers that weren't designed for that use—the labels completely gum up their printers, requiring expensive service calls to remove the label bits and clean the stickum out from the delicate printer innards. Don't let this happen to you!

6. Now **S**elect the label and press OK on the Page format window. If you are in Page or Graphics Mode, you will notice that part of your screen is grayed out now. That remaining space is the portion you have to type your label on.

Creating Your Own Labels

If none of the label formats you see meet your needs, you can create your own custom labels. The most helpful method is to find a label that comes closest and then select **E**dit. Make sure you have your ruler handy and then change the measurements to suit your needs. Follow the instructions in step 6, previous.

Printing on Sheets with Individual Labels

If you have the type of individual labels that come in individual sheets, here's what you'll need to do to use them:

1. Select **P**age from the **L**ayout pull-down menu.

2. Select Paper **S**ize/Type.

3. Select **C**reate.

4. Create a definition for a page the size of your label.

5. Choose OK and Close. You now can start typing your label.

TRICK

If you do have individual labels, it is usually much easier to just type or handwrite them than to print labels from WordPerfect. Many printers will not properly handle individual labels, too. You're better off letting WordPerfect only handle the larger label jobs.

Changing Back

If you changed your environment measurement above, don't forget to change it back to the measurement method you prefer before continuing. Follow these steps:

1. Starting from the main WordPerfect document screen, either press Shift-F1 or pull down the **F**ile menu and then choose Se**t**up

2. Choose **E**nvironment

3. Choose <u>U</u>nits of Measure

4. Select <u>D</u>isplay/Entry of Numbers, and then choose WP 4.2 Units (Lines/Columns)

5. Select <u>S</u>tatus Line Display, and then choose WP 4.2 Units (Lines/ Columns)

Label Groupies

The Label feature in WordPerfect is really meant to print a lot of labels at one time. If you need to print one label, but know that you'll be sending packages to that person in the future, it's easier to use the copy and paste features and make up an entire page of labels for that recipient. Use them at your convenience. Unlike refrigerated pizza, they won't go bad.

If you are making up lots of packages and need one label per package, then see Chapter 14, "Caution: Merge Ahead."

CHAPTER 8

A Word about Files

If there was only one word to describe file management with WordPerfect that word would have to be *nice*. Or maybe it would be *easy*. No, wait, how about friendly? Or, pleasurable, remarkable, congenial. Wow, that WordPerfect thesaurus is fun! Actually, file management isn't all that difficult, and in this chapter you'll read about:

 What files really are, where they come from, and where they go when they retire.

 The good, the bad, and the meaningless in file names.

 How to set up the WordPerfect File Manager to make the most of the way you work. Or, Laziness Made Easy with the WordPerfect File Manager.

 Taking advantage of QuickLists—a WordPerfect exclusive.

FOOD FOR THOUGHT

The discussion on disk drives and directory names assumes you have installed WordPerfect on the C drive in directories that it specifies during the installation. If WordPerfect was installed on a different drive or with different directory names, you need to substitute these names.

What Is a File?

WordPerfect 6.0 runs in the DOS operating system. DOS is really the boss of your computer. For this reason, WordPerfect must follow rules and conventions set by DOS.

FOOD FOR THOUGHT

WordPerfect runs in DOS just like thousands of other programs. The information in this section applies to any DOS file.

A *file* is a group of information—or *data*—stored under one name on your disk or in your computer's memory. The term *document* has been used throughout this book to refer to anything you create in WordPerfect. Each document is stored as a file on your disk as one piece of information. A document can be one word long or one million words long.

The Name Game: Understanding File Naming Conventions

WordPerfect must follow DOS rules for file names, just like any other DOS program. The rules in the file name game are primarily concerned with length and valid characters. You need to know these rules so you can save your work and understand what each file is.

 Length. A file name in DOS cannot be longer than eight characters. In addition, each file name can be followed by a period (called a "dot" in computerspeak) and an *extension*—three characters often used to identify the file. A file name can be shorter than eight characters, but "eight dot three" (in nerd lingo) is the maximum length. DOS understands a file name of "IRSLET" just as well as it does "IHATE.IRS". But "IHATETHEIRS.LET" is way too long.

Valid characters. You can use any alphabetic character and any numeric character in a file name. You can also use the characters ~!@#$%^&()_-{} in your file name. They aren't particularly useful for selecting meaningful file names (which is important), but you can use them.

 Illegal characters. UNDER NO CIRCUMSTANCES do you ever use a space, an asterisk (also called a "star"), a question mark, a forward slash (/), or a back slash (\) in a file name. DOS is confused by these characters in file names, which confuses you and helps no one. When you use one of these characters, you cannot look at your file again.

Good Conventions

A good file name is a descriptive file name. Granted, you can't fit much of a description in 11 characters (eight leading characters and a three letter extension), but you can make helpful names if you think ahead a little.

There is no wrong way or right way to name your files. The only "right" way is the one that works for you. For letters, most people use the extensions .LET, .LTR, or something similar. Many people use dates, an abbreviation, or initials in the file name. Another popular way to name things is incrementally; a number is included in the name that is bumped up one digit each time the user creates a document.

An example of a file name for a letter that uses initials and dates is "RJC0815.93." This is a perfectly valid file name and indicates a letter was written to a person with the initials RJC on August 15, 1993. Another example is "RJC01.LET." This is an example of using a person's initials, a number that will be incremented for the next letter to this person, and an extension of ".LET" to indicate this is a letter.

Names for documents are easier to think of. You can use the initials of the title of the document and maybe combine the initials with a revision number. For example, the first Deed of Trust you type could be called DOT01.DOC. Many people end their document names with a .DOC extension. They reserve a .FRM or .FOR extension for forms.

The Wild Cards

No, you won't find any pointers on poker here, but you can learn and take advantage of WordPerfect's File Manager.

A *wild card* is an asterisk (*) or question mark (?) that replaces a character or number of characters used in searching for a file name. To illustrate this dry idea, suppose you're looking for a letter and you want WordPerfect's File Manager to list all your documents that end in a .LET extension. You might try by asking, "WordPerfect, please list all my documents that end in a .LET extension." WordPerfect can't understand speech (yet), so you have to use a wild card. To see the files, you type ***.LET**. The asterisk tells WordPerfect that you don't care what the file names have before the .LET extension. You can also replace file name extensions with a wild card. To ask for all your documents that begin with the letter "B," for example, you type **B*.***. By using the asterisk, you are telling WordPerfect that you don't care if there are one or five characters, you just want to see all of them.

If you want to find all the documents with a few common characters in their file names, you use the question mark. Suppose you want to see all the Deeds of Trust you have made, and you type **DOT??.DOC**. This finds any document that has a file name that begins with DOT, has two more characters, and a .DOC extension. It will not find a document that has an additional three or more characters after the DOT and before the .DOC extension. If you had a DOT144.DOC, for instance, it wouldn't be listed using the DOT??.DOC entry. To find DOT144.DOC, you'd need to type **DOT???.DOC**.

You can find documents with no extension by using the period. If you request all Deeds of Trust with no extensions, for instance, you type **DOT***. This entry finds any DOT file that has no extension, no matter what it is. That same request also finds directories that begin with DOT, because directory names seldom (almost never) have an extension.

You can mix and match these wild cards in any way you want. In other words, you can use both the "?" and the "*" in one command. An example would be **DOT??.***. That would find all the files that begin with DOT, have five more characters, and end in any type of extension.

Files You Shouldn't Mess Around With

WordPerfect cannot read certain types of files. Other files can be read, but shouldn't be messed around with at all. Those are:

1. Files ending in .EXE or .COM. Those are *executables*, or programs that you run—like the WordPerfect program.

2. Files ending in .SYS, .BIN, .DRV. Those are special programs or files required by DOS, WordPerfect and other programs.

STOP!

Some of the files listed here can be read in by WordPerfect— after it converts them from another file format. BUT, if you read them in by accident, you should NEVER elect to **S**ave them. Just tell WordPerfect you want to **C**lose the files without saving them. If you **S**ave them with WordPerfect, you break them.

STOP!

If you feel comfortable working with your AUTOEXEC.BAT or CONFIG.SYS file, and you use WordPerfect to work with them, remember to save them in the ASCII Text (Standard) format or they will not work. When WordPerfect writes a file in the WordPerfect format, a lot of information is written to the beginning of the file. That information makes any batch file (AUTOEXEC.BAT) or configuration file (CONFIG.SYS) unusable.

If you are looking for a file that you wrote and you cannot remember the filename, it's okay to go ahead and try to read the file with WordPerfect. But if you see that it is not a document that you wrote, then you should just close the file without saving it.

What Is a Directory?

A *directory* is a bit like a label on a filing cabinet drawer. Directories are merely names—a way to help you organize your work.

Directory Tree

The DOS directory structure is often referred to as a *directory tree*. WordPerfect's File Manager displays a directory tree to help you access files. To see a directory tree of your computer:

1. Select **F**ile from the pull-down menu and then select **F**ile Manager, or press F5.

2. Select the Directory Tree button or press F8.

The Directory Tree window pops up and displays a directory tree of all the directories on your disk drive. Figure 8.1 shows the display from a directory tree, but yours will be different.

Figure 8.1:

Your basic directory tree.

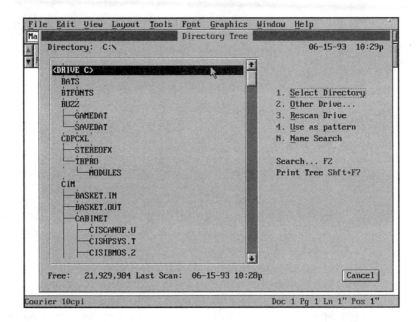

If the depiction in the File Manager window doesn't make sense, look at an upside-down tree or stand on your head and look at a right-side up tree. This may help provide a mental picture of the way your hard disk is organized.

The root and main trunk is the disk without any directories on it. Each directory is represented by a branch, and each file is represented by leaves on the branch. When directories are inside of other directories, they are referred to as subdirectories. Think of those as little twigs growing off a main branch.

Directory Suggestions

If you installed WordPerfect with the defaults (you didn't specify a different directory during the install), you have a directory on your hard disk called WPDOCS. This directory is ready and waiting for all those new files you create. Eventually, however, the WPDOCS directory becomes pretty crowded. With all those files in one directory, it might become difficult to find the file you need. Another problem is numerous unrelated files—a letter to your pen pal stuffed in the same directory as your recipes.

You need to consider making a few directories of your own. Your new directories can be inside of the WPDOCS directory (that would make them subdirectories), or you can create some directories off the root directory on the disk drive on which you installed WordPerfect (usually C:\). The *root directory* is the starting point for creating all your directories. The WPDOCS directory, for instance, is connected directly to the root directory.

You could make a directory for your letters, a directory for your forms, and a directory for your newsletter. If the work you do is more project-based, you could make a new directory for each major new project.

When you go exploring with the File Manager, you'll also see the term *Parent Directory*. That is the previous level up from the directory where you are at the moment. For instance, with the WPDOCS directory, the parent is the root directory. The root directory is as far as you can go and it has no parent. This is perfectly legitimate.

Follow the Right Path

When you ask WordPerfect to find your files, you will need to know the complete path name. The path name consists of three major parts:

 The disk drive letter (A, B, C, D, E, etc.)

 The directory name(s) (WPDOCS, or your directory name)

 The file name (IHATEIRS.LET, for example)

The complete path to the example here would be C:\WPDOCS\IHATEIRS.LET. Notice that all parts are separated by a backslash (\), which is why you cannot use the backslash in a file or directory name.

FOOD FOR THOUGHT

Don't forget that you cannot use a period (.), backslash (\), forward slash (/), question mark (?), or asterisk (*) in a file name.

WordPerfect expects to see a full path name when you ask to retrieve a document, but who wants to do all that typing? For convenience, you can set up the File Manager to do all your work.

Using the WordPerfect File Manager

The WordPerfect File Manager is accessed by selecting **F**ile from the pull-down menu and then selecting **F**ile Manager, or by pressing F5.

Go ahead and open the File Manager. You'll see a dialog box on-screen that reads Specify File Manager List (see fig. 8.2).

Figure 8.2:

The friendly File Manager.

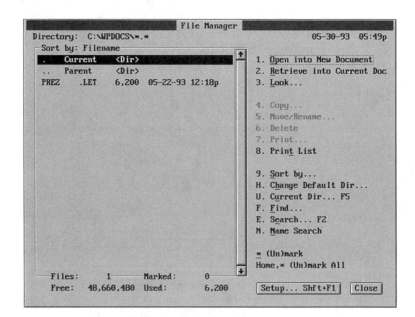

The Specify File Manager List dialog box seems basic, but each button in this dialog box accesses a number of different features. Aside from the Directory field for entering a directory, your choices include:

 QuickList... F6. A super-fast way to access files.

 Use QuickFinder... F4. A super-fast way to access very large groups of files (upwards of about 75 files or more).

 Directory Tree... F8. This gives you the "big picture" on all your files. This isn't nearly as much fun as the "big top," but it will have to do for now.

 Redo... F5. List the same directory that you listed the last time you used File Manager. Particularly useful if you exit File Manager without meaning to.

Accessing the Directory Tree and File Manager

To access the File Manager Directory Tree:

1. Select **F**ile from the pull-down menu and then select **F**ile Manager, or press F5.
2. Select Directory Tree or press F8.

After a second or two the Directory Tree window displays all the directories and subdirectories on your hard disk. As you can see, a number of operations are possible, including:

 Select Directory. Choose a specific directory to work with.

 Other Drive. Look at the contents of a directory on another drive with Directory Tree.

 Rescan Drive. Rescan the current drive (necessary when you add or delete directories).

Use as Pattern. Search for subdirectories or files in a directory with wild cards, using the currently highlighted directory to automatically fill in part of the path name.

 Name Search. Type in a specific name of a directory so you can jump to that location on the directory tree quickly. If you want to search for a subdirectory, it must contain the path name without the drive designator. Example: WPDOCS\BOOK.

 Search. Search for a directory or subdirectory without typing in the path (as in Name Search). Use the Backward Search option to search backwards in the tree from your current highlighted selection.

 Print Tree. Print a copy of the Directory Tree.

 ## FOOD FOR THOUGHT

If you add or delete directories on your hard drive, you want to **R**escan the drive. Once WordPerfect collects the information to show you here, it doesn't do it again unless you tell it to.

3. Highlight the directory you want to open and press Enter.

A new window, the File Manager, appears displaying more options that you may ever need. Your choices include:

 Open into New Document. Open a highlighted document (the default) into a new document. If you already have a document on your screen, this automatically opens a new Window and puts it there without disturbing your existing document.

 Retrieve into Current Doc. Open the highlighted document into the document window that you already have open on your screen. The new document begins at the current cursor location in the document window.

Look. Look at a document on your screen without calling it into the document window for editing. The **L**ook feature saves time because the document does not have to be formatted for the selected printer, as it does when you open a document for editing.

 Copy. Copy files.

 Move/Rename. Move and rename files without making copies.

 Delete. Delete files quickly and painlessly. If you are not sure this is a document you want to delete, use the **L**ook feature first.

 Print. Print files (you don't even have to open them).

 Print List. Make a printout of a directory's contents for reference.

 Sort by. Sort files for easier access.

 Change Default Dir. Change the default directory so that you can access your most often used files more quickly. This is also where you create new directories and subdirectories.

 Current Dir... F5. Change to another directory using the Specify File Manager List dialog box to get there painlessly.

 Find. Find a specific word or phrase in a file or find a file or group of files with wild cards.

 Search... F2. Search for files and directories. Check the Backward Search option when searching backwards in the list of files.

 Name Search. Search for file or directory names by typing in just the first few characters of the name.

 * (Un)mark. Mark or unmark one or several files for copy, move, delete, print, or Find operations.

 Home,* (Un)mark All. Mark or Unmarked all the files in the directory for copy, move, delete, print or find operations.

The Use as Pattern Command

The **U**se as Pattern function looks for directories, subdirectories or files in a directory. You must know the name of the directory in order to search for files. **U**se as Pattern completes a path name by filling in the currently selected directory.

FOOD FOR THOUGHT

If you are not sure what directories your files are in, you need to set up and use QuickFinder to locate them instead of U̲se as Pattern. See the section titled "Using QuickFinder" for details.

To use this time-saving feature:

1. Select **F**ile, **F**ile Manager, or press F5.

2. Select Directory Tree, or press F8.

3. Highlight the directory where you want to look for files.

4. Select **U**se as pattern.

5. In the Specify File Manager List dialog box, you add a backslash to the directory name, and then the exact file name, or a pattern you want to search for in that directory. A sample of what a complete entry in the Directory entry field would look like is `C:\WPDOCS\*.LET`. See the preceding section on wild cards if you're not sure what that asterisk means.

Creating a Directory in File Manager

You may want to create one or several directories to help you organize your documents. Organizing your files helps you find them easier and faster. Putting different types of documents in differently labeled directories and subdirectories is one way to organize.

To create a directory (or subdirectory), follow these steps:

1. Select **F**ile, **F**ile Manager, or press F5.

2. In the Specify File Manager List dialog box the Directory entry field should default to `C:\WPDOCS\`. If not, type it in.

FOOD FOR THOUGHT

If you installed WordPerfect on a drive other than C, or changed the default document directory from **WPDOCS** *to another name, you will need to make the appropriate adjustment as you follow these steps.*

3. Press Enter. Now the File Manager window is on your screen.

4. Select **C**hange Default Dir. The Change Default Directory dialog box is now showing.

5. Press the End key so that your cursor is at the end of the C:\WPDOCS entry.

6. Type in a backslash (\) and your new subdirectory name. For our example, we will use **LETTERS**. The entire entry would look like this: `C:\WPDOCS\LETTERS`.

7. Press Enter or click on OK.

8. You should see a confirmation box that says `Create Directory` `C:\WPDOCS\LETTERS?` or whatever the directory is that you named. Choose **Y**es.

Now you see an entry in your **WPDOCS** directory that looks similar to the one in figure 8.3!

Copying Files in File Manager

Copying your files to disk as an additional means of backing up your work is always a good idea. You may also want to copy files to different names on your hard disk so that you can use them as a head start in typing a new, but similar document. To use the File Manager to copy files:

1. Select **F**ile, **F**ile Manager, or press F5.

2. Tell File Manager what directory the file is located in by typing the entry in the Specify File Manager List dialog box and pressing Enter. As an alternative, use the Directory Tree (F8) and proceed with the **U**se as Pattern function to select the directory.

Figure 8.3:

The new directory.

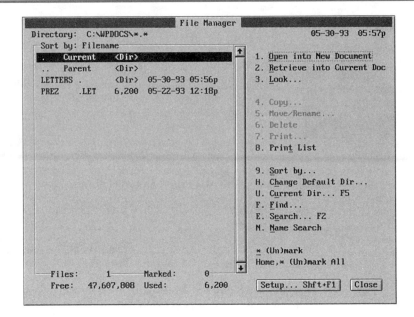

3.   Once you have selected the directory and pressed the enter key, the File Manager screen appears. Highlight the file using the Down Arrow key, the F2 Search, or the **N**ame Search option from the list of options to the right of the window.

4.   Select **C**opy.

The Copy dialog box shows on-screen. The Copy Highlighted File to entry field defaults with the full path name of the file you want to copy. Because you cannot copy a file onto itself, this field needs to be edited.

5.   Edit the Copy Highlighted File to entry field using the Right and Left arrow keys to move around and the Del key to erase the portion not needed. Type in the changes or additions needed to make a full path name.

As an example, you might have a document that would appear in the Copy Highlighted File entry field that reads `C:\WPDOCS\LETTERS\IHATEIRS.LET`. To copy this file to the disk in drive A, the field would need to be edited to read `A:\IHATEIRS.LET`.

6.   After the entry field is edited, press Enter or click on OK.

TRICK

Explore the Directory Tree (F8) and QuickList (F6) options on the Copy dialog box (explained in this chapter) for aid in looking for the directory where you want the file copied.

That's all there is to copying a file.

Deleting Files and Directories in File Manager

It's always a good idea to take care of "housecleaning" on your hard disk periodically. Keep your hard disk clear by either copying files to a disk (and putting that in a safe place) or deleting them, or a combination of both. Doing so will help to keep disk space available for new documents.

The Delete function can delete both files and directories. To do either, just follow the bouncing ball:

1. Select **F**ile, **F**ile Manager, or press F5.

2. Tell File Manager where the directory or file is located by typing the entry in the Specify File Manager List dialog box and pressing Enter. As an alternative, use the Directory Tree (F8) and proceed with the **U**se as Pattern function to select the directory or file.

3. Once you have selected the directory and pressed the enter key, the File Manager screen appears. Highlight the file or directory using either the down-arrow key, the F2 Search, or the **N**ame Search option from the list of options to the right of the window.

4. Select the **D**elete option. You can also press the Del key on your keyboard.

5. WordPerfect prompts you to confirm your selection, just in case you made a mistake when you pressed the **D**elete key. Go ahead and confirm by selecting the **Y**es button.

SAVE THE DAY

If you are not 100-percent positive/sure/certain that you want to delete the file, answer **N**o to this question. Then select the **L**ook option from the option list to view the file prior to deleting it. If you are indeed certain that you want to delete the document, you can select the **D**elete option while viewing it.

FOOD FOR THOUGHT

DOS (and WordPerfect) will not let you delete a directory if there are any files inside the directory. You receive an error message if you attempt to do so.

Opening a File

When you have a file highlighted in the File Manager window, the first two options in the list to the right are **O**pen into New Document and **R**etrieve into Current Document. The difference between these two commands revolves around whether the file you select opens in a new document window or is added to an existing document:

 If you already have a document on-screen, the **O**pen option switches to a new window that has no document in it before it opens the file you requested.

 If you already have a document on-screen, the **R**etrieve option places the file at the spot where your cursor was before you went into the File Manager.

 If you do not already have a document on-screen, there is no difference.

How To Look at Your Document in File Manager

One of the more valuable options on the File Manager window is the **L**ook option. By highlighting a file and then pressing **L**, you can become a Looky-Loo so that you know just what the file contains before you do anything with it. When you use **L**ook to look at a document you can:

 Look at the **P**revious or **N**ext document without returning to the File Manager window.

 Scroll through the document. This quickly scrolls your screen to the bottom of the document you are viewing.

 Delete the document.

 Mark the document.

 Open the document into a new document window.

You cannot edit the document in this window; you have to **O**pen it to edit it.

Move/Rename

STOP!

When you move or rename a file, you are not making any copies of the document—you are working with the original. Until you are really comfortable working with files, you might want to make a copy of a file using the **C**opy command before using **M**ove/Rename so that you always have the original as a backup.

1. Select **F**ile, **F**ile Manager, or press F5.

2. Tell File Manager where the file is located by typing the entry in the Specify File Manager List dialog box and pressing Enter. As an alternate, you could use the Directory Tree (F8) and proceed with the **U**se as Pattern function to select the directory or file.

3. Once you have selected the directory and pressed Enter, the File Manager screen appears. Highlight the file using either the Down Arrow key, the F2 Search, or the **N**ame Search option from the list of options to the right of the window.

4. Select the **M**ove/Rename option.

5. The Move/Rename dialog box appears on the screen. The New Name entry field defaults with the full path name of the file you want to Move/Rename. This field needs to be edited.

6. Edit the Move/Rename entry field using the right- and left-arrow keys to move around and the Del key to erase the portion not needed. Type in the changes or additions needed to make a full path name.

7. Press the enter key or click on OK.

There is no confirmation box to verify the new name or location of the file since this is not a destructive operation. In other words, the file is not deleted, so you can always correct any typo by repeating the operation.

Printing in File Manager

From the File Manager screen, selecting the **P**rint option brings up the Print Multiple Page window. From here you can print the file directly from the disk without having to look at it or open it first. You can even print all or part of a document from this window.

1. Select **F**ile, **F**ile Manager, or press F5.

2. Tell File Manager where the file is located by typing the entry in the Specify File Manager List dialog box and pressing Enter. As an alternative, use the Directory Tree (F8) and proceed with the **U**se as Pattern function to select the directory or file.

3. Once you have selected the directory and pressed the enter key, the File Manager screen appears. Highlight the file using the down-arrow key, the F2 Search, or the **N**ame Search option from the list of options to the right of the window.

4. Select the **P**rint option.

5. The Print Multiple Pages dialog box shows on the screen. Press Enter to print the entire document or select Item 1, **P**age/Label Range and type in the specific pages that you want to print. Individual pages are separated by a comma (example: 1,5,6,9) and ranges of pages are separated by a dash (example: 1-3,5-8,).

The Prin**t** List command prints the list of files shown in the window on the left side of your screen, rather than printing any actual files.

Using Setup and Sort by in the File Manager

The **S**ort by option in the File Manager and the **S**etup button at the bottom of the screen display the same window—File Manager Setup. File Manager Setup helps you display File Manager files in a number of different ways:

 Sort List by. You can sort the list of files by any of these criteria:

File name (default).

Extension type.

Date/time that the file was created or last saved.

Size.

No sort. No sort means the names appear in the order that they are recorded on your disk.

 Display List **M**ode. You will be selecting a DOS file name, unless you decide to use the Document Summary feature when saving all your documents. If you use Document Summary, you can fill in the Descriptive Name entry field and use that name to list all your files with the File Manager. Although DOS and WordPerfect only use 11 characters for a file name, you can use much longer file names by using these options.

D̲escending Sort. No matter what criteria you used in the **S̲ort List by** option, you can show the files in descending order (sorted by ZYX...). The default is ascending order (ABC...).

 W̲P Documents Only. This option only displays documents in the WordPerfect format. It will not show any files that were made with another program. It will also not show documents that were edited with WordPerfect, but stored in another format. It doesn't matter what the document is named, WordPerfect knows if it is a WordPerfect document. Documents made with previous (versions 4.0 through 5.2) of WordPerfect are valid WordPerfect documents.

FOOD FOR THOUGHT

WordPerfect 6.0 can read several different format types, including different versions and types of:

AmiPro
ASCII
Displaywrite
DOS Delimited
IBM DCA
MS Word
MS Word for Windows
Rich Text Format
WordPerfect
WordStar

 Compressed P̲rint for List. If you have a really long list of files, this is a good option to choose. It won't affect the display you see, but when you select the Prin̲t list option this causes your list of files to print in smaller type so that you can fit more files on a printed page.

Current Dir and Changing Default Directory

The Ch̲ange Default Dir option is the answer when you want a specific directory to appear when you call up File Manager.

1. Select **F**ile, **F**ile Manager, Directory Tree, or press F5, F8.

2. Select the directory you want to appear first every time you access File Manager. If your home is mouseless, highlight the directory and press Enter.

3. At the File Manager screen, choose C**h**ange Default Dir.

   The path to the directory you selected appears in the New Directory field.

4. Click on OK or press Enter.

   The Specify File Manager dialog box appears.

5. Click on OK again or press Enter to return to the File Manager screen.

It's a good idea to make the directory you use the most the default directory. No sense in a lot of unnecessary moving between directories.

Use the C**u**rrent Dir option when you want to work in a different directory that you don't want to become the default directory.

Using Find to Search for Specific Words

The **F**ind command in the File Manager enables you to search through all the files in the current directory for a particular word or phrase. If you have many files, this can help you find specific documents much more quickly than looking through all of them.

To access this feature:

1. Select **F**ile, **F**ile Manager, Directory Tree, or press F5, F8.

2. Tell File Manager what directory the files are located in by typing the entry in the Specify File Manager List dialog box and pressing Enter. As an alternative, use the Directory Tree (F8) function.

3. Choose **F**ind.

When you select **F**ind, a window pops up with lots of choices (see fig. 8.4):

 Name. Finds a specific file name when you type only part of the name.

 Document Summary. Searches through document summaries (looks in all the Document Summary dialog boxes) for a particular word.

 First Page. Enables you to search through the first page of every document shown in the file list. If WordPerfect finds the word you're looking for in any of the documents, you will see a new File Manager window with just those documents listed. If WordPerfect doesn't find any documents that contain that word, you see a confirmation box that says no matching files were found. To return to the entire list of files, select **<Current>** at the top of the file list and press Enter to return to the Specify File Manager List dialog box. Press Enter once more to return to the directory.

Figure 8.4:

Quite a Find, eh?

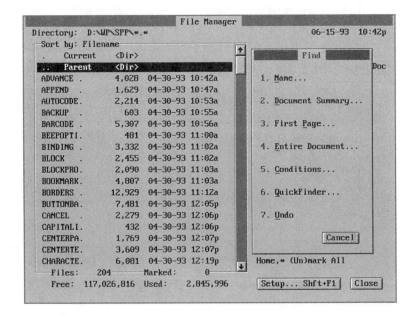

Entire Document. Performs the same search that the First Page search does, except it searches the entire document for a match. Obviously, searching an entire document takes more time than just one page, and if you have a lot of long documents this could take a while.

 Conditions. Helpful for reducing the time it takes to perform separate searches with the First Page, Entire Document, and Document Summary searches. With the **C**onditions search you can narrow down the options by selecting bits and pieces from all or part of the other types of searches so you don't have to do two or three separate searches to find just what you are looking for. Enter the same word or phrase you would if you were performing separate searches.

 QuickFinder. See the section on **Q**uickFinder later in this chapter. On large groups of documents (upwards of about 75 or more) QuickFinder can perform searches faster. It creates an index of documents that is faster for the computer to read.

 Undo. Undoes (that's not a word!) the search you just performed.

Search and Name Search in File Manager

The **S**earch and **N**ame Search commands do the same job they do in the Directory Tree. That is, S**e**arch finds the first match that has the letters you type anywhere in the word, and **N**ame Search finds the closest match to the beginning of what you typed.

1. Select **F**ile, **F**ile Manager, Directory Tree, or press F5, F8.

2. Double-click on the directory you want to examine. If your home is mouseless, highlight the directory and press Enter.

3. At the File Manager screen Choose S**e**arch or **N**ame Search to quickly select the file you want to work with.

FOOD FOR THOUGHT

$\underline{S}$earch and $\underline{N}$ame Search are useful replacements for using the down- and up-arrow keys for selecting files to work with in File Manager. If there are only a few files in a directory, the arrow keys are a faster way to select your files.

TRICK

If your currently highlighted location of the list of files is below the one you want to search for, don't forget to check the Backward Search checkbox when you use $\underline{S}$earch.

(Un)mark in File Manager

If you want to $\underline{C}$opy, $\underline{D}$elete, $\underline{M}$ove/$\underline{R}$ename, or $\underline{P}$rint a whole lot of files, you can mark them with an asterisk. You can mark an individual file or a group.

TRICK

Sometimes it is easier to mark the entire directory and then unmark the ones you don't want.

1. Click on $\underline{F}$ile, $\underline{F}$ile Manager, Directory Tree, or press F5, F8.

2. Tell File Manager what directory the file(s) are located in by typing the entry in the Specify File Manager List dialog box and pressing Enter. As an alternative, use the Directory Tree (F8) function.

3. Once you have selected the directory and pressed the enter key, the File Manager screen appears. Highlight the file using either the down-arrow key, the F2 Search, or the $\underline{N}$ame Search option from the list of options to the right of the window.

4. To mark a file, highlight the first file to be marked and press the asterisk key (*****) or press the Spacebar.

    You'll see the asterisk appear next to the file name.

5. You can continue marking files this way until all the desired files are marked. To mark or unmark all the files in the current list, press Home, *****, or Alt-F5.

Once you've marked the files you want to work with, you can **C**opy, **M**ove/**R**ename, **D**elete, or **P**rint them all at once.

Using the QuickList

WordPerfect includes a file organization tool called the *QuickList* that lets you define groups of files, and then tell WordPerfect where those files are located and how they are named. With the QuickList window you can quickly access all your letters (or faxes, or whatever) that fit in a particular group.

To really make the File Manager useful, you will want to keep the QuickList as up-to-date as necessary. You can add to or delete entries from the QuickList information about directories whenever you want.

To add a new LETTERS subdirectory to your Quicklist, for instance, follow along:

1. Select **F**ile (from the pull-down menu) and then **F**ile Manager, or press F5.

2. Select QuickList by pressing F6.

3. Select **C**reate. The description can be as long as the entry field window allows. For this example, type **Important Letters**, then press Enter.

4. At the Filename/Directory: entry field, type in the path of the file or directory you want to add to the Important Letters group. For example, type **C:\WPDOCS\LETTERS** and press Enter. Click on OK or press Enter again.

You just added the description "Important Letters" to the QuickList. When you select "Important Letters," you automatically access the LETTERS subdirectory. That's all there is to adding to the QuickList!

FOOD FOR THOUGHT

Of course, the QuickList entries will only be useful if the directories they refer to actually exist. See the section on "Creating a New Directory in File Manager" for details on creating the directories.

TRICK

Make the most of QuickLists. If you keep different types of documents in one directory, but have standardized on a naming convention (that is, Deeds of Trust = .DOT, Promissory Notes = .NOT, etc.), then make more than one entry in QuickList for the same directory using wild cards. For an example you can use one description for Deeds (Deeds of Trust) and the directory entry would be C:\WPDOCS\FORMS*.DOT. Another entry for the same subdirectory would have a description of "Promissory Notes" with a directory entry of C:\WPDOCS\FORMS*.NOT.

Using your QuickList entries is as easy as:

1. Pressing F5 to access File Manager, then F6 to access QuickLists.

2. Double-clicking on Important Letters, or highlighting it and pressing Enter.

3. Blammo, you're there! Find that important file and get to it.

TRICK

You probably will use the QuickList frequently. You may have noticed that the display on your QuickList is sorted alphabetically. To help make the QuickList even quicker, **E**dit the descriptions in the QuickList so that your more frequently used entries appear at the top and the entries you almost never use appear at the bottom of the screen. You can do this by adding a number—or a letter of the alphabet—as the first character you type in the Description entry field.

CHAPTER 9

Get Serious with Styles and Other Fancy Stuff

You can bet that if our nation's Founding Fathers had used WordPerfect to prepare the Declaration of Independence, they wouldn't have needed to rewrite the whole thing several times to perfect it. Just think—if they had used WordPerfect, their document might have been ready several weeks earlier, in time for kids to get another school holiday!

Well, you can't rewrite history with WordPerfect, but that doesn't mean you have to rewrite your document every time you want to make a change or two.

In this chapter you can see some amazingly simple-to-use features that ensure a professional-looking document every time! Just send $99.95 to... oh, that's right, you already did. (We hope you got your Ginsu knives, too.)

The features covered include:

 Stylish outlines (one size doesn't have to fit all)

 How to save the widows and orphans

 Neatening up your document by getting rid of widows and orphans

 Protecting your blocks of text

The Latest in Styles

Styles are similar to Document Initial Codes in that you can define a whole bunch of formatting codes and apply them all at once. The difference is that you can create the codes you want for only one line or one paragraph, as well as for a whole document. Once the codes are created, you can use them anywhere in a document, at any time, without having to constantly retype them. You can keep using the same codes, in fact. For example, if you constantly have to shift back and forth between using text that is bold, underlined, italic, and small caps, and regular normal text, you could use styles to automate the process. If you have certain sets of formatting codes that you frequently use, setting up styles will save you a lot of time because you can apply the style that contains all those formatting codes very quickly—far more quickly than formatting step-by-step.

Another nice thing about styles is that if you use a style in several places in a document, you can change the style if you change your mind, instead of having to change individual codes throughout the document. For instance, you create a style to center, bold, and underline a heading, and later decide that the heading should not be underlined. You can simply take the underline code out of the style and the change will take place everywhere that particular style code was used. This eliminates having to go back through your document and make the same edit over and over again.

Creating a Style

Styles aren't that hard to create if you know exactly what the style is supposed to do. Before you start clicking buttons, think about the purpose of each style. In addition, think of a good naming scheme for each style. WordPerfect enables you to designate each style with a three-letter heading or a few words.

To illustrate creating styles, use an example. Create a style that centers, bolds, and underlines your text.

1. From a blank document, select **L**ayout,**S**tyles or press Alt-F8. You see a screen just like the one in figure 9.1.

2. Select **C**reate from the Style List window.

3. In the Style Name entry field, type **CUB** (for Center, Underline, Bold) and press Enter.

Figure 9.1:

Getting into Styles.

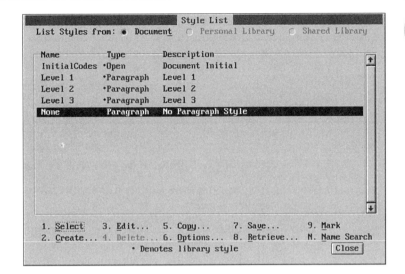

Now you need to decide the Style type. Your choices for style types include:

 Paragraph Style. A paragraph style affects one entire paragraph, or all the text between two hard returns (places where you pressed Enter). In fact, this is the definition of a paragraph as far as WordPerfect is concerned. Headings are a good example of a place to use the paragraph style because WordPerfect sees a heading as a complete paragraph, albeit a short one. You also can apply a paragraph style to a chunk of blocked text.

 Character Style. Affects blocked text or text you are about to type, and is useful mainly for words and phrases.

 Open Style. Affects all text from the cursor to the end of the document.

4. Because you want to use the CUB style for headings (at least you do in this example), select the Paragraph style. Because this is the default, you can leave this alone.

The **C**reate from Current Paragraph checkbox uses whatever set of formatting codes that are being used at the present time and makes those codes part of the style code that you're creating. That's not necessarily a good thing to do, however. If you create a style that makes a paragraph underlined and bold, for example, and then use that style in a different document, the new document will get all of the formatting that was in the original document, including things like the font, margin settings, and so on. Depending on what you want your style to do, this may or may not be your intention.

5. Click on OK or press Enter to begin creating the style.

6. Select **D**escription, type **Center/Underline/Bold** in the **D**escription field, and press Enter.

7. Now select Style **C**ontents. Hey, your screen changes to show you all the types of codes you can put in your Style code! As a matter of fact, your screen should look just like the one in figure 9.2.

Figure 9.2:

Calvin Klein never had it this good.

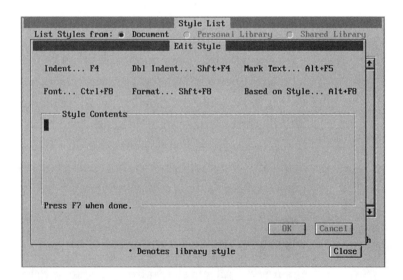

The two types of formatting codes that you need for your style are Format and Font.

8. Press Shift-F8 to select Format.

Yet another window pops up with more choices than you'd have on *The Price Is Right!*. The itsy-bitsy Format dialog box contains options for formatting any type of textual element you can have in a document.

9. Select **L**ine.

10. Select **J**ustification, and then select **C**enter.

11. Press Enter or click on OK and then close the Format window. The **[JUST]** code appears in the Style Contents window.

12. Press Ctrl-F8 to select Font.

13. Select **A**ppearance, and then **B**old. Select **A**ppearance and then **U**nderline. Click on OK to exit the Font dialog box.

Now your Style window looks like the one in figure 9.3.

Figure 9.3:

Eat my dust, Oscar de la Renta!

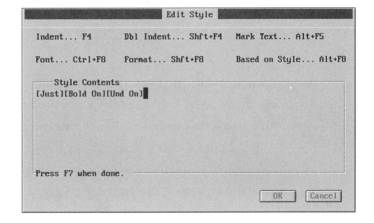

14. Press F7 to tell WordPerfect you are finished entering your codes.

15. Just to see what happens, click on the Show Style **O**ff Codes checkbox (or press O).

This will pop up a little window that will show you what codes will be inserted into your document when the style is turned off.

Off codes for bold and underline (the [Bold Off] and [Underline Off] codes) do not appear at this point. A good use for Show Style **O**ff Codes is if you want a one-time code put in your document after you finish using the style. Something like a hard page break maybe.

16.   Click on **E**nter Key Action... Off/On.

The **E**nter Key Action... Off/On option displays a mini dialog box that you can use to customize what happens when you press Enter when a style code is active. Your options include:

 Insert a Hard Return. This selection is available if you are working with a Character Style or Paragraph Style. Because these types of styles are used for a few words or phrases, you probably do not want a hard return to appear every time you press Enter.

 Turn Style Off. If you want to be able to turn off the style by pressing Enter, this is a handy feature. This moves the cursor past the style code.

 Turn Style Off and Back On. This option causes the style to turn off when you press Enter, and then turn back on for the next paragraph. Although it may sound as though this will put a lot of extra codes in your document, this is the best way to work with outlines. By using this option, you can go back and insert regular text easily and still have the style on in the places you want.

 Turn Style Off and Link to. This option enables you to jump into another style when you press Enter.

For your pretend CUB style, choose the Turn Style Off option. When you press Enter, the style will turn off and you won't have to do it manually.

17.   Select Turn Style Off and then click on the OK button.

18.   Now click on OK in the Edit Style window.

19.   You're finally finished creating a style! You now can save it by clicking on Sa**v**e (press 7) in the Style List window. Save your new style with the name CUB.STY. (WordPerfect uses .STY as the extension on styles.) Click on OK after you name your new style.

20. Click on Close to exit the Style List window. Now type **DOCUMENT'S TITLE** (or whatever) and press Enter. Notice that the cursor moved over to the far left margin, and when you type, the type is not centered, underlined, or bold.

Applying a Style to Text

If you followed the steps in the preceding section and created a style called CUB, you can apply the style to new text you type right after you close the Style List window. If you want to apply a style to text that already exists in your little masterpiece, you need to follow these steps.

If you are using the ribbon:

1. Locate the second field from the left on the ribbon bar. Normally, it says "None."

2. Click on the small down arrow to the right of that field.

3. Either scroll through the list until you find the style you want and select it, or type the name of the style you want.

TRICK

If the handy Ribbon isn't on-screen, pull down the <u>V</u>iew menu and choose <u>R</u>ibbon.

Another method to access styles without the ribbon bar is almost as easy:

1. Select <u>L</u>ayout,<u>S</u>tyles or press Alt-F8.

2. Highlight CUB and choose <u>S</u>elect.

3. Now type **DOCUMENT'S SUBTITLE** (or whatever) and press Enter.

Great! You can see how styles sure save a lot of keystrokes normally made by selecting all those options individually.

Changing Styles

Besides saving lots of keystrokes, styles also eliminate the need to make individual changes to every place you used one particular style. Suppose, for example, you create a style called CUB (Center, Underline, Bold) for all the headings in your 238-page report, and you decide the underline isn't such a good idea. To get rid of the underline, you only have to make a change in one place—the Edit Style window. To do that, follow these steps:

1. Select the **L**ayout pull-down menu and choose **S**tyles, or press Alt-F8.

2. Highlight CUB and choose **E**dit.

3. Select Style **C**ontents.

4. Use the right-arrow key to move the cursor until it's on the **[Und On]** code, then press Del.

5. Press F7 to tell WordPerfect you are finished with your editing.

6. Press Enter twice or click on OK in the Edit Style window and then click on Close in the Style List window.

That's it! Every place where you used the CUB style no longer has the underline. This certainly is an easy way to make fast changes!

Hopefully this example illustrates how easy it is to change existing styles. Now if only changing your vices were that easy!

Stylish Outlines

Before you begin to work on your latest masterpiece, it's always wise to prepare an outline of the structure and flow of the text. One of the nice styles WordPerfect has already created is an Outline style. WordPerfect also put that style in a special Outline menu function and provided a whole bunch of outlining choices.

If you're starting a brand-new document, you probably have an idea about the main subject matter, but you might not know how you want it to begin or what type of structure it will have. A basic outline may help you get started. To create an outline:

1. Select **T**ools,**O**utline,Out**l**ine options, or press Ctrl-F5. A bunch of options will appear, as shown in figure 9.4.

Figure 9.4:

The new national craze: outlining.

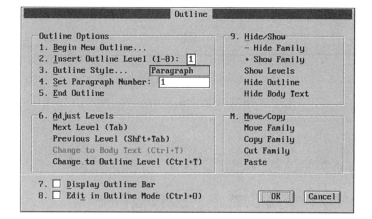

```
┌─────────────────────── Outline ───────────────────────┐
│ ┌─Outline Options────────────────┐ ┌─9. Hide/Show──────┐ │
│ │ 1. Begin New Outline...        │ │  - Hide Family    │ │
│ │ 2. Insert Outline Level (1-8): 1│ │  + Show Family    │ │
│ │ 3. Outline Style...  Paragraph │ │    Show Levels    │ │
│ │ 4. Set Paragraph Number: 1     │ │    Hide Outline   │ │
│ │ 5. End Outline                 │ │    Hide Body Text │ │
│ └────────────────────────────────┘ └───────────────────┘ │
│ ┌─6. Adjust Levels───────────────┐ ┌─M. Move/Copy──────┐ │
│ │   Next Level (Tab)             │ │    Move Family    │ │
│ │   Previous Level (Shft+Tab)    │ │    Copy Family    │ │
│ │   Change to Body Text (Ctrl+T) │ │    Cut Family     │ │
│ │   Change to Outline Level (Ctrl+T)│ │  Paste          │ │
│ └────────────────────────────────┘ └───────────────────┘ │
│ 7. □ Display Outline Bar                                  │
│ 8. □ Edit in Outline Mode (Ctrl+O)    [ OK ]  [Cancel]   │
└──────────────────────────────────────────────────────────┘
```

2. Select **B**egin New Outline. A list of all the outline styles will appear.

3. Using the up arrow, highlight the name **Outline** and then **S**elect it (press Enter). You will return to your document, which will already have an 'I' inserted for your first line.

Yep, as easy as 1-2-3! Now type **Learning to Use Outline** and press Enter. As you can see, when you press Enter, WordPerfect moves you to the next line, with the proper outline letter all ready for your next item! What if you want to type the next level of the outline right here? Simply press Tab and the number II suddenly turns into an A. If you change your mind about making this an A item, use the Shift-Tab combination and ta-da! There you are, at the Roman numerals again!

4. To end working on your outline, select **T**ools,**O**utline, and then **E**nd Outline. This turns off the outline and lets you continue typing.

Understanding Widows and Orphans

In word processing lingo, a *widow* is the first line of a paragraph left all alone at the bottom of a page. An *orphan*, conversely, is the last line of a paragraph left all alone at the top of a page.

Believe it or not, WordPerfect even has a dialog box for widows and orphans. Before you begin a long document, you might want to engage this option by checking the Widow/Orphan protect checkbox in the Other Format window. To get there:

1. Select **L**ayout,**O**ther or press Shift-F8,O.

2. Choose **W**idow/Orphan protect, then press Enter.

With this option selected, your document won't have any sentence stragglers on the top or bottom of pages.

WordPerfect's Special Formatting Features

WordPerfect considers a paragraph to be text separated by a hard return. Two common situations exist in which WordPerfect interprets text as a paragraph that we consider something else.

TRICK

WordPerfect 6.0 includes something called "drag and drop" editing. This name may conjure up all sorts of awful images, but this feature is actually very handy, er, helpful. With drag and drop, you can move text in one quick sequence of mouse events. If you have a mouse, try it out:

1. Highlight a block of text with your mouse and then release the mouse button.

2. Move your mouse pointer over the marked text, so that the tip is inside the marked area.

3. Press down on your left mouse button and hold it down. While you are holding it down, move to another place in the document. In Graphics mode, your mouse pointer will change to indicate that you are dragging text.

4. When the small vertical bar that follows your mouse is in exactly the place where you want to move the text, release the mouse button.

Presto! Your text is moved with very little hassle.

Conditional End of Page Feature

What if you want to put two headings in your document separated by two hard returns? You want to keep both lines of the heading together along with two lines of the following text, so that you don't have any lonely headings all by themselves at the bottom of a page. The **W**idow/Orphan Protect option, which keeps paragraphs together on the same page, isn't of much use here.

For this example, use the **C**onditional End of Page feature in the Other Format dialog box. To access and engage this feature:

1. Position your cursor at the line just above where you want the text to be together (even if there is text on that line).

2. Choose **L**ayout,**O**ther.

3. In the Other Format dialog box, select the **C**onditional End of Page checkbox. Now specify how many lines you want to keep together. In this particular example, you want to connect six lines. The blank lines count as a line even though there is no text on them.

4. Press Enter twice.

Now your special heading section will always be together and won't wrap.

Using the Block Protect Feature

Another type of textual element that isn't protected from being split in two when some of it moves to another page is a short list, column, or table. The **W**idow/Orphan Protect option is supposed to keep paragraphs together so that the first or last sentence doesn't appear on a page all by itself. **W**idow/Orphan Protect doesn't protect lists, columns, or tables, however, from being split in two. Suppose you want to include an address in your document. The address would look pretty dumb if you had part of it on one page and part on the next. Fortunately, you can prevent these embarrassments.

WordPerfect provides the Block Protect feature to group together long lists and irregularly formatted text. To take advantage of Block Protect, you have to highlight the text you want to hold together:

1. Block (highlight) the text you want to keep together.

2. Select **L**ayout,**O**ther.

The all-purpose Other Format window appears.

3.   Select **B**lock Protect.

Headers, Footers, and Watermarks

A *header* is text or a graphic that is printed at the top of each page of your document, automatically. A *footer* is exactly the same, except it prints at the bottom of your pages. For example, this book has headers that identify the chapter and section that you're currently reading. These headers are handled automatically by the production software that the publisher uses. You can do much the same thing with WordPerfect.

A *watermark* is a figure or text that prints in very light grey type on your document, with the real text of your document printed normally and "superimposed" on top of the watermark. While not all printers can print watermarks that will look good, most laser printers can do a credible job with them. Watermarks are not generally called for in most personal or business correspondence, however, and are rarely used.

All three of these things, headers, footers, and watermarks, are called *insertions*.

Creating a Header, Footer, or Watermark

Headers, footers, and watermarks are all created the same way in WordPerfect. To create one of these in your document, follow these steps:

1.   Pull down the **L**ayout menu and choose **H**eader/Footer/Watermark. (How's that for a menu item name? Yuck!)

2.   The Header/Footer/Watermark dialog box will appear, as shown in figure 9.5.

Under each of the three sections on the dialog box (**H**eaders, **F**ooters, and **W**atermarks), you will find the options to create up to two different insertions. For example, under **H**eaders, you will find an option for Header A and for Header B. **F**ooters and **W**atermarks have this same capability. This is so that you can define alternating insertions. For example, you might want to have different headers, footers, or watermarks on odd and even pages.

Figure 9.5:

The Header/Footer/
Watermark dialog box.

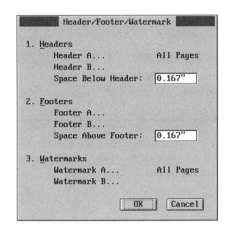

When you select option A under either of these three sections, a dialog box appears; WordPerfect will ask you if you want to create the insertion on **A**ll Pages, **E**ven Pages, or **O**dd Pages. If you want the same header, footer, or watermark on every page, then just define option A and tell WordPerfect to create it for **A**ll Pages.

You will also notice that the **H**eaders section has an option called **S**pace Below Header, and that **F**ooters has an option called **S**pace Above Footer. These control how much space WordPerfect will keep between the header or footer and the text of your document.

After you choose to create a header, footer, or watermark, you will be taken to what appears to be a blank document. In fact, it is a separate area where you type what you want to use for your insertion. You can even import graphics, just like in a normal document! When you have finished typing the text you want to use, just press F7 to return to your real document. When you press F7, your insertion is created, and can be seen by previewing your document (Shift-F7,V).

FOOD FOR THOUGHT

Headers and footers don't appear on your editing screen in Text or Graphics viewing modes. They only appear when you are working in the Page viewing mode.

*You can see watermarks only when you preview your document with Shift-F7,V, or by pulling down the **F**ile menu and choosing Print Pre**v**iew.*

Footnotes and Endnotes

A *footnote* is a numbered note at the bottom of the page that contains a reference to a note in the text. Some books also use *endnotes*, which place all the notes at the end of the chapter or book.

To create a footnote or endnote in your document, follow these steps:

1. Move your cursor so that it is at the end of the word that will be explained in your note.

2. Pull down the **L**ayout menu, choose **F**ootnote or **E**ndnote and then **C**reate.

3. You will be taken to a blank document screen where you can type your note. You will also see a small number right next to your note; this is the number of the footnote or endnote.

4. Type your note or reference and press F7.

5. When you return to your document, you will see that the number of the note has been automatically inserted by WordPerfect. Your footnote will appear at the bottom of that page when you print, or at the end of your document if you chose to use an endnote.

TRICK

To make sure a "continued" message prints at the bottom of a footnote that has to go to more than one page, be sure to select the checkbox option called Print **C**ontinued Message in the **O**ptions selection of the **F**ootnote or **E**ndnote menu option.

Inserting Comments

When you are editing someone else's work, you may need to insert comments into the document that your writer can read, but that will not print. To do this in WordPerfect:

1. Move your cursor to where you want the comment to appear.

2. Pull down the **L**ayout menu and choose Comme**n**t and then **C**reate.

3. Type your comment and press F7.

Your comment will be inserted into the text, surrounded by a double line border.

FOOD FOR THOUGHT

Comments can only be seen when you are in the Text or Graphics viewing mode. Page mode will not show comments.

Bonus! Bonus! Bonus! The Filename Feature

WordPerfect 6.0 includes a real treat called the Filename feature. Anyone who uses WordPerfect and has more than three documents on their disk should use this nifty feature as an aid to finding documents.

At the end of your document, follow these steps:

1. Select **L**ayout,**O**ther,Insert **F**ilename, or press Shift-F8,7.

2. Select Insert **F**ilename or Insert **P**ath and Filename, depending on which type of marker you want to include.

A [filename] code is inserted in your document at the cursor's location. When you print the document, the name of the file will be printed there. Many folks make the font for the [filename] code small so that it doesn't draw too much attention. After all, this is a tool for you, not your audience.

CHAPTER 10

What Is a Macro and How Much Weight Will I Lose?

M acro is not a new diet craze—you won't lose any weight. What you will lose though, if you use macros, are all those unwanted keystrokes.

Macro is actually short for a nerdy term: *macro instruction*. This means that with one tiny keystroke you can tell WordPerfect to perform a whole bunch of keystrokes.

Any keys that you can press on the keyboard, including function keys, Shift, Alt, Ctrl, and Backspace, as well as alphabetic and numeric keys, can be recorded in a macro. You can "play back" those keystrokes just as you do an audio cassette. This capability is especially useful for repetitive words and phrases, and for tasks.

Fly-By-Night Macros

One of the most convenient macro "tricks" is the variable. *Variable* means that the meaning can be changed anytime. You can use macro variables to record words or phrases you have to type many times.

Suppose you typed a letter to the I.R.S. and you found that you typed the term "red tape" thirty times in the same letter. What you could have done was put that phrase in a variable macro, and just hit one key combination to type the phrase rather than type all those letters all those times. Here's how you create a variable macro:

1. Select **T**ools,**M**acro,**C**ontrol from the pull-down menus, or press Ctrl-PgUp.

2. Select **A**ssign Variable.

3. In the Variable entry field type any digit from 0 to 9. Try typing **1**. Now press Enter.

   Notice how WordPerfect fills the entry field for you with VAR1.

4. Select the **C**ontent entry field.

5. Type the word or phrase you want. In this case it is **red tape**. Press Enter.

   Now your screen looks like figure 10.1.

Figure 10.1:

Cutting through red tape.

Assign Variable	
Variable:	VAR1
Content:	red tape
	OK Cancel

6. Press Enter or OK twice to exit.

7. Now press Alt-1 (the number 1). Note that if you use the numeric keypad, you will get a different character.

TRICK

If you block some text before you begin the preceding step 1 to assign a variable macro, the text in the block is automatically used in the variable macro; you are not prompted to type anything in the **C**ontent entry field.

Sundry Variable Info

The following list contains everything you always wanted to know about variable macros:

 Variable macros can only be assigned to the 10 numeric keys, 0 through 9. You can assign variables to as many or as few of these keys as you want during any WordPerfect session.

 The length of the Content field is 30 characters. If you have a phrase that's longer than that, see the next section on permanent macros, which are far more flexible.

 Variable macros are only active for that session of WordPerfect. When you exit WordPerfect, the macros exit also (they are eliminated). Scientists have tried for years to find out where they go, but no one knows for sure. You need to re-create them if you want the same ones again for your next WordPerfect session.

 You can reassign a variable to a key that already contains a variable simply by "recording" over it.

TRICK

When you record a phrase in a macro, don't put a space at the end of the word or phrase. That way, if you need to make it plural by adding an "s" at the end of it, or want to use the phrase at the end of a sentence, you don't have to backspace to put in the period or "s" or whatever.

What if you want a macro that has a longer lifespan and is available to you every time you use WordPerfect? Funny you should ask; that's covered next!

Using Permanent Macros

You don't seriously think that we, the authors, actually typed the word "WordPerfect" every place it appears in this book, do you? Not on your life. A variable macro (described earlier) for the word "WordPerfect" would have been helpful, but variable macros are deleted every time you exit WordPerfect. To avoid having to retype the same macro every time, we chose to use a permanent macro. Permanent macros are just as easy to create as variable macros, plus they have staying power.

Before you begin recording your permanent macro, you need to make an executive decision: What alphabetic key are you going to assign to your macro? You can use any letter of the alphabet for this purpose, but it's a good idea to think of something that would be a helpful mnemonic. If you create a macro that produces a fax form, for example, an assignment of the letter "b" would be no help at all in remembering what that macro did. Something along the lines of an "x" might be more helpful.

STOP!

Do NOT assign the letters F, E, V, L, T, O, G, W, or H for your macro. These letters are used to access each of the pull-down menus. If you assign a macro to one of these letters and then press one of these letters with the Alt key to access the menu, your macro will execute instead. The pull-down menu won't work. If you always use a mouse to activate pull-down menus, you can use these letters.

Sundry Permanent Macro Info

Macros are very flexible and versatile. This chapter only scratches the surface of what you can do with macros, but here are some points to consider about permanent macros:

Macro names need to comply with the DOS 8.3 character naming convention (refer to Chapter 8, "A Word about Files," for more information on DOS file names), but WordPerfect automatically assigns an extension of .WPM to any macro.

You do not need to assign a macro to a character key on the keyboard to play it. To play a macro of any name, select **T**ools,**M**acro,**P**lay from the pull-down menu or press Alt-F10. Type in the name of the macro you want to play. You may type the file name extension (.WPM), but it is not necessary.

You can record as many macros as you want and store them on your hard disk, but only 18 can be assigned to the keyboard at any one time. This is the 26 letters of the alphabet less the 8 letters assigned to the pull-down menus. Since you want to have some flexibility in assigning macros to the 18 letters, you might want to record macros with full names and then assign them to keys as you need to. This point is best illustrated with an example. What we will do is assign the calculator macro that comes with WordPerfect to the Alt-C key combination:

1. Select **T**ools,**M**acros,**R**ecord from the pull-down menus, or press Ctrl-F10.

2. At the Macro entry field in the Record Macro dialog box, either type in **ALTC** or press the Alt-C keys.

3. Press the Enter key or click on the OK button.

4. Select **T**ools,**M**acros,**P**lay from the pull-down menus, or press Alt-F10.

5. At the Macro entry field in the Play Macro dialog box, type in **CALC**.

6. Press the Enter key or click on the OK button. Notice the lower left-hand status line now reads `Recording Macro`.

7. Select **T**ools,**M**acros,**S**top from the pull-down menus, or press Ctrl-F10.

That's it! Now press Alt-C and the WordPerfect calculator pops up on your screen! Press the Esc key when you want it to go away.

Macros can call other macros. See the assignment we just did.

 When you are recording a macro, you can use a mouse to select menu items, but you cannot position the cursor on the editing screen with the mouse. To position the cursor, you must use keyboard keystrokes.

Making a Permanent Macro

Everyone wants to save time throughout their workday and using a macro is a great way to see an immediate return on your macro-writing investment. Here's how to write a permanent macro that can be used anytime, in any WordPerfect document:

1. Select **T**ools,**M**acros,**R**ecord from the pull-down menus, or press Ctrl-F10.

2. In the Macro entry field, type the name of your new macro, then press Enter. The name can consist of the Alt key in combination with one alphabetic key—for example, ALTN, ALTZ, or ALTR. If you want to assign the Alt-N key combination, you would type **ALTN** in the field or simply press the Alt-N keys.

Notice that the left-hand side of the status line changes to read "Recording Macro." Every keystroke you make from now until you stop recording will be in your macro.

3. Type the word or phrase you will be using often. Maybe your name would make a good macro.

4. Select **T**ools,**M**acros,**S**top, or press Ctrl-F10.

You have just stopped recording all your keystrokes; notice the status line went back to its usual display.

5. Press your new Alt-*key* combination to see if it works.

That's how you do it!

Call Me Macro Master

You aren't limited to just the Alt-*key* keys on your keyboard. You can also use a full name for your macro. To create a macro with a full name:

1. Select **T**ools,**M**acros,**R**ecord, press Ctrl-F10.

2. In the Macro entry field, type the full name of your new macro, then press Enter. For example, if you want to assign the macro name BIOTIC, type **BIOTIC** in the Macro field.

3. Type the word or phrase you will be using often.

4. Select **T**ools,**M**acros,**S**top, or press Ctrl-F10.

You have just stopped recording all your keystrokes; notice the status line went back to its usual display.

When you assign a full name to a macro, you run the macro by following these steps:

1. Press Alt-F10

2. Type the name of your macro

3. Press Enter

The best strategy for naming macros is to assign your most frequently used macros to Alt-*key* key combinations, and to assign names to less frequently used macros.

FOOD FOR THOUGHT

Notice that when you stop recording a macro, you see a box on your screen that reads "Compiling Macro." To refresh your memory on "compiling" refer to Appendix A "(Im)Perfect Computers."

Recycling and Updating Macros

Just like variable macros, you can reassign the same key to a new macro if your existing macro isn't being used much. If you assign a key to a new macro and the key is already used for an existing macro, you will receive a confirmation box asking whether you want to replace the existing macro. If you want to keep the new macro and change it to a different name, just press Cancel.

To browse through your existing macro names, click on the File List button in the Record Macro dialog box (press F5). One of the things you can do here is go straight into the File Manager. Once there, you can rename your macro before using the same letter again by renaming the file just like any other file. WordPerfect always assigns the extension of .WPM for macros. If you copy your macro to another file name, make sure it ends in .WPM.

Editing a Macro

Although many of your macros may be straight-forward, you may want to make adjustments to them. There is an alternative to re-recording all of the keystrokes in your macros, and that is to edit the recorded macro.

To edit a macro:

1. Select **T**ools,**M**acro,**R**ecord, or press Ctrl-F10.

2. In the Macro entry field type the Alt-*key* combination of the macro you want to edit, then press Enter.

3. Select **E**dit.

Now you see a regular editing screen just like the one where you type your documents. This screen shows all the commands that WordPerfect uses "behind the scenes." Your screen should look something like the one in figure 10.2.

4. In the example shown in figure 10.2, you would position your cursor anywhere between the quote marks (" ") and add or delete text as necessary. You can also add and delete keystrokes on the document screen. Refer to the WordPerfect Manual (or use Help) for complete information on editing macro keystrokes.

5. Press F7 when you are finished editing. Just like saving any document file, answer **Y**es to the question of saving your revised macro.

6. Answer **Y**es to the question of exiting the document.

Now your edited macro is ready to use!

Figure 10.2:

A macro revealed.

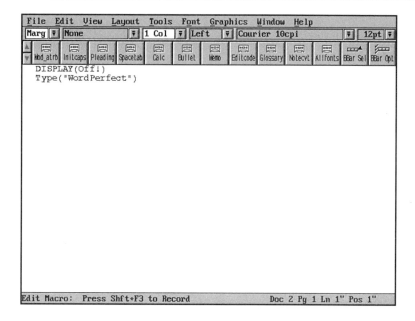

Macro Suggestions

Macros are so versatile you probably will never stop thinking of new ways to use them. Any series of keystrokes that you find yourself typing over and over again are good candidates for making into macros. Here are some suggestions:

 Date macros. If you type lots of letters throughout the day, make a date macro. Start recording your keystrokes with the Ctrl-F10 keys and assign this macro to the letter "D" for date. Next, press all the keys that you normally press to put in a date in code format. Stop recording (Ctrl-F10) and that's it! By using the commands to use date codes (Shift-F5,C) rather than date text (Shift-F5,T), you'll always get today's date rather than a fixed date.

 Typeface macros. What if you want to switch quickly from normal type to underline type and back again? Assign the "U" key (for underline) to a macro and perform all the keystrokes you need to get underline type. Stop recording. Now you just have to press the Alt-U key to get underline type and Alt-U again to turn it off. (Remember that font attributes are toggles—you have to turn them on to use them and then turn them off again to revert to normal attributes.)

 Signature block macros. If you type letters for yourself or someone else, make a macro for the signature block.

Prerecorded Macros

WordPerfect has thoughtfully included a number of prerecorded macros for you to use. When WordPerfect was installed on your computer, the macros were installed in the macro directory, `C:\WP60\MACROS`.

FOOD FOR THOUGHT

You may need to adjust the drive designator or even directory names for your particular installation.

To find out what these macros do, you can:

1. Select **T**ools,**M**acros,**P**lay from the pull-down menus, or press Alt-F10.

2. Press F5 or F6 to locate the `\WP60\MACROS` directory.

3. Select the macro you want to play by highlighting the name, and press the Enter key. The macro will then "play."

If you have a mouse, you can play the macros from the button bar that WordPerfect included. The button bar is named MACROS. To change the button bar to the Macro button bar:

1. Select **V**iew,Button Bar **S**etup,**S**elect.

2. Highlight MACROS and press Enter.

If you are already using a button bar, just find the one marked BBAR Sel and press there to make your selection. You may need to use the little down arrow on the button bar to find the BBAR Sel button.

We suggest that you play with some of these macros. If you find one or two that are particularly useful, you can access them without the button bar. You can record a macro to call the one(s) that you will use, or just use the Play Macro function, or copy them to a different name with the help of the File Manager. You might want to copy MEMO.WPM to ALTM.WPM, for instance.

CHAPTER 11

Caution: Rated PG (Perfect Graphics)

W ordPerfect has more graphics features than you can shake a graphic artist at. In this chapter, you learn about the following:

 Placing borders around paragraphs and pages

 Spiffing up documents by adding horizontal and vertical lines

 Using WordPerfect's line-drawing feature

 Incorporating graphic images into documents

This chapter focuses on WordPerfect's most commonly used graphic features. WordPerfect has a ton of tricks for working with images, but this chapter focuses on the standard features that you can use immediately.

Creating Borders

Ready grappling hooks! All hands on deck to repel borders! Man the cannon! (Oops. Wrong book. Ahem.)

You can make your work look sharper by placing borders around certain parts of your document. WordPerfect lets you put a border around the following:

 Paragraphs. You can place a border around a paragraph to draw attention to a particular passage. WordPerfect also lets you add shading within the borders.

 Pages. An entire page can have a border around it. A brochure or an invitation, for example, can look classy with a full-page border.

 Columns. If you're working in a multicolumn document, such as a company newsletter or a newspaper, you might want to place a border around some or all of the columns.

You can customize the borders to include a *drop shadow*, which is a black area that makes the bordered text look like it is "raised" off the page. You also can add shading inside a border. *Shading* is a percentage of grey used to fill in the area inside the border. You can use different kinds of borders, ranging from single hairline borders to thick borders to combinations of thin and thick.

Setting Up

Instead of typing a document that has multiple paragraphs, you are going to copy and paste several paragraphs from the PRINTER.TST file. You won't modify the actual file; you'll merely "borrow" a few paragraphs for your own use.

Loading the Test Document

Begin by using a new document. Close any open documents by choosing **C**lose from the **F**ile menu. Once you have a fresh document, take the following steps to load the PRINTER.TST document and copy out the paragraphs you want:

1. Press Shift-F10 to load a new document.

2. In the **F**ilename field, type the letter of the drive where you installed WordPerfect (this is probably the C drive), a colon (:), a backslash (\), the name of the directory where WordPerfect is installed (typically WP or WP60DOS), another backslash (\), and finally (whew!), the name PRINTER.TST. If you installed WordPerfect in the WP60DOS directory, the entry looks like the following:

```
C:\WP60\PRINTER.TST
```

   If you installed WordPerfect in the WP directory, type this:

```
C:\WP\PRINTER.TST
```

3. Press Enter to load the file. If a dialog box appears that tells you that the file could not be found, very carefully check the file name that you just typed. Make sure that you didn't use the forward slash (/) rather than the backslash (\).

The WordPerfect printer test document appears, as shown in figure 11.1.

Copying and Pasting the Text

Now you're going to copy a few paragraphs of text from the PRINTER.TST document into a new, blank document:

1. Press the down-arrow key until the cursor is on the first letter of the first paragraph.

2. Press Alt-F4 to begin marking a block.

3. Hold down Ctrl and press the down-arrow key three times. Three paragraphs are highlighted. If you want to use your mouse, then click and drag downwards until three paragraphs are highlighted.

4. Pull down the **E**dit menu and select **C**opy. Alternatively, you can press Ctrl-C.

5. Press Shift-F3 to switch to the blank document. If Shift-F3 doesn't work, pull down the **F**ile menu and select **N**ew to open a new document.

6. Pull down the **E**dit menu and choose **P**aste to paste the copied paragraphs into the new document.

Figure 11.1:

The printer test document.

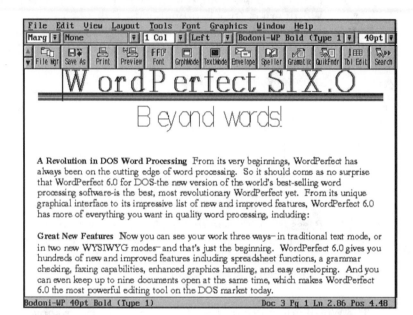

FOOD FOR THOUGHT

When you paste the paragraphs into the blank document, they will lose their formatting from the original document. That's OK, it is what you want for this section.

If all went well, your screen should resemble figure 11.2.

Figure 11.2:

The new document
with the copied text.

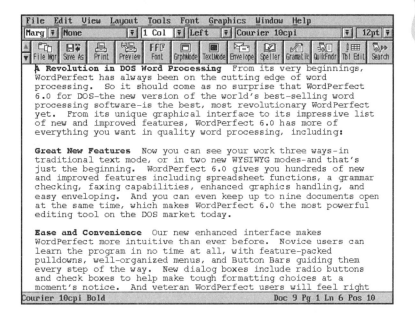

```
 File  Edit  View  Layout  Tools  Font  Graphics  Window  Help
 Marg ▼ None          ▼ 1 Col ▼ Left  ▼ Courier 10cpi           ▼  12pt ▼
 ▲  ⌘    ☐     ⎙    ⎙   FFF   ☐      ■     ⊞     ⌘    ⌘    ⌘    ⊞    ⌘
 ▼ File Mgr Save As Print Preview Font Grphikbde Textlkbde Envelope Speller Gramatik QuikFndr Tbl Edit Search
 A Revolution in DOS Word Processing  From its very beginnings,
 WordPerfect has always been on the cutting edge of word
 processing.  So it should come as no surprise that WordPerfect
 6.0 for DOS-the new version of the world's best-selling word
 processing software-is the best, most revolutionary WordPerfect
 yet.  From its unique graphical interface to its impressive list
 of new and improved features, WordPerfect 6.0 has more of
 everything you want in quality word processing, including:

 Great New Features  Now you can see your work three ways-in
 traditional text mode, or in two new WYSIWYG modes-and that's
 just the beginning.  WordPerfect 6.0 gives you hundreds of new
 and improved features including spreadsheet functions, a grammar
 checking, faxing capabilities, enhanced graphics handling, and
 easy enveloping.  And you can even keep up to nine documents open
 at the same time, which makes WordPerfect 6.0 the most powerful
 editing tool on the DOS market today.

 Ease and Convenience  Our new enhanced interface makes
 WordPerfect more intuitive than ever before.  Novice users can
 learn the program in no time at all, with feature-packed
 pulldowns, well-organized menus, and Button Bars guiding them
 every step of the way.  New dialog boxes include radio buttons
 and check boxes to help make tough formatting choices at a
 moment's notice.  And veteran WordPerfect users will feel right
 Courier 10cpi Bold                           Doc 9 Pg 1 Ln 6 Pos 10
```

Placing a Border around a Paragraph

When you place a border around a paragraph, the border command applies to all of the paragraphs that follow the cursor, unless you block the only paragraph you want. For this exercise, we'll just select one paragraph to get a border.

Perform the following steps to create a border around the paragraph:

1. Place the cursor on the first letter of the second paragraph, or on the line immediately preceding the second paragraph.

2. Block the paragraph. To do this, you can use the mouse to quadruple-click on the paragraph. If you prefer to use the keyboard, press Alt-F4 and then hold down Ctrl and press the down-arrow key once to select the paragraph.

3. Press Alt-F9 to open the Graphics window. Using your mouse, pull down the **G**raphics menu.

4. Press O or 3 to select the Borders option, or click on B**o**rders.

5. Press 1 or P to select **P**aragraph, or click on **P**aragraph. A dialog box appears and displays the following three options:

Border Style. Border Style enables you to choose from a list of different border styles, from single line borders, to thick borders, to combinations of thick and thin borders.

 Fill Style. Fill Style enables you to choose the percentage of gray shading for the area inside the border. The shading appears as the background for the entire area within the border.

 Customize. Customize enables you to modify one of the included border styles by adding shadows, rounded corners, and other special features.

6. To keep this simple, use just a single line and a shaded background. Because the Single border option is already selected, all you need to do is select **F**ill Style. Press F. Use the arrow keys to highlight 10% Shaded Fill and press Enter to close the Fill Style window.

7. To close the Create Paragraph Border dialog box and apply your change, click on the OK button or press Enter.

Figure 11.3 shows the paragraph surrounded by a border.

Placing a Border around an Entire Page

You add a full-page border in much the same way you add a paragraph border. In the following example, you'll put a border around the whole page by using a border style that places lines at only the top and bottom of the page.

FOOD FOR THOUGHT

A page border applies to the page your cursor is on and any following pages. Because you're working with only a single-page document here, you don't have to worry about turning the border off because of extra pages, but you learn how to do that anyway at the end of this section.

The paragraph with a border and shading.

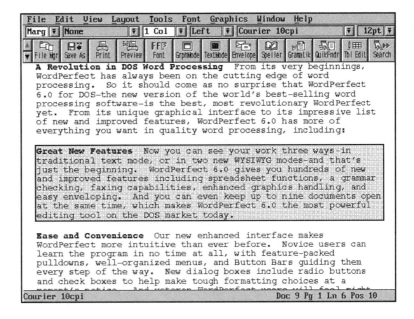

To add a border around the entire document, take these steps:

1. Open the **G**raphics menu by pressing Alt-F9, or pull down the **G**raphics menu.

2. Select B**o**rders.

3. Select P**a**ge border.

4. Select **B**order Style.

5. Use the arrow keys to scroll through the list and highlight Thick Top and Bottom Border, and press Enter.

6. Close the Border window and apply the code by pressing Enter, or by selecting OK with your mouse.

The page looks like figure 11.4 (you can either press Shift-F7 and then press V, or pull down the **F**ile menu and choose Print Pre**v**iew from the menu, to see what it looks like on your system). See the thick lines at the top and bottom of the page? When you're done looking at the image, press F7 to return to the document.

Figure 11.4:

The page with top and bottom borders added.

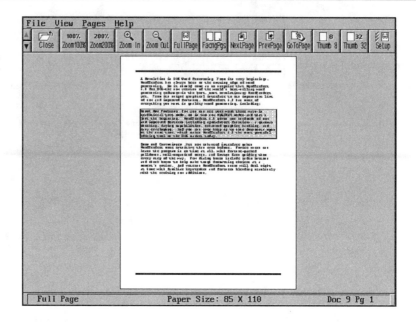

Adding Lines

You also can make a document more attractive by adding horizontal or vertical lines.

Adding a line is similar to adding a border, but different options control the line's position, length, width, and so on. Graphic lines apply to only the page on which you define them. If you want the lines to apply to more than one page, you have to apply them to each page.

In the following example, you add a vertical line to the left edge of the sample document:

1. Press Alt-F9 to bring up the **G**raphics menu, or pull down the **G**raphics menu with your mouse.

2. Select Graphic **L**ines, and then select **C**reate. The Create Graphics Line dialog box appears, as shown in figure 11.5.

3. Select Line **O**rientation and then **V**ertical.

4. Select the OK button to create the line.

5. Press Shift-F7 and then press V to view the document with the line inserted, as shown in figure 11.6. Note the new line against the left edge of the page.

Figure 11.5:

The Create Graphics Line
dialog box.

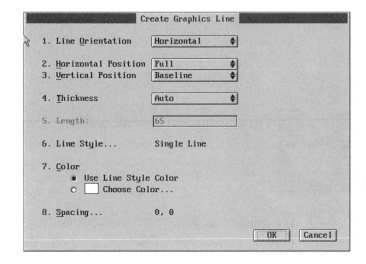

Figure 11.6:

A vertical line added to
the page.

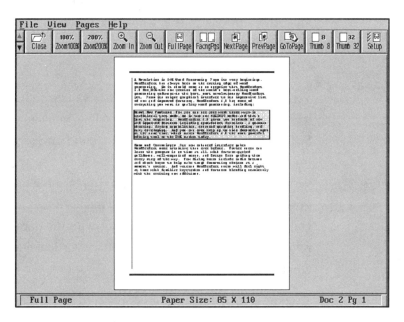

Other Options for Creating Lines

The Create Graphics Line dialog box contains a variety of options. Although
you won't be using any of the other options right now, here's a description
of each one, in case you want to use them another time:

Line Orientation. You can choose either **V**ertical or **H**orizontal. The line is drawn in the direction you select.

 **FOOD FOR THOUGHT**

The following two settings have slightly different options depending on whether you have selected Vertical or Horizontal lines.

 Horizontal Position. This option enables you to choose from **L**eft, **R**ight, **C**entered, **F**ull, or **S**et. **F**ull makes the line the full width of the page, while **S**et lets you specify a measurement for the line's width. The other options specify where the line is to begin. If you are working with a vertical line, you also can position the line **B**etween Columns.

 Vertical Position. Vertical Position is similar to **H**orizontal Position. If you are working with a horizontal line, you can choose between **S**et and **B**aseline. **S**et enables you to enter an absolute measurement from the top of the page (or the left edge if you are working with a vertical line). **B**aseline enables you to place the line at the current position relative to the text, which means if you put the line at the end of a paragraph, the line remains with the paragraph, even after reformatting. If you are working with a vertical line, then you can choose between **S**et, **T**op, **B**ottom, **C**entered, and **F**ull.

 Thickness. Use the **T**hickness option to specify line thickness. **A**uto uses the last line thickness and **S**et enables you to specify a measurement.

 Length. **L**ength is available only if you have not chosen **F**ull as the horizontal or vertical position. Otherwise, you can specify a length.

Line Style. Line Style brings up a window that lists 10 line styles, similar to the line styles that you saw when you worked with borders at the beginning of the chapter.

 Color. Line color usually depends on the line style (you can edit line styles to specify a color). If you want to deviate from the predefined line color, choose **C**olor.

 Spacing. If you use horizontal lines, **S**pacing enables you to specify an amount of space above and below the line. If you use a vertical line, **S**pacing lets you specify the amount of space between the line and the right or left edge of the page.

Line Drawing

A totally different line feature in WordPerfect is the Line Draw feature. You can use Line Draw to draw all sorts of interesting things, rather than a single, boring line. I like to redraw my company's organization chart (showing me as the president, of course). Line Draw also is a useful tool for doing simple diagrams and flow charts.

STOP!

You must be using a monospaced font before you can use Line Draw. In a *monospaced* font, each letter takes up the same amount of horizontal space. This is different from a *proportional* font, where each letter takes up only the space it needs. For example, in this book, you can see that lowercase letter *i* takes up less space than uppercase letter *G*. That's because this paragraph is printed in a proportional font.

Courier is a monospaced font, as are all fonts specified by cpi (characters per inch) rather than point size. The fonts you can use depend on your printer. This paragraph is printed in a monospace font.

To begin using Line Draw, perform the following steps:

1. Select a monospaced font. Courier is good.

2. Move your cursor to where you want to begin drawing.

3. Press Ctrl-F3, or choose Line **D**raw from the **G**raphics menu. The Line Draw window appears, as shown in figure 11.7.

Figure 11.7:

The Line Draw window.

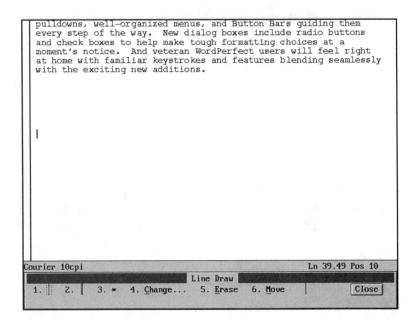

Select a line-drawing character by pressing 1, 2, or 3. Press 4 to select a line-drawing character from a list of eight other characters, or specify your own character (you could draw by using the letter w, although why would anyone?). Once you have Line Draw activated, the following keys are used.

Table 11.1
Keys Used for Line Drawing

Option Chosen	Funky Function
1	Selects single line
2	Selects double line

Option Chosen	Funky Function
3	Selects asterisk drawing
4	Chooses a specific character for drawing
5 (**E**rase)	Changes to erase mode
6 (**M**ove)	Allows you to reposition your cursor
F7	Exits Line Draw

After you choose a line-drawing character, use the arrow keys to draw in the desired direction. You also can select **E**rase to make whatever area you draw over disappear. Or, you can use **M**ove to reposition your cursor without drawing anything.

I drew something using the Line Draw feature and was going to include it as a screen image in this book, but my agent told me it would cause panic in the New York art world. My lawyer told me I might have to deal with massive lawsuits for collapsing the world's fine art market. And then my therapist told me I wasn't ready to deal with the media attention that would inevitably result. So you'll just have to draw your own stuff to look at!

Creating a Simple Line Drawing

If you need to create a simple line drawing, such as drawing several small boxes, follow these steps:

1. Start with a fresh document (pull down the **F**ile menu and choose **N**ew).

2. Change to the Courier font by pressing Ctrl-F8, F**o**nt, and then choose Courier. Press Enter to make this change active.

3. Press Ctrl-F3,L or pull down the Graphics menu and choose Line **D**raw from the menu. Your screen should look like figure 11.8.

4. Choose single line by pressing 1 on your keyboard.

5. Press the down arrow key five times, then the right arrow key five times, the up arrow key five times, and finally, the left arrow key five times. When you are done, you should have a box drawn on your screen.

6. Now move your cursor without drawing anything. Select **M**ove and then press the down arrow key seven times.

7. Switch to double line drawing by pressing 2 on your keyboard.

8. Press the down arrow key five times, followed by five presses each of the right arrow, the up arrow, and the left arrow.

Figure 11.8:

The Line Draw Window.

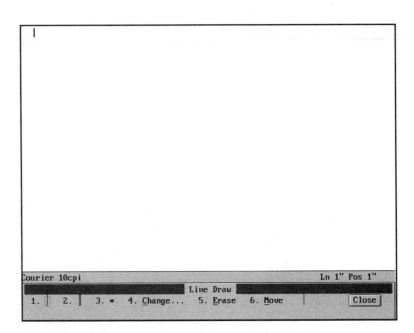

When you have followed these steps, your screen should look like figure 11.9.

Look at the Pretty Pictures!

I usually say this after I ram my head into a wall (don't try this at home!). But you'll be saying it after you see WordPerfect's graphics feature. Or you can ram your head into a wall. If you really want to party, do both!

WordPerfect makes it easy to add pictures to your documents. There are even 40 images included with WordPerfect at no extra cost!

WordPerfect's own graphics files use the extension WPG, which stands for *WordPerfect Graphic.* WordPerfect can also retrieve and use images created in other formats. WordPerfect supports most popular graphic file formats, such as the PCX files created by some paint programs.

Figure 11.9:

Two complete boxes.

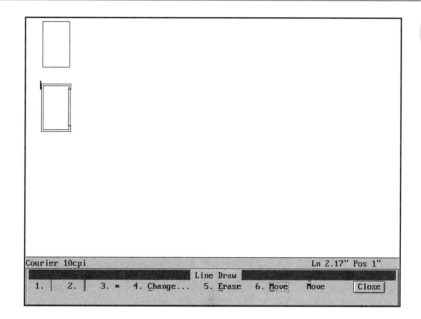

STOP!

The WordPerfect graphic images must be installed before the following exercise can work. If they're not, and you want to install them, refer to Chapter 1, and look in the section on performing a custom installation.

Loading an Image into Your Document

To retrieve an image that is included in WordPerfect, take the following steps:

1. Move to the top of the sample document by pressing Home, Home, up arrow.

2. Select **R**etrieve Image from the **G**raphics menu.

3. If you know the name of the file you are retrieving, type it and press Enter. Otherwise, press F5 and then press Enter to get the list of included WordPerfect pictures.

4. Use the arrow keys to highlight the file HOTROD.WPG, then press Enter to select it.

In graphics mode, the figure appears at the right end of the first paragraph, as shown in figure 11.10. In text mode, a box marked BOX 1 appears. BOX 1 represents the location of the picture. In text mode, you can view the picture by pressing Shift-F7 and then selecting **V**iew.

Figure 11.10:

Hot dog! No, hot rod!

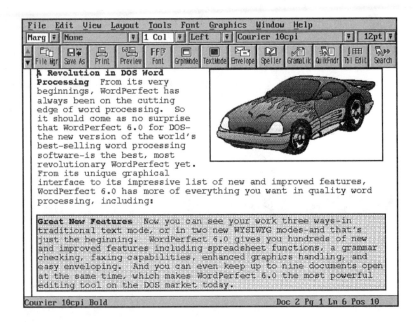

Working with an Image

You have innumerable ways to adjust the way an image appears. A highlighted tour follows. To edit the characteristics of an image, do the following steps to get to the editing window:

1. Pull down the **G**raphics menu and select Graphics **B**oxes, then select **E**dit.

2. At the next dialog box, choose the box you want to edit. Because your document has only one box, you can just go ahead and select the **E**dit Box button. If you have more than one box, select Document Box **N**umber to choose the box you want to edit, and then choose the **E**dit Box button.

3. The Edit Graphics Box dialog box appears, as shown in figure 11.11.

Figure 11.11:

The Edit Graphics Box dialog box.

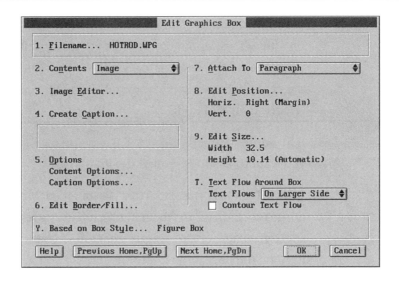

The Edit Graphics Box dialog box offers the following options:

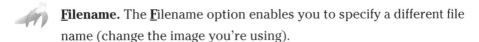

Filename. The **F**ilename option enables you to specify a different file name (change the image you're using).

Contents. Co**n**tents lets you choose from a number of different contents, ranging from equations to text. If you change the setting of Co**n**tents, the current image is lost because you redefine the kind of image the box contains.

Image Editor. The Image Editor is used to change the characteristics of the image. You can do tricks like make the color fills transparent, flip the image in different directions, shrink or expand the image, and so on.

Create Caption. Choose this option if you want to give your image a caption.

Options. Here, you get two choices. Content Options enables you to change how the image is sized within the box. Caption Options changes the position of the caption and lets you determine whether the caption number should be automatically generated (the Caption Counter). The Caption Counter can automatically number each of your figures, and automatically put the figure number in as part of the caption. For example, the caption might say something like: "Figure 1. My Hot Rod."

 Edit Border/Fill. Edit **B**order/Fill lets you choose the kind of border you want to use to surround the graphic box.

 Attach To. This is an important option. It enables you to attach an image to a paragraph (the default), a fixed page position that you specify, a page, or a character position. If you want the image to be fixed on the page, attach it to the page. If you attach the image to the page, no matter how you reformat the document, the image stays in the same place on that page.

 Edit Position. Here you can choose where to put the graphic image within your **A**ttach To choice. For example, if you attach an image to a paragraph, Edit **P**osition enables you to put the image on the left or right side of the paragraph, as you please.

 Edit Size. If you don't like the size of an image, you can use Edit **S**ize to expand or shrink it. Typically, you specify a width or a height. If you specify a width, WordPerfect automatically determines a height that maintains the proportions of the box, and vice versa.

 Text Flow Around Box. Another important option, **T**ext Flow Around Box, enables you to decide how text flows around the box. You can flow text around the image's larger side (that is, the side that has more room), the left side, the right side, both sides, neither side, or even through the box. This option enables you also to Contour Text Flow the text around the image. Contour Text Flow is useful if the image is not square or rectangular and you want the text to follow the image rather than the box.

To remove a graphics box, Reveal Codes (Alt-F3), find the code for the box, and press Del once it's highlighted.

Wrapping Text around a Figure

In this section you'll learn about wrapping text around a picture, as well as relocating the picture and observing how WordPerfect automatically adjusts the text.

Starting with the image that you loaded in the previous section, follow these steps:

1. Type several sentences of text into your document. If you're not feeling very creative today, use the following text:

   Sure, WordPerfect is a complex, big program, that does everything but walk my dogs and take out the trash. Initially, I was concerned about my ability to learn WordPerfect, and I really felt like a wimp. But with this book, I now look straight into the WordPerfect screen with a sneer on my face, and a baseball bat in my hand. This program isn't going to get the better of me!

Your document should now look like figure 11.12.

Figure 11.12:

An example of wrapped text.

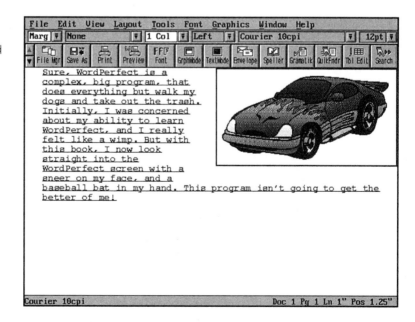

Moving the Image

There are two methods that can be used to move an image. If you are working in graphics mode, follow these steps:

1. Position your mouse pointer inside the graphic image.

2. Press and hold down the left mouse button.

3. Drag your mouse to a new position. When the figure is positioned where you want it, release the mouse button. For this example, move the image until it is centered on the page and release the mouse button.

That's all there is to it! If you have text that wraps around your graphic box, then the text will automatically adjust to wrap around the new image location. More on this in a minute.

Controlling Text Wrap

To change the way text wraps around your image, follow these steps:

1. Pull down the **G**raphics menu.

2. Select Graphics **B**oxes and then **E**dit.

3. On the screen that appears, choose the number of the image you want to edit by choosing Document Box **N**umber and then typing in the number of the image you want to change. After this number is set correctly, select the button **E**dit Box.

4. You will now see the Edit Graphics Box dialog box.

5. Choose **T**ext Flows Around Box.

6. Choose **T**ext Flows. You will be offered these choices:

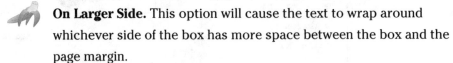

    On Larger Side. This option will cause the text to wrap around whichever side of the box has more space between the box and the page margin.

On Left Side. Choosing this option will force the text to only wrap on the left side of the box.

On Right Side. This choice will force the text to flow on the right side of the box.

 On Both Sides. Here, the text will flow on both the right and left side of the box. Each line will continue, but will be interrupted by the image. In other words, each line is still read across the page; you just have to jump your eyes over the box as you read.

 On Neither Side. This will make the text only show up above and below the box. No text will appear on either side of the box.

 Through Box. Choosing Through Box will force the text to be super-imposed on the graphic image.

7. Choose On **L**eft Side.

Examine figure 11.13 carefully. Notice that the border around the box consumes space that could otherwise be used for your text. WordPerfect lets you put text in this extra space with the Contour Text Flow checkbox. To see how this works, continue with step 8.

Figure 11.13:

Text wrapped to left of image.

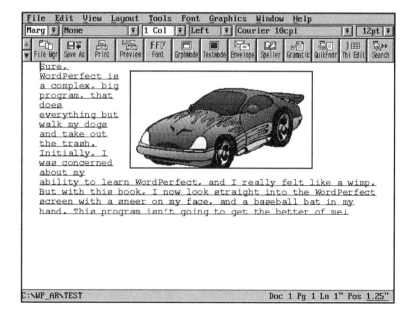

8.   Again, choose **T**ext Flows Around Box.

9.   Choose **C**ontour Text Flow.

10.   Press Enter to apply these changes.

As you can see in figure 11.14, the Contour Text Flow option can give your work a more professional polish.

Figure 11.14:

Example of **C**ontour Text Flow.

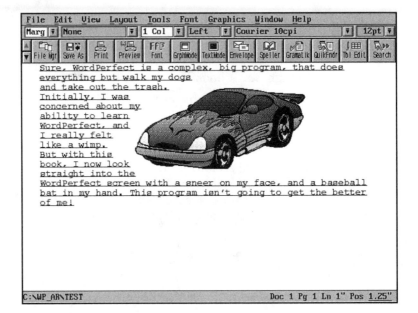

Word Perfect

CHAPTER 12

Mighty Columns

Columns in word processing programs are a little funny; you will probably rarely use them (if at all), but when you do need columns, it is extremely useful to be able to do them easily. This chapter will teach you about using WordPerfect's column features. With WordPerfect columns, you can create:

 Newspaper columns, useful for generating newsletters. You can have up to 24 separate columns (although on normal paper, each column would be extremely narrow).

 Parallel columns, which can be used to create textual tables, scripts, and other tabular types of data.

In this chapter you learn how to set up both types of columns, along with their different flavors.

Setting Up Columns

In most word processors, it's hard to set up columns of text or numbers. Instead of trying to create real columns, most people try to "cheat" by using lots of tabs and extra spaces to line up their information across the page. If you do this, however, you'll pay for it if you have to change anything, because you'll wind up creating a whole new set of tabs and extra spaces. WordPerfect's column feature makes it easy to set up columns of words or numbers and then change them as much as you want.

STOP!

Don't ever try to set up pseudo-columns using tabs, spaces, and indents unless it is for information that is only a couple of lines long. For anything longer than that, learn to use the WordPerfect column feature to avoid major irritation.

The easiest way to use the newspaper column feature is to type your information without columns and then put it into columns, as in the following exercise.

Entering Text To Be Set in Newspaper Columns

You'll begin this example by typing a grocery list. WordPerfect's default settings are perfect for your needs. Remember: As you type this list, use the F4 key rather than the Tab key to indent. If you use Tabs and a line must wrap down to the next row, the line won't wrap properly for a column. F4 sets up the lines to wrap properly in columns.

Now type the following list:

Meats:
> **5 lbs. hamburger**

Breads:
> **Some kind of yummy dinner bread**

Seasonings/mixes:
        4 packages Hamburger Helper
        1 package chili seasoning mix

Canned goods:
        1 can beans for chili
        2 cans tomato sauce for chili

Selecting the Column Options

After you type the list, all you have to do is set it up in columns. To create the columns, take these steps:

1. Position the cursor at the beginning of the top item of the list.

2. Select the **L**ayout pull-down menu.

3. Select **C**olumns.

The Text Columns window appears, as shown in figure 12.1.

Figure 12.1:

The Text Columns window.

```
┌──────────────── Text Columns ─────────────────┐
│                                                │
│  1. Column Type                                │
│     ● Newspaper                                │
│     ○ Balanced Newspaper                       │
│     ○ Parallel                                 │
│     ○ Parallel with Block Protect              │
│                                                │
│  2. Number of Columns:          [2  ]          │
│                                                │
│  3. Distance Between Columns:   [0.5"]         │
│                                                │
│  4. Line Spacing Between Rows:  [1.0 ]         │
│                                                │
│  5. Column Borders...                          │
│                                                │
│                                                │
│  [Off]  [Custom Widths...]  [ OK ]  [Cancel]   │
│                                                │
└────────────────────────────────────────────────┘
```

First you must decide what kind of columns you want. You have four choices:

Newspaper. Newspaper columns flow down one side of the column and then continue on the next column just like a real newspaper.

Balanced Newspaper. The Balanced Newspaper format is like Newspaper format, except it ensures equal column length. Figure 12.2 shows this.

Figure 12.2:

Balanced Newspaper Columns.

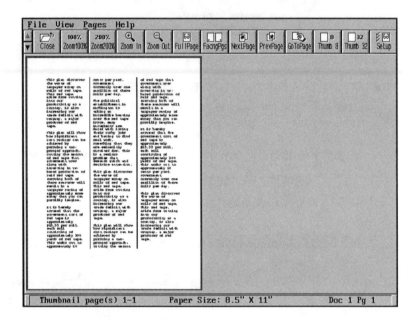

 Parallel. Parallel columns group the text across the page in rows. This is especially useful for typing tabular text, such as a script. See figure 12.3 for an example of parallel columns.

 Parallel with Block Protect. This feature keeps each paragraph of the column together so if the information is too long to fit on one page, the text is kept together and grouped on the next page. Notice how, in the last figure, one of the paragraphs is split between the first and second page. By setting this same document to Parallel with Block Protect, that problem is avoided—WordPerfect makes sure that each block, or paragraph, is on a single page. See figure 12.4 to see how this looks.

Figure 12.3:

Parallel columns.

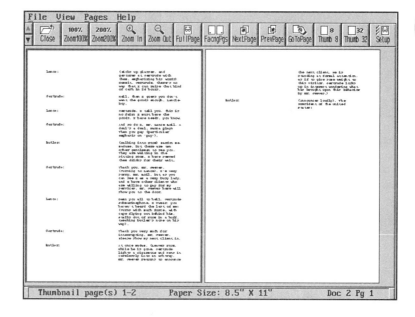

Figure 12.4:

Parallel with Block
Protect columns .

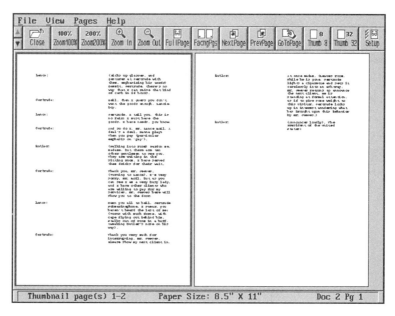

Choose the Parallel with Block Protect option for your grocery list. If you use
Parallel, you might end up with one item from the Seasoning/mixes category
in one column and the rest of the items in another column, and that's
intolerable.

The default <u>N</u>umber of Columns is two, a good choice for your list. The default <u>D</u>istance between Columns is five spaces, which is fine. Line <u>S</u>pacing Between Rows is 1.0, a setting you'll probably never have to change, unless you want your lists to be scrunched up and hard to read.

The last option is Column <u>B</u>orders. You don't need column borders for the grocery list, but a section further on will show you how to add them.

The Custom <u>W</u>idths button enables you to customize the columns if you want one column to be fatter and one narrower, but a plain grocery list doesn't require customization. Just select OK.

Putting Your Text in Columns

Aha! Nothing happened! Well, something happened. Your list didn't go into two columns, but some of the words wrapped. To divide the information into columns, position the cursor at the desired beginning point of the second column (in this case, at the beginning of the `Seasonings/mixes` section) and press Ctrl-Enter. Your list should look like figure 12.5.

Figure 12.5:

The grocery list takes shape.

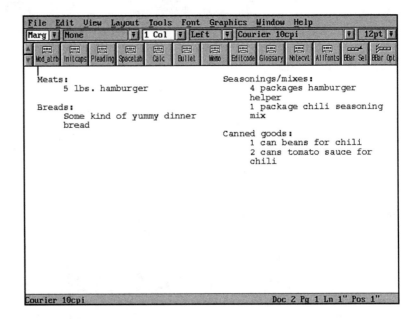

Now you need to turn off the column feature, in case you need to type information at the bottom of the list that you don't want in columnar format. To turn off the column feature, follow these steps:

1. Move to the bottom of the column area, past all of the text that is in columns.

2. Select the **L**ayout pull-down menu, select **C**olumns, and choose O**ff**. Now you're in business.

Creating Parallel Columns

Parallel columns are not the columns that you are used to. Rather, they are a means of working with tabular data, where you have a number of headings going down the page, along with associated comments or text on the right side of the page. See figure 12.3 for an example of this.

If you are working with data like this, it is far better to set up the columns first, and then enter the information. This section will show you how to do that.

1. Positioning your cursor where you want the parallel columns to begin, pull down the **L**ayout menu and then choose **C**olumns.

2. Choose Column **T**ype, and then choose either Parallel or Parallel with Block Protect. As you can see in figure 12.3 and 12.4, these two options are very similar, except that Parallel with Block Protect ensures that none of your paragraphs span two pages.

3. You will typically want to use parallel columns with only two columns. Select **N**umber of Columns, type 2, and press Enter.

4. If you need to adjust the **D**istance Between Columns or the Line **S**pacing Between Rows, do that here by choosing each one in turn and entering the measurement that you want to use.

5. Select the OK button to return to the document.

6. Type the first heading, which will appear on the left side of the screen. When you have finished typing it, press Ctrl-Enter. This will move you to the second column, starting on the same line as the heading.

7. Type in as much text as you need, and press Ctrl-Enter again to return to the left column to add the next heading. Continue in this fashion until you are done.

When you are finished entering the parallel column information, turn the column feature off by:

1. Pulling down the **L**ayout menu and choosing **C**olumns.

2. Choosing the O**f**f button.

Working with Existing Columns

Any person who works with documents frequently will tell you that getting the perfect document is largely an iterative process. You set it up, print it, decide you don't like how something looks, and then go and change it, print it again, and so on. Some people think that computers cut down on the use of paper but, if anything, they increase it! This section will show you how to change and rearrange your existing columns, hopefully with a minimum of wasted paper. After all, everyone wants to be environmentally friendly!

Getting around in Columns

WordPerfect lets you move around quickly between columns. See table 12.1 for all the right moves.

Table 12.1
Moving around in Columns

These Keys...	Move You Here...
Ctrl-Home,Right arrow	One column to the right
Alt-Right arrow	One column to the right
Ctrl-Home,Left arrow	One column to the left
Alt-Left arrow	One column to the left
Ctrl-Home,End	To the last column
Ctrl-Home,Home,Right arrow	To the last column
Ctrl-Home,Home,Left arrow	To the first column
Ctrl-Home,Up arrow	Top of column in current row
Ctrl-Home,Down arrow	Bottom of column in current row

Note that Ctrl-Home brings up a window on-screen that says `Go to:` followed by an entry field. Ignore the entry field and press the key you need to finish the operation.

Adding and Deleting Column Stuff

What if you forget that the Frozen Food section is between the Bread and the Seasoning sections at the grocery store? No problem. Position the cursor where you want to add or delete material.

Changing the Number of Columns

What if you initially set up a section of columns using two columns, but later decide that you want to see how this section looks with three or four columns? Fortunately, WordPerfect makes it easy to do this.

1. Make sure your ribbon is active. If you don't see the ribbon (it should be between the button bar and the pull-down menus), activate it by pulling down the **V**iew menu and then choosing **R**ibbon.

2. The third field from the left on the ribbon will indicate how many columns you currently have. To change it, simply click on the small button at the right of the field (called a spin button) and then choose the number of columns you would like from the list that appears.

Presto-chango, different columns! If you don't like the results, simply click on the spin button again and put it back to the previous setting.

Adding and Deleting Column Borders

Some documents can profit by adding lines to segment the columns, much like a newspaper does. To add these lines:

1. Pull down the **L**ayout menu and choose **C**olumns.

2. Choose Column **B**orders.

3. Choose **B**order Style. A window appears with a variety of different line styles. For a simple look, choose Column Border (Between Only), which will place a vertical line between your columns. To fully enclose each column with lines, choose Column Border (Outside and Between).

4. Choose OK and then OK again.

To delete column borders:

1. Pull down the **L**ayout menu and choose **C**olumns.

2. Choose Column **B**orders.

3. Choose **B**order Style. A list appears with many different line styles. Scroll the list to the top and choose [None] to delete the lines.

CHAPTER 13

Data on the Table

When WordPerfect 5.1 shipped, a new feature in it caused much rejoicing among WordPerfect users: tables. The tables feature has been enhanced in WordPerfect 6.0.

Tables let you quickly set up "grids" in your document. These grids, or tables, can be used to set up forms, small spreadsheets, lists, and many other things. In this chapter, you read about:

 How to set up a proper table, no special napkin folding skills necessary

 How to revise table settings

 Proper grocery store etiquette

Setting a Proper Table

Suppose you have a list of items—say a grocery list—and you want to enter the prices for each item and then total them. Hey, you can sum up your total and know the amount for your second mortgage before you go to the grocery store. How about that? A table is more appropriate for such a task than a column. This section will show you how to create tables. Later on, you'll learn about the cool things you can do with tables, such as set up forms and do more advanced math. You'll also learn about the tricks for formatting tables to make them pleasing to work with and to view. After all, style counts!

Table Talk

Before you set up a table, you need to know a little table terminology:

 Table. A *table* is a collection of data that is divided into rows and columns. A common data table is a collection of people's names, addresses, and phone numbers.

 Row. In a data table, a *row* is a horizontal line of information. In a table, a row may contain all the information about one thing, such as a person's name, address, and phone number.

 Column. In a data table, a *column* is a vertical line of information. In your imaginary table, one column may contain all the people's names, the next one may contain all the addresses, and so on across the page.

 Cell. A table is made up of a series of little squares; each square is where a row and a column meet. Each square is called a *cell*.

Figure 13.1 shows an example table.

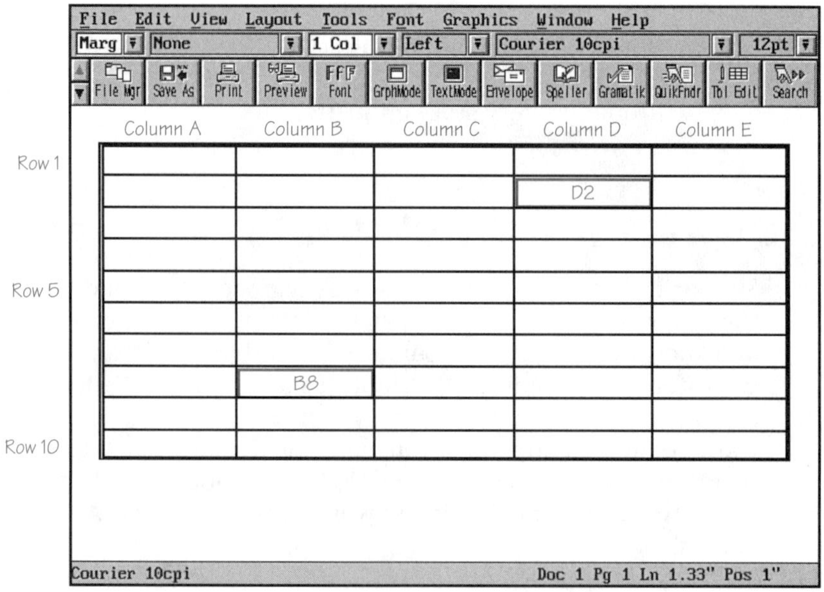

Figure 13.1:

A simple table.

Like most software programs that deal with tabular data, WordPerfect has a standard labeling system for the rows and columns. Each column is named for a letter of the alphabet; the far left column is always labeled with letter "A," and it goes from left to right, so that the next row to the right is "B," then "C," and so on. Each row is named with a number, and the top row is always labeled with number "1."

A character and a number are required to refer to an individual cell. The top left-hand cell is A1. The next horizontal cell (or, the next cell in the first row) is B1, and so on. The next vertical cell (or, the next cell in column A) is A2, and so on.

TRICK

You can refer to rows, columns, and individual cells in a manner less akin to a rousing game of bingo by naming the cells. You can name cells by using the Name button in the Table Edit window. You don't need Names in your grocery list table because it's small, but if you want to, go ahead. Select useful names for referring to the different cells. If you're creating a table of year-end sales, names like Harry and Sheila are not useful. Harry and Sheila are more appropriate if you're drawing up a stat sheet for your softball team.

Creating a Table

Now you can create a table for your shopping list. In this example, you'll create a two-column table. The first column will hold the names of the items you want to buy. The second column will hold the price of each item. At the bottom of the table, the last row will automatically add up the prices of all the items, so that you can see how much you need to spend at the store.

Take these steps to start setting up the table:

1. Begin by using a clean page. Press Shift-F3 to bring up the Document2 window.

2. Select the **L**ayout pull-down menu, then select **T**ables.

3. Because you are making a brand new table, select **C**reate. The Create Table window appears.

At the Create Table window, you decide (or preferably, already know) how many rows and columns the table needs. For this example, your table will have two columns and ten rows. You can always add more later, if you want. After you select OK, the table appears; beneath the table, the Table Edit window should be visible (see fig. 13.2).

Figure 13.2:

Setting the table.

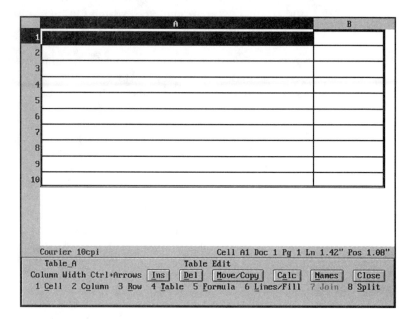

Setting Column Widths in a Table

By default, the columns are equal in size. In this example, however, you want column A to be wide for the product descriptions, and column B to be narrow for the prices.

At the bottom of the screen the Table Edit window shows that you can use the Ctrl key and the left- or right-arrow key to adjust the size of a column. Press Ctrl-right arrow until column A is wide enough and column B is narrow enough. In this case, the column widths don't need to be exact; just use figure 13.2 as a rough guide for setting the column widths.

To actually set a column width by entering a measurement, follow these steps:

1. Start at the Table Edit window. If you are not there, position your cursor inside the table and press Alt-F7,T,E to go there immediately. You can also pull down the **L**ayout menu, choose **T**ables, and then **E**dit.

2. Using your arrow keys, move to the column whose width you want to set.

3. Select C**o**lumn and then **W**idth. Enter in the measurement, and then press Enter.

4. Choose OK.

Exploring Table Options

Before you exit from the Table Edit window, take some time to explore a few of the options. These options are explained throughout the rest of this chapter. For now, press the right-arrow key to move the cursor to the right-hand column. You'll need to make one change to the settings in the second column, and you need to place the cursor in that column to make it active.

Cell Formats

The first option in the Table Edit window is **C**ell. As the name implies, this option lets you format the text you put into your table's cells. Select **C**ell now; the Cell Format window should appear as shown in figure 13.3.

Figure 13.3:

Cell Format dialog box.

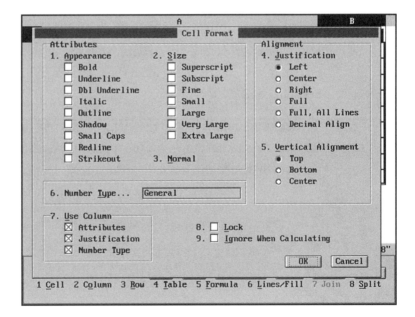

The Cell Format window provides these options:

 Appearance. Here you can change the formatting for the data that the cell or cells contain. Unlike normal editing mode, in which you format the text itself, here you format the cell and all text that goes into the cell will automatically get whatever appearance attributes that you choose.

 Size. If you want a cell to have a larger or smaller font size than the other cells, choose **S**ize and then choose from the available relative sizing options.

 Normal. When you choose **N**ormal, all formatting attributes are turned off, as well as any special size attributes.

 Justification. In many tables it is important to be able to justify different cells differently. For example, if you were designing a form, you might want the labels for the blank cells to be right justified so that the label was right next to the blank cell, or field. When you choose **J**ustification, you can choose from the normal WordPerfect justifications of **L**eft, **C**enter, **R**ight, **F**ull, and so on, as well as **D**ecimal Align, which will cause all of the numbers to line up on the decimal point.

 Vertical Alignment. Within the cell, you can use this option to have the data appear lined up with the top or bottom of the cell, or to be centered between the top and bottom lines.

FOOD FOR THOUGHT

When you set the vertical alignment for a cell, you will not see the effect until you print or look at the print preview. Until then, all text appears aligned at the top of each cell.

Number Type. Number **T**ype gives you much control over how numbers appear in your table (see fig. 13.4). You can choose from eight different formats for displaying numbers, and see what they will look like in the Preview window below. For any of those formats, you can modify them by using the choices found in the **O**ptions box.

With the **O**ptions, you can change how many digits to display after the decimal point, whether or not to use commas, how to represent negative numbers, and how to deal with currency symbols. Also, when you choose **D**ate from the Standard Formats, you can then click on the S**e**lect Date Format button to choose from 12 different methods for displaying dates.

Figure 13.4:

The Number Type Formats dialog box.

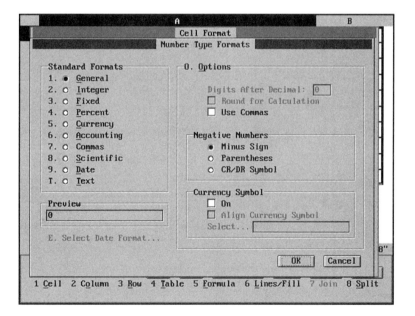

Use Column. The **U**se Column box lets you choose to have this cell inherit the attributes, justification, or number type for the entire column. (You can set many of these formatting parameters for an entire column at once by using the Column formatting feature.)

<u>U</u>se Column is useful when you want most of a column to be formatted in a particular way, but some individual cells to have a different format. By using these checkboxes, you can choose to either set unique formatting for the cell, or to use the settings for the entire column.

 <u>L</u>ock. Use the <u>L</u>ock box to prevent yourself from entering data in a particular cell. It may sound silly, but you might want to put locks on several cells you want to use later. Or, if you design a form for others to fill out, you can make the process easier by locking the cells you don't want them to edit.

 <u>I</u>gnore When Calculating. Use the <u>I</u>gnore When Calculating box when you've formatted a row or column for calculations and you want to exclude a specific cell from those calculations. For example, you might want to put a subtotal in a particular cell, but not want the subtotal added to the other numbers for the total of the column or row.

TRICK

The block and edit commands you use on regular text can also be used on data in tables. For instance, if you want to format a number of cells at one time, press the Block key (Alt-F4 or F12), mark out the cells you want to format, and then choose the <u>C</u>ell option. Whatever formatting changes you make will then apply to all marked cells.

Now, select Cancel to close the Cell Format window.

Column Formats

You should now be back at the Table Edit window. Choose C<u>o</u>lumn, and the Column Format window should open, as shown in figure 13.5. This window lets you format all the cells in a column at the same time.

Figure 13.5:

Column Format
dialog box.

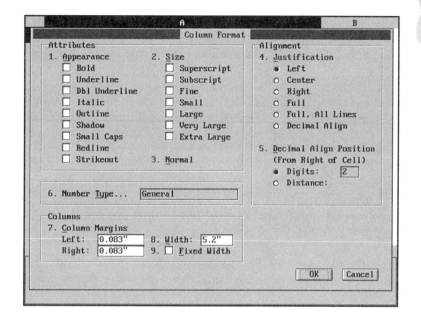

This window is just like the Cell Format window, but features the Column Margins section. These margin settings indicate how close to the edge of the box you want the text to be during printing. The defaults usually are pretty good selections.

However, you need to change the default **J**ustification setting for the second column, so that the numbers line up on the decimal points for this example. (Remember that the second column will contain prices.) To align the prices, select Decimal Align. The default decimal alignment of two digits is perfect for your grocery list prices, so you don't need to change anything else. Select OK; WordPerfect sets up the price column and the Column Format window closes.

Row Formats

You should now be back at the Table Edit window; select **R**ow. The Row Format window appears, and offers several options.

The Row Margins and Row Heights options are used to format the way text appears in relation to the cells. The defaults are fine and you don't need to change them often. What you might want to look at is the Lines of Text. Do you want the row limited to one line of text per row, or do you want to be able to enter multiple lines per row? The default of multiple lines is more flexible, but if you're designing a form, this might screw everything up, so you might want to force some rows to only contain a single line of text.

The **H**eader Row is a nice feature to use for long tables. If you designate a row as a header row, whatever headings you type automatically print at the top of the table if it needs to be printed on two or more pages. You don't need the **H**eader Row feature for your shopping list, but you might find it useful in the future.

Close the Row Format window. In the Table Edit window, select **T**able. Any settings you make in the Table Edit window affect the entire table. Of course, you can override any table-wide settings by using settings in the Row, Column, and Cell windows.

Time to close the Table Edit window and type information into your table. Select Close to return to your table and enter data.

Entering Table Information

You can't enter information into the table in the Table Edit window. The window is strictly for formatting the table layout. Place the cursor in cell A1 and begin typing in the grocery list. Use figure 13.6 as your guide.

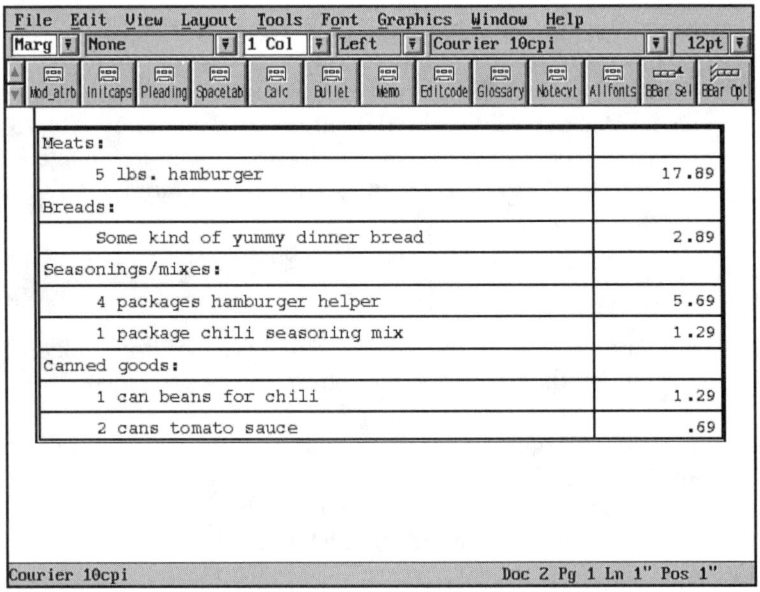

Figure 13.6:

The shopping list table.

As you type, use table 13.1 to find movement keys that will help you get around.

Table 13.1
Moving around Tables

These Keys...	Move You Here...
Down arrow	Down one cell
Shift-Tab	Left one cell
Tab	Right one cell
Up arrow	Up one cell
Enter	Creates a new line within the cell; all other cells on that row are also affected by this
Ctrl-Home, up arrow	Beginning of text in cell
Ctrl-Home, down arrow	Last line of text in cell
Ctrl-Home, Home, up arrow	First cell in column
Ctrl-Home, Home, down arrow	Last cell in column
Ctrl-Home, Home, left arrow	First cell in row
Ctrl-Home, End	Last cell in row
Ctrl-Home, Home, Home, up arrow	First cell in table
Ctrl-Home, Home, Home, down arrow	Last cell in table

The keystrokes shown in table 13.2 work only in the Table Edit window.

Table 13.2
Moving in a Table from the Table Edit Window

These Keys...	Move You Here...
Ctrl-Home, Cell address or Cell name	Specific cell
Ctrl-Home, Column name	Specific column
Ctrl-Home, Row name	Specific row
Ctrl-Home, Table name	Another table
Ctrl-Home, Cell, Column,	Cell/column/row in another or Row name table

To indent information in a table, press F4.

After you finish entering your shopping list, it should look like the table in figure 13.6.

Adding a Row to a Table

Oops! You still need an extra row for the total amount of the second mortgage. Better do it. Here's how:

1. Make sure that the cursor is in row 10.

2. Press Alt-F7,T,E to return to the Table Edit window.

3. Select **T**able, then **E**dit.

4. Select **I**ns from the Table Edit window.

5. The Insert window opens, and asks if you want to add columns or rows to the table. For this example, select **R**ows.

6. At the **H**ow Many? prompt, make sure that the answer is **1**.

7. Select **A**fter Cursor Position to place the new row after row 10.

8. Choose OK, and the new row appears at the bottom of the table.

Totaling Up

The last task in the Edit Table window is to total up the price column (column B). The prices are estimates, but they should be close. Especially the last digit. Everything in the grocery store ends in a "9." To total up column B, perform the following steps:

1.   Position the cursor in the cell where you want the total, probably B11 or the last cell in the last column.

2.   Select **F**ormula. The Table Formula window appears.

3.   In the Formula entry field, type **Sum(B1:B10)** and select OK. The Sum formula adds the values in the cells you specify in the parentheses. In this case, B1:B10 specifies for WordPerfect to add up the numbers in cells B1 through B10. The total (29.64) appears in cell B11.

4.   Close the Table Edit window.

5.   Move your cursor to cell A11 and enter the word **TOTAL**.

FOOD FOR THOUGHT

All the math functions you can use on tables are in the button marked Functions...F5 in the Table Formula window. Sum is one of the functions you'll find. Functions accompanied by the word "list" require a list of the cells to be included in the function.

SAVE THE DAY

To use any of the functions in your columns, you must *always* have an opening and a closing parenthesis. If you don't, you get an error message.

Great! Now your table looks like the one in figure 13.7.

Figure 13.7:

More of shopping list
table.

File Edit View Layout Tools Font Graphics Window Help		
Meats:		
5 lbs. hamburger		17.89
Breads:		
Some kind of yummy dinner bread		2.89
Seasonings/mixes:		
4 packages hamburger helper		5.69
1 package chili seasoning mix		1.29
Canned goods:		
1 can beans for chili		1.29
2 cans tomato sauce		.69
TOTAL		29.74

Courier 10cpi   Doc 2 Pg 1 Ln 1" Pos 1"

Creating Forms with Tables

One of the most useful things you can do with tables is create forms that
others can then fill in and print. If you work in an office that has standardized on WordPerfect, this is a real time-saver. Just create the forms that
people need to fill in, put them on the network or distribute to others via
floppy disks, and voilà, you have electronic forms that never run out, and
don't cost you any money from the printers.

In this section, you'll learn how to create a basic form that people can use
to order office supplies. It will be small because it's a learning example, but
you'll learn enough to be able to apply these techniques to virtually any
form you might want to design using tables. Along the way, you'll learn
about:

 Working with borders, lines, and fills to spiff up your form

 Using Join to make the table grid conform to your form design

 Using the Cell Lock feature to make the form easier to use—and
harder for others to mess up

 Using simple math and formulas

When you are finished with this exercise, your sample form will look like figure 13.8.

This section will cover a lot of ground, so rev up your engines and go!

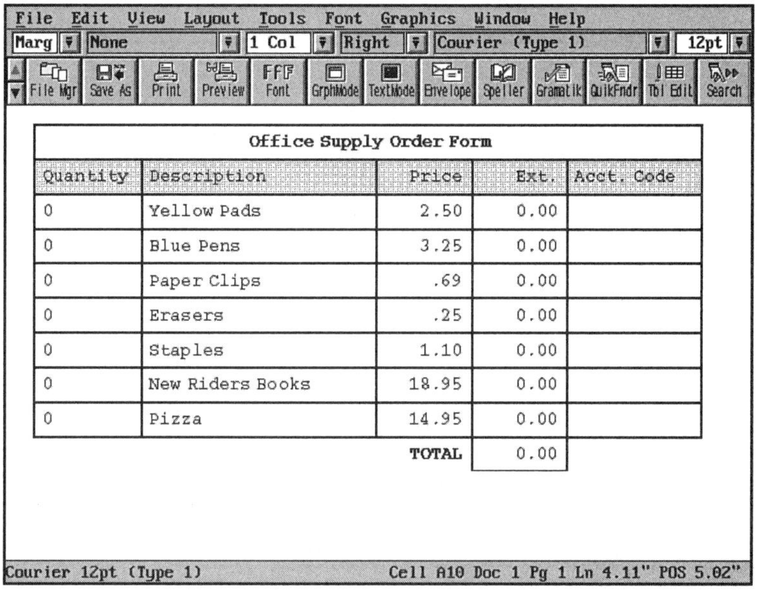

Figure 13.8:

The finished product.

Creating the Basic Table

Follow these steps to create the basic table:

1. Pull down the **L**ayout menu and choose **T**ables.

2. Choose **C**reate.

3. WordPerfect will ask you how many columns and rows your table will contain. Choose 5 columns and 10 rows and press Enter.

You will see your new table in the Table Edit window.

Joining Cells

One very powerful feature in WordPerfect's tables is the capability to join cells to create one large cell. In this way, your table doesn't have to be a simple square grid, but can be customized so that it appears to have different shapes. For example, notice in figure 13.8 how the top row has been converted to be one large cell. Here's how to create that one large cell at the top of the table:

1. Move your cursor so that it is in cell A1.

2. Press the Block key (Alt-F4 or F12), and move your cursor to the far right of the table. All of the cells on the top row will be blocked.

3. Choose **J**oin from the list of commands below. A dialog box will appear asking if you are sure you want to do this; choose **Y**es.

The large cell that was created will hold the title for your form.

Changing the Table Border

On-screen you will see that the table has a double-line border around it. You'll be doing some tricks to hide some of the cells, which means that this border is in your way. To get rid of the double border, follow these steps:

1. Choose **L**ines/Fill from the list of options at the bottom of the screen.

2. The Table Lines dialog box appears. The top two settings, **D**efault Line and Bord**e**r/Fill, control these two parts for the entire table. For this example, you want to turn the border of the table off. Select Bord**e**r/Fill, then choose **B**order Style, and then None.

3. Choose the OK button, and then the Close button to return to the Table Edit dialog box.

Hiding Cells

If you look carefully at figure 13.8, you will see how it seems that the TOTAL label is hanging outside of the body of the form. In reality, all tables must be square, and the TOTAL label is actually inside of a cell. How is this possible? Simple: the cell was made so that it is joined, *and then made invisible*. Here's how to set this up:

1. Move your cursor to cell A10.

2. Press Block (Alt-F4 or F12) and move your pointer to cell C10.

3. Choose **J**oin and then select the OK button to confirm the join.

4. Choose **L**ines/Fill. The **L**ines/Fill dialog box will appear, as shown in figure 13.9.

Figure 13.9:

Lines/Fill dialog box.

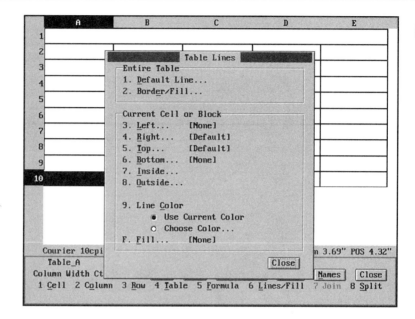

5. Turn off the bottom and left lines. Select **B**ottom, and then choose None from the list. Then select **L**eft, and choose None from the list.

TRICK

You can affect the lines for multiple cells by blocking the cells before choosing **L**ines/Fill.

6. Choose the Close button to close the Table Lines dialog box.

7. To continue with the example, you also want to make cell E10 invisible using this same technique. Move your cursor to cell E10 (bottom right cell), choose **L**ines/Fill, and set the **B**ottom and **R**ight lines to None. Select the Close button to return to the Table Edit screen.

At this point, your table should be taking shape, and should look like figure 13.10.

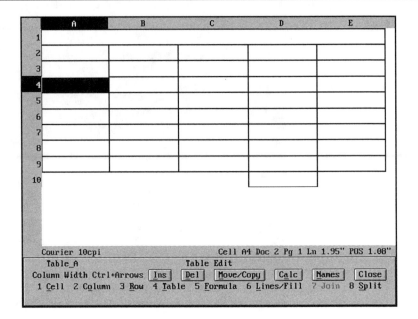

Adding Shading to Cells

One thing that really makes a table stand out is the use of shading. In the example form that is being used to illustrate tables (see fig. 13.8), you'll notice that the entire second row is shaded. To add this effect:

1. Move to cell A2.

2. Press Block (Alt-F4 or F12) and move your cursor to cell E2.

3. Choose Lines/Fill.

4. From the Table Lines dialog box, choose Fill.

5. From the Fill Style and Color dialog box, choose Fill Style. A list of fill styles will appear. Choose 10% Shaded Fill and press Enter.

6. Choose the OK button and then the Close button to return to the Table Edit window.

TRICK

Different printers print different levels of shading. To find out which level of shading your printer prints best, set up a table that contains 10 cells and shade each one a different Shaded Fill percentage, from 10% to 100% and then print the table. This shows you how each one looks on your specific printer. Adding some text to the shaded cells also shows you how well text reads with each shade percentage.

Adding Labels

You've gone about as far as you can go without adding the labels for the form you're designing. You can't enter text into a table while you're editing the table itself, so press F7 to return to the document, which will have your table thus far all ready for filling. Use table 13.3 to enter each of the labels for each cell in the sample table you create in this section. As you are entering text, some of it wraps around inside the cell or does not format exactly as shown in figure 13.8. Don't worry about that now; you'll learn how to fix it in a minute. Just enter all the information into the cells.

TRICK

The cell number where your cursor is located is shown in the status line at the bottom of your document.

Table 13.3
Labels for Sample Form

Cell Location	What You Type
A1	Office Supply Order Form
A2	Quantity
B2	Description

continues

Table 13.3
continued

Cell Location	What You Type
C2	Price
D2	Ext.
E2	Acct. Code
B3	Yellow Pads
C3	2.50
B4	Blue Pens
C4	3.25
B5	Paper Clips
C5	.69
B6	Erasers
C6	.25
B7	Staples
C7	1.10
B8	New Riders Books
C8	18.95
B9	Pizza
C9	14.95
A10	TOTAL

Final Formatting

Now that all the labels are in your table, it's time to do the final formatting and spiff up everything. After that's done, you'll learn how to add the formulas so that the form automatically totals the order. This final section will walk you through all of these final steps.

Adjusting Column Width

The easiest way to adjust the column width for your form is to use the Ctrl-arrow keys and adjust the column widths until everything looks good. To do this:

1. Go back into Table Edit mode. Press Alt-F7,T,E to do that.

2. Move your cursor to any cell in column A. Because you don't need such a wide column A, you can reduce its width. Press Ctrl-left arrow until the word "Quantity" just barely fits. If you move too far and "Quantity" gets wrapped onto two lines, just press Ctrl-right arrow to correct the problem.

3. Move to any cell in column C. You don't need quite as wide a column for Price as the default width. Narrow the column by pressing Ctrl-left arrow repeatedly. Again, if the word "Price" or any of the numbers below gets wrapped onto two lines, simply press Ctrl-right arrow to straighten things out again.

4. Using the same procedure, narrow the column for Ext. so that it is just a bit wider than the Price column (just estimate this visually). Also shrink the Acct. Code column.

5. The Description column could use some more space. Move to column B and press Ctrl-right arrow to widen it about 50 percent. You will know when it is wide enough when "New Riders Books" all fits on one line.

Justifying Cells

Now that you have your column widths adjusted, you can set the alignment for the various cells. There are several adjustments to make:

1. Move to cell A1.

2. Select **C**ell.

3. Choose **J**ustification and then **C**enter.

4. Choose the OK button.

Typically, in forms such as this, the headings for the numeric columns are right-justified. Follow these steps to do this:

1. Move to cell C2.

2. Press Block (Alt-F4 or F12) and move right one cell, to cell D2.

3. Choose **C**ell, **J**ustification, **R**ight and select the OK button. This will cause the headings for Price and Ext. to be right justified.

Notice how all the numbers in the Price column are aligned in a haphazard fashion. Generally, you'll want columns of numbers to be aligned on their decimal points. Also, in anticipation of adding the formulas later, you'll want to align the Ext. column in the same way. Lastly, you can make your form neater by specifying the numeric format for the cells that contain numbers. The **C**ell format dialog box lets you set both of these attributes (decimal alignment and numeric format) at the same time. To do this, follow these steps:

1. Move to cell C3.

2. Press Block (Alt-F4 or F12) and mark all cells down to C9.

3. Choose **C**ell, **J**ustification, **D**ecimal Align to cause the range of cells to align on the decimal point. While you're in the **C**ell dialog box, choose Number **T**ype, choose **F**ixed, press Enter, and then select the OK button.

4. Move to cell D3.

5. Press Block and mark all cells down to D10 (you want to format the cell where the total will go, too).

6. Choose **C**ell, **J**ustification, and **D**ecimal Align. Then, choose Number **T**ype, choose **F**ixed and press Enter.

7. Select the OK button to close the Cell Format dialog box.

Lastly, you will want to justify the cell that contains the TOTAL label so that it is right justified. To do this:

1. Move to cell A10.

2. Choose **C**ell, **J**ustification, **R**ight and then select the OK button.

Locking Cells

In forms that you're designing with WordPerfect that others will fill out, you can make it more convenient for them by making the cursor avoid all the label fields. By avoiding the label fields, the user cannot screw up the form labels accidentally. To lock the cells, follow these steps:

1. Move to cell A1.

2. Choose **C**ell, **L**ock. You will see an 'x' appear in the **L**ock checkbox. Choose the OK button.

3. Repeat the above for cells A2 through E2 (you can block that entire range), cell A10, and cell E10.

If you ever need to unlock these cells, perhaps to change the data in them, repeat the above procedure so that the **L**ock checkbox is unchecked. After you've made your changes, you can relock them in the same way.

Adding Formulas

Because you're using a computer to fill out this form, wouldn't it be nice if you could get the computer to do all the math for you? If you're designing a form for others to use, automatic calculation helps ensure that the other users won't make math mistakes and create a nightmare for the Accounting department. The example table created in the section "Creating the Basic Table" can be used to add a formula for each order line that takes the quantity and multiplies it by the price. Follow these steps:

1. Move to cell D3.

2. Choose **F**ormula.

3. Type in **A3*C3** and press Enter.

FOOD FOR THOUGHT

A computer doesn't have a distinct multiply key or divide key, so it uses an asterisk (*) for multiply and the forward slash (/) for divide.

At this point, you could repeat the above for each row of your table, but that would be pretty laborious, wouldn't it? Fortunately, WordPerfect provides a cell copy feature that automatically adjusts the formula for each line. To copy your formula to the other lines:

1. Starting in cell D3, choose **M**ove/Copy.

2. The Move dialog box appears. Because you want to copy rather than move, choose the Co**p**y button.

3. You now have the choice of copying the cell contents to a single cell (To **C**ell), to the **R**ight, or **D**own. You want to copy this cell down, so choose **D**own.

4. WordPerfect will ask How Many? It is asking how many cells down you want to copy the cell contents. Type in **6** and press Enter twice.

After a moment of thinking, your formula will be automatically copied into each line of your form and you will return to the Table Edit window. WordPerfect is even smart enough to make sure that each line contains the formula that refers to that particular line and not to the line you originally copied the formula from. So, for example, cell D6 contains the formula A6*C6, cell D7 contains A7*C7, and so on.

Adding a Total

The final touch to add to your form is the formula for the total at the bottom of the form. To add this:

1. Move to cell D10.

2. Select **F**ormula. Type in the formula **SUM(D3:D9)** and press Enter twice.

SUM is the name of the function. The parentheses contain information the function needs to calculate, in this case the range of cells to total. The range of cells is indicated by entering the starting cell and ending cell, separated by a colon.

Calculating Your Form

You're now finished setting up your form (and aren't you glad!). Press F7 to return to your document, where you should find your form all ready to fill out. Before you mess with it, though, make sure to save it by pressing F10, type in a file name (like OFFSUPP.FRM) and press Enter.

When you use your form, you'll enter in a quantity for each item you want to order. However, you'll notice as you enter in those quantities that the formula portions of the form don't automatically calculate. This is because you have to tell WordPerfect when to calculate the form. To do this:

1. While the cursor is anywhere within the table, press Alt-F7.

2. Choose **T**ables, C**a**lculate All.

That's all that's required to get an up-to-date total for your table formulas.

CHAPTER 14

Caution: Merge Ahead

One of the most powerful and useful features of modern word processors is the capability to take information, such as a mailing list, and merge that data with a letter or form to create a large number of automatic copies. Now you can annoy many more people with much less work!

This chapter shows you how to use WordPerfect's merge functions. You do the following:

 Create a list of names and addresses

 Create a standard letter for your merge

 Perform a merge that automatically creates envelopes for every letter

Once you master WordPerfect's merge capabilities, you can become a direct-mail tycoon!

Creating a Data File

Before you can do a merge, you must have a file that contains specific data for the merge: a *data file*. You create the data file, inserting the necessary data for WordPerfect to perform the merge properly.

Data File Definitions

Before you create your data file, take a couple minutes to familiarize yourself with a few terms from database software: field, record, and database.

Imagine a database set up with a list of all your friends. Each entry for each friend is a *record*. So, let's say for your database you have, er, two records (that's a lot, right?). Each record is divided into *fields*. The entry that contains your friend's name is one field, his or her street address is another field, and the city, state, and ZIP code are still more fields. You also may have a field that specifies how much money they owe you. You can call this your "field of dreams."

All of the records together are stored in a single file on the computer. This is the *database*.

Setting Up the Data File

Before you create a data file, you need to iron out your fields. To understand this whole merge business, try an example. The following fields are for today's lesson:

Name
Address
City
State
Zip
Salutation

You want to include the field *Salutation* because you're merging a letter and you want the right kind of greeting for whomever you're sending the letter. For example, you might address some people by first name (Dear Barney), while you might address others more formally (Dear Mr. Rubble). Still others you might address uniquely (Dear Bonehead). Including salutation as a field enables you to designate appropriate greetings. You see the idea clearly when you create the letter.

To prepare a data file for WordPerfect, you have to indicate the end of each field and the end of each record. You prepare data files by using a couple of special keys.

To begin to create a merge document:

1. Open a new document.

2. First, you need to tell WordPerfect what type of merge document you're using. Press Shift-F9 or pull down the **T**ools menu, click on M**e**rge, and then click on **D**efine. The Merge Codes window appears (see fig. 14.1).

Figure 14.1:

The Merge Codes window.

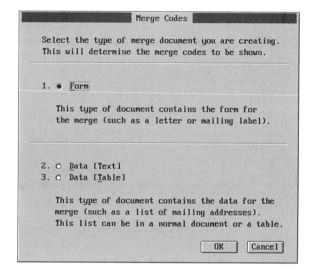

3. Because you're defining a data file, click on **D**ata [Text] or press D.

    The Merge Codes (Text Data File) window appears (see fig. 14.2).

    The box on the left shows common merge codes you can choose to insert into the document automatically. The box on the right enables you to define how you want WordPerfect to display the merge codes. The default is Show Full Codes. Leave it. You want to see what you're doing, after all.

4. Before you create your data file, you need to name the fields you'll be using. Select Field **N**ames or press N.

The Field Names window appears. At the top you enter new field names; a list box also appears (the Field Name list box) showing field names that are already defined.

Figure 14.2:

The Merge Codes
(Text Data File)
window.

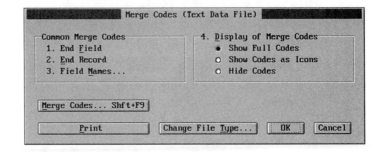

5.   Type the field names listed here, and press Enter after each one.

Name
Address
City
State
Zip
Salutation

After you're done, your screen looks like figure 14.3.

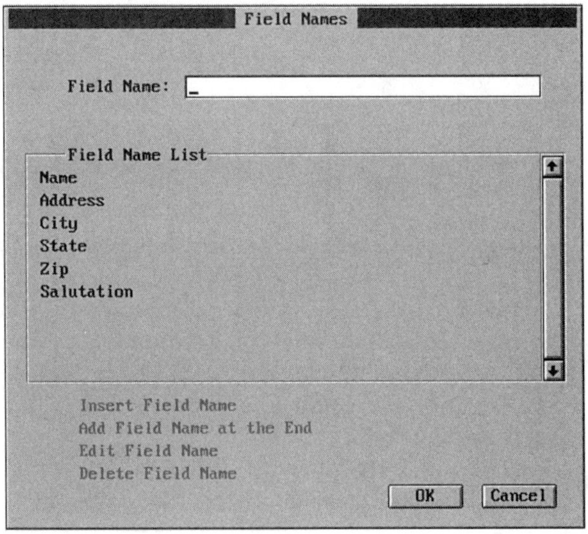

Figure 14.3:

The completed Field
Names window.

If you make any mistakes and need to fix any entries, press Tab or click on the entry you want to change. The editing items at the bottom of the window (Insert Field Name, Add Field Name at the End, and so on) become active.

6. If you screw up an entry, select Edit Field Name to fix it.

7. After you finish, select OK to save the field names you've entered (use the Tab key or click on OK).

After you return to the document, it looks like figure 14.4.

Figure 14.4:

The Data file document.

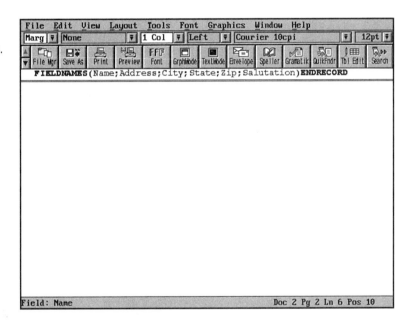

WordPerfect created a record at the top of the document. It defines the names of the fields you type. WordPerfect uses it to figure out which field is which when you do the merge.

Entering Data into the Data File

The preceding section shows you the steps you take to create a merge document. After you are done naming the fields, you are ready to enter the data into the merge document. It's time to get on with merging your friends!

1. Now that you have defined the names of the fields that you'll be using, it's time to enter the actual data. Enter the first data field by typing **Barney Rubble**.

2. Press F9 to tell WordPerfect that you have finished typing the first field and are ready to move on to the next field. The code **ENDFIELD** appears right after Barney Rubble and the cursor moves to the next line, ready for the next field.

FOOD FOR THOUGHT

The ENDFIELD code defines where one field (like the name) ends, and where the next one (like the address) begins.

STOP!

For a correct merge, you need to use F9 at the end of each field rather than pressing Enter. WordPerfect needs to know where the field ends, and it uses the ENDFIELD code to do that. If you press Enter rather than F9, WordPerfect will think that you're still working on the same field; it's not smart enough to know if you are just using multiple-line fields or not, which is why using F9 is critical here.

3. Enter the rest of the Barney info, as listed here. Type the following lines and press F9 after each line, including the last line.

111 Rocky Road**ENDFIELD**
Boulder**ENDFIELD**
CO**ENDFIELD**
55555**ENDFIELD**
Barney**ENDFIELD**

TRICK

If you type a record, but don't fill in a field you've defined, you still need to use ENDFIELD (F9) on a blank line for the missing data, so that WordPerfect doesn't get confused about which field is which. For example, if you define two address lines, but only need one line, put **ENDFIELD** on the blank line.

The reason you do this is that WordPerfect counts the number of fields for each record, and if you miss one of the fields in a record, it gets all confused as to where everything is supposed to be. Hey, nobody said computers were actually smart!

After you complete the full record for Barney, you need to tell WordPerfect you're finished and are ready to do the next record. To tell WordPerfect you're finished with this record, you need to insert the **ENDRECORD** code:

1. Press Shift-F9 to pull up the Merge Codes window.

2. Click on **E**nd Record or press E.

The added **ENDRECORD** appears immediately following the salutation, as well as a hard page break (the hard page line also shows you the end of the record). See figure 14.5.

Figure 14.5:

A completed record.

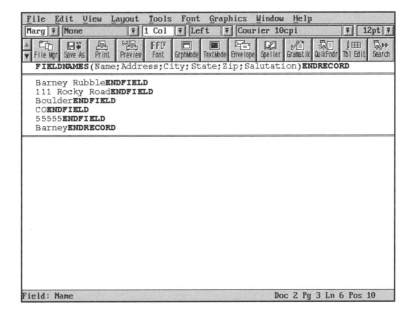

3. Enter the following records, and refer to the preceding exercise if you have any trouble. Remember to press F9 after every field, and press Shift-F9,E at the end of every record. If you get lost, the status line tells you which field you're in; this is displayed in the lower left-hand corner of your screen.

    The Honorable Bullwinkle Moose
    505 Circus Lane
    Washington
    DC
    11111
    Honorable Moose

    Betty Boop
    123 Boop-Boop-Dee-Doo Lane
    Beverly Hills
    CA
    90210
    Ms. Boop

    Wile E. Coyote
    5 Acme Road
    Phoenix
    AZ
    90231
    Mr. Coyote

After you finish the data file, save it.

4. Press F10 to save it, and name the file **DATAFILE.WP.**

Creating a Form File

Next, create the form file. The *form file* is the letter you want to send to everyone in your data list. By the way, how about a big round of applause for WordPerfect for the names of the files in WordPerfect 6.0. In WordPerfect 5.1, the data file was called the Primary file and the form file was called the Secondary file. Nobody could ever remember which file did which! Data file and form file are much easier to keep straight, don't you think?

You're going to write a brief letter and set it up to be a form letter.

1. To begin, open a new document and close the DATAFILE.WP document if you need to (remember to save!).

2. In the new document, press Shift-F9.

    The Merge Codes window appears because you have a new file (see fig. 14.1).

3. Select **F**orm if it isn't already selected and click on OK. The Merge Codes (Form File) window appears, as shown in figure 14.6. Note the way the box on the left is different from the one in figure 14.2. The reason is the merge options for a form are different from the merge options for a data file.

Figure 14.6:

The Merge Codes (Form File) window.

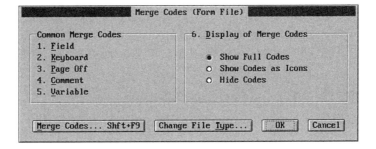

The functions in this window include:

 Field. You use the **F**ield function to insert a particular field at the current cursor position.

 Keyboard. The **K**eyboard function enables you to decide at what point in the form you want WordPerfect to pause for each record and ask for your input to be incorporated in the document.

 Page Off. In most merges WordPerfect forces a hard page break between every form. By using **P**age Off, you can let all the merged forms run together.

Comment. If you work on a complex mail merge, **C**omment enables you to insert a comment into the form file to help you figure out what you did when you come back later to look at the document. Comments don't print; they exist purely for your benefit (or for the poor sucker who has to figure out your work!).

 Variable. Advanced users create merge documents more like programs than simple mail merges. **V**ariable enables you to include a variable from a macro or another document.

4.   You don't need to insert codes for your task, so click on OK to close the window.

You have now designated this new document as the one that will contain your form letter, and set any options that you need. The next step is to actually type both the letter itself as well as the special insertion codes that tell WordPerfect where to put the names and addresses for your letter.

Creating a Merge Letter

Before you can run off a thousand form letters to all the people you want to pester, you need to create a merge codes document. The steps you use to create this are in the section "Creating a Data File," earlier in this chapter. The example used here—a merge list of all your friends—illustrates the most commonly used parts of merging a letter. Refer to earlier sections to create this example.

If you already have a data file, you can create merge letters to your heart's content. To create the documents into which the merge codes will be placed:

1.   Unless your document is already on-screen (it should be from the last exercise if you've been following along), press Shift-F10 to load it. Enter the name of your form file and then click on OK to load the file.

Your cursor should be at the top of the page. If necessary for your form letter, create your letterhead at the top of the page and move your cursor to where you want the person's name and address to appear.

Inserting a Data Field Code in a Document

You now want to insert a code indicating the name from the data file to fill in the first line of the name and address when you merge. Do the following steps:

1. Press Shift-F9 to pull up the Merge Codes (Form File) window. If you have not yet designated this document as being a form file, then select **F**orm and click on the OK button.

2. Select **F**ield—click on it, or type **F**.

3. A window appears, prompting you for the field to insert. Type **NAME** and press Enter.

    The code **FIELD**(*NAME*) is inserted into your document. When WordPerfect performs the merge, the name from your data file replaces the code.

4. Move to the next line and insert the code for the address line. Press Shift-F9,F and type **CITY**, then press Enter to insert the code. Press Enter again to move to the third line of the address.

    The third line is tricky because you use three (count 'em, three) merge codes on one line: City, State, and ZIP.

5. Press Shift-F9,F and type **ADDRESS**, then press Enter to insert the code. Next, type a comma (,) and a space. To insert the State code, press Shift-F9,F, type **STATE** and press Enter. Finally, type a single space (between the State and ZIP codes) and enter the code for ZIP (you know what to do by now, right?).

6. For the final merge code, Salutation, press Enter twice to move down two lines.

Observe the following steps to insert the Salutation merge code:

1. Type **Dear** followed by a space.

2. Insert the merge code for Salutation. Press Shift-F9,F and type **SALUTATION**, then press Enter.

3. To finish, enter a comma (,) and press Enter twice to move to the beginning of the letter body.

4. It's time for the easy part. Type the body of your letter.

5. After you finish the form, save it, using the file name FORM.WP.

Merging: Watch Out for That Tree!

After you set up and save to disk your data file and form file, merging the two documents is cake. Merging is so easy, in fact, that you're going to complicate it a little bit and learn the way to not only merge your form, but also generate envelopes for every letter!

To begin actually merging two documents:

1. Press Ctrl-F9 and select **M**erge from the window that appears.

   The Run Merge window appears (see fig. 14.7).

Figure 14.7:

The Run Merge window.

Run Merge
Form File: ▼
Data File: ▼
Output: Unused Document ◆
Repeat Merge for Each Data Record: 1
Display of Merge Codes   Hide Merge Codes   ◆
Data File Options...
File List... F5   QuickList... F6   Merge   Cancel

2. In the field for the form file, type **FORM.WP** (or the name of the file you used for your form) and press Enter.

3. In the Data File field, type **DATAFILE.WP** (or the name of the file you used for your data file) and press Enter.

4. If all you want to do is merge the letter, just select the Merge button. You're finished, unless you want to merge envelopes too.

TRICK

If your printer can't print envelopes, you might want to skip the next part and click on the Merge button to complete the merge. Go ahead and follow along so that you know how it works, but remember that not all printers can handle envelopes. See Chapter 7, "Printing Your Letter," for more information on printing and using envelopes in a printer.

Merging Envelopes

One nice feature that was added in WordPerfect 6.0 is the capability to have WordPerfect automatically generate an envelope for each form letter it merges. This section assumes that you have done everything in the preceding section, because the envelope option is available only during the entire merge process.

1. To generate envelopes select the Data File Options button. The Run Merge window expands, showing more options (see fig. 14.8).

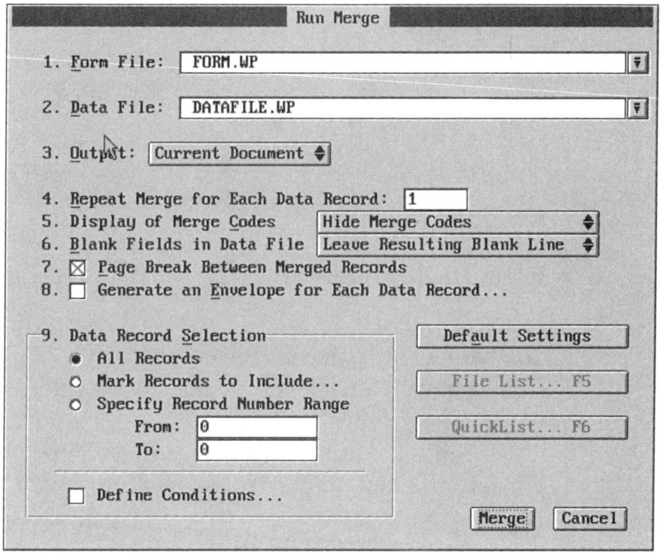

Figure 14.8:

The expanded Run Merge window.

```
                         Run Merge
  1. Form File:    FORM.WP                                  ▼
  2. Data File:    DATAFILE.WP                              ▼
  3. Output:  Current Document ◆
  4. Repeat Merge for Each Data Record:  1
  5. Display of Merge Codes      Hide Merge Codes          ◆
  6. Blank Fields in Data File   Leave Resulting Blank Line ◆
  7. ☒ Page Break Between Merged Records
  8. ☐ Generate an Envelope for Each Data Record...
  ┌─9. Data Record Selection──────┐   ┌Default Settings┐
  │  ● All Records                │
  │  ○ Mark Records to Include... │   ┌  File List... F5 ┐
  │  ○ Specify Record Number Range│
  │       From: │0        │       │   ┌ QuickList... F6 ┐
  │       To:   │0        │       │
  └───────────────────────────────┘
  ☐ Define Conditions...
                                       ┌Merge┐ ┌Cancel┐
```

2. Select Generate an **E**nvelope for Each Data Record.

The Envelope window appears, as shown in figure 14.9. Yep, you define the information for your envelope in the Envelope window.

Begin by typing the return address for every envelope.

3. Select **R**eturn Address. The cursor moves to the box for the address. Type your address.

4. When you're done entering the return address, press F7 to finish editing it.

Figure 14.9:

The Envelope window.

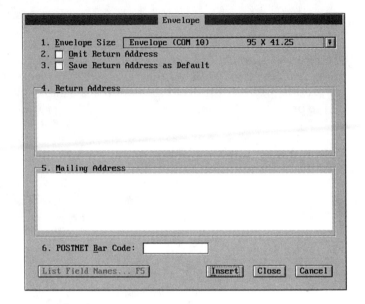

5. Select **M**ailing Address.

    Now you want to use merge codes to automatically take the name
    and address from the merge file. To do this, follow these steps:

6. Press Shift-F9,F to insert a merge field. Type **NAME** and press Enter.
    Move to the next line by pressing Enter again.

7. Again, press Shift-F9,F, then type **ADDRESS**. Press Enter twice.

8. Fill in the third line yourself. Use all three merge codes (CITY, STATE
    ZIP). Press F7 when you're finished editing. Your screen should look
    like figure 14.10.

9. Select the **I**nsert button to save your envelope information. You
    return to the Run Merge window.

    OK, everything is done and you're ready to merge.

10. Cross your fingers and click on the Merge button to have
    WordPerfect perform the merge.

Figure 14.10:

The completed Envelope window.

After the merge is complete, you are taken to a new document, which is the result of the merge. You find a copy of your letter for everyone on your list. And further down, you find an envelope for each one of them!

11. If your merge didn't go right, and the names and addresses got mixed up, check two important things, both in the data file:

 Make sure every record has the same number of fields. If any record has an extra field or is short a field, the merge doesn't work right.

 Make sure **ENDFIELD** and **ENDRECORD** are in the right places (the end of all fields and the end of all records, respectively). If they are in the wrong places, delete and reinsert them.

12. If the document resulting from the merge is fine, print it, save it, or both!

Other Uses for Merging

A number of other uses for merging exist:

 Set up a form for labels. Merge your address list or perhaps a list of file folder titles onto labels.

 Create a form and use the Keyboard merge code to prompt you (or someone else) for all the pertinent data.

 If you have your address list in a data file, you can purchase Rolodex cards for your printer and print all your Rolodex cards!

Doubtless, quite a few other uses for merging exist. Let your imagination run wild!

Word Perfect

GLOSSARY

Nerdy Words

Application. The programs you bought to make your life easier, like the WordPerfect word processor, spreadsheets, and games.

ASCII. American Standard Code for Information Interchange. Even though this sounds pretty important, it's really just a way of saying basic text. In other words the numbers 0 through 9, basic punctuation characters, and the letters of the alphabet. See also *Extended ASCII character set*.

Attribute. Any characteristic you assign to a character. That can be things like **bold**, <u>underline</u>, and so on.

AUTOEXEC.BAT. This is a batch file that gets executed each time you start up your computer. It contains commands that can be personalized to your computer setup and tells the operating system and other programs where to find your files and what to do when you first start the session.

Backup. An extra copy of your program and data files. Back up often, back up regularly, and don't let an unexpected problem back *you* up against the wall.

Batch file. A series of instructions that you (or some nerd) have typed and saved in a file so that they can be done all at one time by your computer.

Block. Text or graphics that is highlighted and will be affected by the next action such as moving, deleting, or reformatting in some manner.

Buffer. A fluffy cloth used to polish the wax on your car. This is really the magic area where your last deletion went; you can recover it by using the undelete function in WordPerfect. The buffer is also the area where the words go when you want to move, copy, or paste them somewhere else. The buffer area is in RAM, so if you lose power you lose the words in the buffer.

Button Bar. Where all the single buttons go to hear live jazz. The Button Bar is actually a nice arrangement of icons (pictures and/or words) that can be arranged on-screen to invoke some functions by using a mouse. Some people prefer using the Button Bar for their most commonly accessed functions as a replacement for calling them with pull-down menus or keystrokes.

Cell. The little box in a table where you imprison a bit of text or numbers.

Click. When you want your mouse to perform a function, like open a file or start a program, press down on one of the buttons on top of your mouse. This action is called a click. When you press down twice real fast, you double-click. A click usually refers to the left mouse button.

Clip-art. Little ready-to-use pictures that come with WordPerfect and other software packages that you can use in your documents or letters. These are really handy for the person who writes better than they draw. You can size these pictures to your needs.

Clipboard. The clipboard is similar to the buffer, but words put into a buffer disappear into deep space when you exit WordPerfect or block new text. Words or pictures can be put in the clipboard and then used in another document, even though you've closed the old one. Like the buffer area, anything in the clipboard also departs to deep space once you lose power or turn off your computer.

Codes. Codes used in WordPerfect are no secret, they're just shorthand notations for the instructions you put in your document that don't actually show up in the printed product. They include all sorts of things like attributes that you have given a word or character (bold, underlined, etc.), the kind of type you have chosen, whether you want a decimal tab or a regular tab and things like that.

Command. An instruction you give to your computer or the WordPerfect program.

Compiler. A special program that turns a human-readable file into a file the computer can read and process faster.

CONFIG.SYS. This file is executed when you power on your computer. It is where commands such as how to load device drivers and other setup stuff is located.

CPS. Characters Per Second. The speed (or lack thereof) of a dot matrix printer is measured in how many characters it can print in one second.

CRT. Cathode Ray Tube. A popular blues singer. Actually, it's another name for your computer monitor.

Cursor. A person who has a narrow vocabulary and a bad outlook on life. On your computer, it's the little blinking line or box on your screen and acts as a placement to let you know where the next character you type is going to go.

Data. Information that you generate from your application programs. Letters, spreadsheets, and files are all data.

Data file. Information that you generate from your application programs that you save to disk.

Decimal tab. A decimal tab makes it so that your columns of numbers line up in a nice, neat row by the decimal point. With a regular tab, everything you type goes to the right of the tab. Since you can use *proportional spacing* with WordPerfect, numbers don't line up properly with a regular tab.

Delimiter. A character that tells a record or field or action to *begin here*, and after you type what you want, to *end here*.

Device Driver. An unassuming program that lets your application talk to the devices attached to your computer, like your screen and printer.

Dialog box. A means of communicating your choices, selections, or desires to the WordPerfect program.

Directory. A place on your disk that you designate for certain types of files and programs. By using directories you can keep your disk orderly and usually find what you are looking for.

Disks. The place where your programs and data are stored. Hard disks and floppy disks store information in the same way.

DOS. Disk Operating System. This is the program that helps your applications software talk to your computer hardware. The three major flavors of DOS are MS-DOS (Microsoft Corporation), IBM-DOS (International Business Machines) and Compaq-DOS (Compaq Computer Corporation).

Dot matrix. A type of printer that prints by putting teensy-weensy dots on the paper to form the characters.

Drag. A race involving funny cars. Actually, this is an action you can take with an object by clicking down on a mouse button and moving the mouse. You can drag text and drop it elsewhere in WordPerfect 6.0.

Drive Designator. An alphabetic character (A through Z) that is used to identify to the computer what physical disk drive, or drive partition, is being referenced. A and B are used for floppy disk drives; C through Z are used for hard disk drives.

Driver. See *Device driver*.

End field. A delimiter that tells WordPerfect that the word(s) just before this marker belong in one field, or place, in the document.

End record. A delimiter that tells WordPerfect that the field(s) before it marks the end of the record, or the information that goes in one document.

Executable. A software program that you "execute" or "run" on your computer.

Extended ASCII character set. Symbols and characters that you can make in WordPerfect Documents in addition to the regular American Standard Code for Information Interchange characters. Extended ASCII characters do not appear on your PC keyboard, and include some foreign language characters (Ñ, $), mathematical symbols (¼,¾), and simple line drawings to brighten your day (✿) or put a song in your heart (♥). See also *ASCII*.

Fax modem. A modem that has the capability to fax documents directly from your computer's disk. Not all modems are fax modems. See also *Modem*.

Field. A logical grouping of information, such as a name and three or four address lines, within a record. Two or more records form a file of information that can then be used to make several different documents from the same file.

File. A group of information that is stored in one place, like that all important letter to Mom. Sometimes called a data file.

File compression. Some computer programs or utilities are capable of compressing files by means of stripping out spaces and doing other tricks so that the file takes up less disk space. When the file is decompressed, the spaces are added back in and the tricks are reversed.

File names. A file name can be eight characters, followed by a period, followed by up to three more characters. The characters after the period are called the *file extension* and can be used to identify different types of files.

Floppy disk. A removable disk that you can store information on and carry with you. A disk in your pocket is the perfect complement to a pocket protector and accessorizes the nerdy look nicely.

Font. In printing, a font is a size and style of type. Check your printer documentation to find out what kinds of fonts it can print.

Form file. A file created as the template for merges. This file contains the main text and/or graphics and is the controlling file for merges.

Global. An action you take affecting your entire document. If you do a "global search and replace" to search for all occurrences of one word to replace it with another word, it takes effect on the entire document, not all the documents in the world.

Graphics. Pictures or drawings. Computers are picky and handle text and graphics differently. You can incorporate graphics into your WordPerfect document. Whether you can print them or not depends on your printer.

GUI. Graphical User Interface. Pronounced "gooey." All those pretty pictures on your screen that make an operating system or program easy to use.

Hard disk. The disk inside your computer that holds your operating system, programs, and data.

Hardware. If you can kick it, it's hardware.

Highlight. Menu selections and other choices—as well as blocked text—are often highlighted. A highlighted area appears on-screen as contrasted, or in some manner standing out, from the other stuff on the screen.

Icon. A little picture that represents a program, a file, or an action that will be taken when you click on a button.

Initial codes. The main controlling codes that affect the entire document. Document Initial Codes control the current document; Initial Codes Setup controls the formatting for all documents. All types of initial codes can be superseded in the document itself.

Ink jet. A type of printer that prints by squirting tiny amounts of ink directly onto the paper. A nice low-cost alternative to laser printers.

Interface card. A piece of hardware that goes inside a PC, enabling the PC to "talk" or interface with an external piece of equipment. Monitors, external tape backup units, and hookups to networks all require different types of interface cards.

Justification. A really good excuse for turning in your work late. In word processing lingo, there are four types of justification. Full justification is when the text is aligned on both the left and right margins. Left justification is when only the left margin text is aligned and the right margin is "ragged." Right justification is when the right margin text is aligned and (you guessed it) the left margin text is ragged. Center justification just means the text is centered in between the margins.

Kern. It comes on an ear and they make breakfast flakes with it. Actually, this refers to the way in which letters can be packed together. For example, if you have a 'P' and an 'a' together, you can make things look nicer by pushing the 'a' under the upper part of the 'P' just a little bit. In fact, this book uses kerning; just look, Pa.

Landscaped. Printing a page with the orientation of the paper being horizontal.

Laser. The best type of printer for word processing, offering the best quality at the fastest speed. Capable of printing superb graphics.

Macro. A series of keystrokes or a file containing lots of keystroke instructions and/or text that is recorded and then used by typing one simple name or keystroke. It's sort of like your computer using shorthand and is important for automating repetitive tasks.

Magnets. Something to keep away from your hardware and software.

Merge. Combining two or more files to make one file.

Microprocessor. The chip that is the "heart" of your computer.

Modem. A piece of hardware that enables you to send your computer's information directly to another computer by using telephone lines. This word was created from the original name: MOdulator/DEModulator.

Monitor. Your computer screen. Also often called a CRT.

Monitor card. The piece of hardware that enables your computer to "talk" to your monitor. See also *Interface card.*

Mouse. The device that hooks up to your computer that you use to "point and click." It makes it easy for the typing-impaired to operate their programs.

Mouse button. When you want to take an action with your mouse, you have to tell the program by clicking on one of the buttons on your mouse. (See also *Click.*)

Operating system. The special program that runs on your computer that plays traffic cop. It directs how your application programs and hardware work together, and also gives you tools for managing your computer.

Path name. A map that points DOS and WordPerfect to the location and name of your files. The full path name is made up of three parts: the drive designator, directory name(s), and file name. All parts are separated by a backslash (\).

Peripherals. Hardware that is external to your main system unit. The monitor, printer, mouse, and modem are all peripherals.

Pixel. Picture element, or one of those teensy weensy dots on your screen.

Port. On a ship, this is left. Nerds prefer the computer definition which is the place on the back of your computer where you hook up your printer, modem, and other devices.

Portrait. A painting or photograph of a person, or, in the computer world printing a page with the orientation of the paper as vertical. See also *Landscaped.*

PPM. Pages Per Minute. The speed (or lack thereof) by which laser printers are measured.

Print queue. When you print something, the queue grabs it at the full speed of your program, and then takes care of feeding it to the printer at the printer's slower rate. The queue can also hold more than one print job. This keeps you from having to wait on the printer all of the time.

Printer device driver. A software program that lets your computer "talk" to the printer. See also *Device driver.*

Program. A set of instructions that accomplish any given task. Your operating system is a program, as are the applications that you run everyday like your word processor or spreadsheet.

Proportional spacing. When a character takes up space in proportion to its size. The letter 'i' takes up less space than a letter 'm', for instance. You can only use proportional spacing if your printer can print that way.

RAM. A bighorn sheep. No, it's really Random Access Memory, which is what your computer uses to run your operating system and programs properly. Your programs use this area to store the information that you type in. When you turn off your computer or lose power, that information is lost.

Record. A set of fields that form one logical grouping of information that can be re-used without having to retype the same information every time. From a file that contains name and address records, for instance, you could write letters, address envelopes, and print Rolodex cards and only have to type the name and address one time.

Ribbon. For those with a mouse, the ribbon is a nice way to dress up the editing screen, but it also provides fast access to the functions that affect size and appearance of text.

Root or **Root directory.** The main directory of your hard disk or floppy disk. So named because a pictorial representation of the DOS directory structure is often shown as a tree, with the roots of the tree as the starting point.

Software. If you can't kick it, it's software. It's the zeros and ones that live on your disk and actually make your computer do something.

Spool. A verb meaning to send a printout to the print queue (which is also called a spooler, but means the same thing).

Subdirectory. A directory that lives inside another directory.

Variable. Each field in a merge record is a variable—the data in the field will change from one record to the next. Variable macros are those that are not permanently recorded on disk.

Video monitor. Your computer screen is a *video monitor*, also known as a *monitor* and a *CRT*.

Window. A window is a viewing area on your screen. You can make the window smaller (minimize) or larger (maximize) depending on what you want to do at the moment.

APPENDIX A

(Im)Perfect Computers

People new to computers have all sorts of misconceptions and worries about what their computers can and cannot do. Or maybe they're worried about pressing the wrong key and erasing everything or something. This appendix will cover:

 Just what is this hunk of metal and plastic on my desk?

 Software? Is that what husbands buy wives on their birthdays?

 How do I avoid making my computer explode?

 Where do all the files I'm going to create for my Great American Novel go? How do I keep track of them?

Okay, we're going to be totally serious here and address those concerns. First of all, if you make a mistake, what's the very worst that can happen? You erase a file? A program? The operating system and all the programs from your hard disk? So? What's the big deal here? If you *learn* something from your mistakes, it's not a big deal. You may have to get help from your favorite nerdy friend to get everything back to the way it was, but so what? You think *they* never made a mistake? Ha! And, in reality, it's very difficult to erase important files and things like that; you have to try to do it.

Pressing the wrong button or making a wrong change in a file is *not* going to make your hardware explode or endanger Western Civilization As We Know It. We make jokes about that sort of stuff, but we are really *just kidding*. The best way to learn is by doing, and remember this important thought for the day:

> *No one was born knowing anything about computers. We all have to start at the beginning.*

We're glad you wanted to start; now let's get down to business and talk about all those terms that are confusing to you now, but won't be by the time you finish reading this appendix. So stop feeling intimidated because your neighbors' six-year-old has mastered some computer game and can kill all the bad guys in the universe five times over before you can say "All kids should play in the middle of the street."

What Computers Really Can and Cannot Do

First of all, let's talk about what computers really can and cannot do. Here is another thought for the day (or tomorrow):

> *Computers and programs do exactly what you tell them to do.*

Unfortunately, computers cannot read your mind. Although Albert Kamenski of Akron, Ohio, is working on a new addition to the keyboard, a "Do what I mean, not what I say" button, he hasn't perfected it yet. For now we all have to settle with what we've got.

Computers are really pretty stupid when you get right down to it. They only understand two things: on or off. That's right. That's it! They can't chop firewood or even contemplate the Meaning of Life, the Universe, and Everything.

The only reason that computers can do some pretty amazing things is because they can do what we instruct them to do incredibly fast. Sometimes it may *seem* incredibly slow, but they really are quite fast.

Smooth Sailing with Hardware and Software

There are three essential parts that go into making your computer useful to you (and something more than just an expensive boat anchor). Those things are the hardware, operating system, and software. Actually, we may have stumbled onto a good analogy here. Think of your hardware as a sailboat, your operating system as the sails, and your software as the wind. Without either the sails or the wind, your sailboat just sits there, rusting. So just what does hardware and software and all that stuff mean and what does it do? In this section you will learn that:

 If you can kick it, it's hardware.

 If you can't kick it, it's software.

 There are several different types of software.

 An operating system is a special class of software.

 A program is a series of instructions.

 You are a programmer everyday. When you use your microwave or set your alarm clock, you are programming it to perform sets of instructions.

Don't Stub Your Toes on the Hardware

If you can kick it, it's hardware. Not that we actually recommend that you *do* that, you understand. You could cause harm to yourself and your hardware if you did do it, but you get the idea.

The main box that holds all the good stuff like the *microprocessor*, the *hard disk*, the *floppy disk drives*, the power supply, and other things is called the System Unit. It does just what its name implies: It's the box where all the system gunk is wired together.

FOOD FOR THOUGHT

If you break down the word *microprocessor*, you actually find out it's a pretty simple term. *Micro* just means teensy-weensy and *processor* just means that instructions (from software) are processed or interpreted and carried out.

A *hard disk* is a disk that is rigid, or hard, and sits permanently inside the System Unit. If you take it out of its protective case, it doesn't flop around like a *floppy disk* does when you take it out of its protective covering. (Kids! Don't try this at home.) All of the information that makes your computer useful is stored on the hard disk (and on floppy disks).

Things like your monitor (the display screen), keyboard, mouse, and printer are also hardware. Those things are classified as *peripherals*. They are auxiliary items to the main System Unit.

Software: The Invisible Stuff

If you can't kick it, it's software. There are different classes of software, but let's just lump them all together for the moment.

You can't see software because it is recorded on your hard or floppy disk with little magnetic signals, just like on a music cassette. The magnetic signals represent either **on** or **off**; that's the on or off we were talking about earlier (the two things a computer understands).

STOP!

Since all of your software is recorded by magnetic signals, it is VERY, VERY important to keep any magnets or anything that is magnetic away from your computer disks at all times. Keep magnets away from your hardware also, since metal can very easily become magnetized from being near something that is magnetic.

People have been known to keep a disk handy by attaching it to their metal filing cabinet with a magnet. Of course this confuses the information on the disk and you end up with unusable information, or what nerds call *garbage*.

Some common objects that are magnetic: telephones, speakers, hand tools, and even the top of your computer screen. Don't put disks near those things.

A piece of software is also known as a *program*. A program is merely a series of instructions that is given to your computer. Programs are written by, as you might have guessed, *programmers*. Programmers are strange people who don't have many social skills, but love Chinese food. Socialize with programmers at your own risk.

Actually, everyone is a programmer of one sort or another. When you decide to cook your delicious heat 'n serve TV dinner in your microwave oven, you select Time Cook, High, set the timer for 3 or 4 minutes, and then press Start. Hey! You're not only a chef, but a programmer as well! You just programmed your microwave oven—you gave it a series of instructions to *execute*. You do the same thing with a program: you execute, or run it.

Operating in the Clear

The most important piece of software on your computer is the operating system. In this case, we are talking about *DOS*, or the Disk Operating System. Your brand might be from Microsoft (MS-DOS), IBM (IBM-DOS), Compaq Computer Corporation (Compaq DOS), or from Achmeds Magic Carpet and DOS shop, but it all functions about the same way for purposes of this discussion.

What DOS, or any operating system, does is provide several important functions that make your other software and your hardware talk to each other properly. It handles the nitty-gritty details of keeping track of which files it stores where, how it writes them to disk, how it finds them again, and so on. Think of the operating system much like you do the innards of your car. You don't actually have to know *how* it works (this doohickey drives that sprocket and then...), you just want to be able to tug on the steering wheel and have it turn. DOS takes care of all the messy details for you.

DOS is not exactly a Cadillac in terms of operating systems, but it does the job and gets you from point A to point B. And after all, that's its purpose in life. But let's face it, it's not pretty, and most certainly not very pretty for beginners. Don't worry, we'll go over the things you need to understand about DOS a little later in this chapter.

Application Software

The stuff that really makes your computer useful is called *Application Software*, *Application Programs*, or just *Applications*. (Those nerds just can't make up their minds, can they?) This is the whole reason you bought your computer in the first place. Applications are programs you buy to solve needs, or "apply" to solve problems. Things like the WordPerfect word processing program, accounting programs, home budget programs, and so on are all applications software.

Applications come in all sizes, shapes, and colors and you should look carefully at the hardware requirements and the features of the program before you buy it.

A Different Breed of Application Software

There is a type of software you can "try before you buy." This is called *shareware*. Shareware is so named because it is intended that you share it with your friends and neighbors. You have thirty days to try it out. If you like it, you mail the author a check. If you think it's the worst thing since the Edsel, erase it and be done with it. Shareware is software on the honor system.

Shareware is written by people who are working on their own instead of a Big Business who will nail you to the wall if you try it without paying for it. These people have real jobs and no marketing budget, so having people pass along the program is the only way for them to "get the word out."

There is some really excellent shareware software available from many different sources. Over the years, there has actually been some shareware that was so astoundingly successful that the nerd who wrote the program quit his real job and went into the software business full-time.

STOP!

WordPerfect is NOT shareware. You gotta buy it!

A Backseat Driver

Another type of software that you need to know about is called a *driver*. Drivers are pretty important, especially with WordPerfect. Drivers do what the name implies, they *drive* the peripheral device and make it work with the software you are using. They drive your printer, your monitor, your mouse, and any other peripherals you have attached to your computer. They might also drive you crazy if you don't have the right one.

STOP!

Each hardware manufacturer makes their equipment different from others. Even the same manufacturer keeps improving on their product and so each model has slightly different hardware. Make sure you have the right drivers for your particular mix of hardware.

If you were to print just a plain text file from DOS, you don't usually need a printer device driver because most printers can handle plain text. But with a product like WordPerfect, where you can print your text bold, underlined, centered, justified, with pictures, and all sorts of different ways, you need a device driver to act as an interpreter between the software, the operating system, and the printer hardware.

Device drivers are not mix and match. There is no such thing as a Universal Printer Driver, for instance. That's why, when WordPerfect was installed on your machine, you had to know what type of printer, monitor, mouse, and other equipment you had.

It's pretty easy to tell if you have the wrong device driver installed. Whatever peripheral you are trying to drive either won't work at all or it will work in a pretty flaky way. That's not always the reason for flakiness, but it's certainly a good place to start looking.

FOOD FOR THOUGHT

Installing the wrong device driver, just like pressing the wrong key, will not cause anything to blow up. Well, maybe your ego a little bit, but it happens.

Batch Files and Macro

Batch files and *macros* are yet another type of program. These are a little different than most software programs because these are in straight *ASCII* text format.

FOOD FOR THOUGHT

ASCII stands for American Standard Code for Information Interchange. ASCII characters are the range of characters that all computers can type, and most printers can print, without any special drivers. Those are the digits 0 through 9, the standard punctuation marks, and the letters A through Z. (Also, the letters a through z. Remember: computers need to be told everything in detail, even when a letter is in upper- or lowercase).

FOOD FOR THOUGHT

All programs start out life as straight ASCII text files. But your other software programs (operating system, applications, and drivers) are then run through yet another program, called a *compiler*. A compiler translates the text file into something only the computer can read. It can also process the instructions much faster than it can a regular text file that a human can read.

Batch files and macros are a sort of automation tool for you. In DOS, you can type a bunch of commands into a file, which ends up getting called a batch file. After you (or some nerd) has done this, you can run the batch file to execute all of those commands at once.

In a program like WordPerfect, you type in a series of keystrokes and use a special feature to record and save those keystrokes. This is called a macro. When you call on your macro, WordPerfect goes off and performs each instruction without any intervention from you, and a lot more quickly than you can type it, even if you're a really fast typist.

Data

Data isn't something you can kick either, but it isn't really software in the sense that it's a program of any type. Data is the stuff that *you* create. It is information. A letter to the president is data. The numbers in a spreadsheet are data. Any output that you create from a program you run are data. Data are grouped together into a logical beginning and ending, called a *data file*, or more commonly, just a *file*. One memo or letter is a file, for instance.

FOOD FOR THOUGHT

People often get confused by the word data. *Data is a plural word. The singular form of data is datum. We're telling you this so that you can act smug with all of the people that screw this up.*

NerdSpeak

A lot of people think that nerds are speaking nerdspeak just to thwart real people from understanding what they say. Actually, there is no conspiracy, no Senate committee investigation, and the FBI has found that nerds really are Americans.

It's just that nerds need to have some way of measuring things, just like cooks (teaspoons and tablespoons), astronomers (light years), and electricians (ohms and volts). Unfortunately, while teaspoons is a common measurement that most people know about, it's really hard to measure a file in those terms. "I've got a 3 teaspoon letter" or "That disk holds about 4 pounds of data" just doesn't work.

So, nerds measure things in bits and bytes and megabytes. Now before your eyes cross and you begin to feel faint, let's take a look at what those terms mean. You'll find they aren't really mysterious words after all.

A *bit* is short for *bi*nary digi*t*. Bi means two. Humans use decimal digits (zero through nine), but computers can't count that high (you may have noticed their lack of fingers and toes), so they only use a zero or a one. Zero means off and one means on. So, a bit has a value of either a zero or a one. Ha! See? That wasn't so hard. Now you are well on your way to understanding nerdspeak!

OK, when the PC was developed, some engineer decided that eight bits would be a sufficient amount of bits to be able to represent just about any character or number they wanted to use. So, in your computer, eight bits strung together equal one *byte*. This is similar to the logic that says that four teaspoons equal one tablespoon—because somebody *said* so, that's why! One byte of information is roughly equal to one character (like the letter "a" or the number "4").

The next measurement that nerds use is *kilobytes*, or one thousand bytes, abbreviated *K*. To put this in perspective, an average printed page is about 3K of data, which is approximately 3,000 characters.

The last measurement we will talk about is *megabytes*, or one million bytes, abbreviated *M*, or sometimes *MB* (and pronounced *meg* by those in the know). 1M would be roughly equal to about 330 printed pages.

So, by this time you might be asking yourself just why you want to know about kbytes and megabytes when you can't actually do anything *useful* with them, like add a dash of kbytes to your chili recipe that blows the top of your head off and brings tears to the eyes. After all, you've managed to get through life just fine so far without it, right? Right. But... if you want to be able to follow along with more discussions in this chapter, you need to know the preceding information. We're not doing this to be sadistic. Honest!

More Hardware Stuff

OK, now that we've bored you to tears with all that stuff about software and data, we're now going to bore you to tears about hardware. Don't get tears on the book!

Baaahhh... Humbug!

The first item we will look at here is *RAM*. This is not a male sheep (fooled ewe, huh?), but stands for *Random Access Memory*.

There are two places where information is kept in your computer. You already know about disks (both hard disks and floppies); data kept on disks stays there until you deliberately erase it.

The other place is RAM, which is where your computer keeps information *only while you are working with it*. It is temporary storage used by the computer. When you work with a document, it is kept in RAM until you save it to the disk. Until you have saved it, though, it can be lost if your computer gets turned off (or has a glass of water spilled into it). So you can see that it's pretty important to save your work frequently so that if you should accidently lose power before you save your file you won't lose the whole document.

SAVE THE DAY

WordPerfect has a setup option that will save your file automatically to disk every so often (you can choose how many minutes between each automatic save). We recommend that you set it to 10 minutes or less so that you never lose more than 10 minutes of work at a time.

Most other application software doesn't have that option, so you need to remember to save your work frequently.

It's also a good idea to save your work to a floppy disk once or twice a day, so that if something bad happens to your hard disk, you have something else to Save The Day for you.

RAM is measured in both kilobytes and megabytes. Older machines have 640K; newer models tend to come with 2M, 4M, and so on. The more memory you have, the better off you are. It means you can run larger programs and have more data in memory at any one time. It can make your computer run faster, too.

Hard Disks

Hard disks are also measured in megabytes. Just like RAM, the more, the merrier. Some nerds like to say things like "Well, I'd like to load that program, but I just don't have enough real estate." They are not talking rental properties here, this is nerdspeak for hard disk space. If you are setting out to buy your own computer, we recommend that you don't settle for less than about 200M of hard disk space. Trust us, you'll use it.

Becoming a Hard Disk Tycoon

If you find yourself running short of disk space, there are a couple of products that can help you stretch it out.

If you're using DOS 6.0, it includes a utility that will magically let your disk store almost twice as much data, through the magic of *file compression*. What file compression does is automatically use special computer programs that can take extra space out of files, use codes for frequently used words, and so on, to make your files smaller, while still keeping all of the information in them. There are also third-party utilities available that do that (a popular one is a product called Stacker by Stac Electronics). Check with your favorite nerd or computer store for more information. Before you actually install such a program, though, be *VERY SURE* to make at least two complete backups of your hard disk, as such utilities have been known to cause problems with some computers. Not often, but it does happen. Most people are very happy with their disk compression software.

Floppy Disks

Floppy disks are so named because if you take them out of the vinyl or plastic covering that they come in, they flop around. Definitely do not try this with a report you just wrote that your job depends on. If you have an old disk around that you don't want anymore, go ahead and cut it open and look at the floppy disk inside. That disk is called a *cookie*, but don't eat it!

Floppy disks are usually measured in megabytes also, but some are still measured in kilobytes. Table A.1 shows some of the sizes and capacities of floppy disks:

Table A.1
Floppy Disk Capacities

Disk Size	Nerds Call It	It Holds
5 1/4"	Double-density	360K
5 1/4"	High-density	1.2M
3 1/2"	Double-density	720K
3 1/2"	High-density	1.44M
3 1/2"	Very high-density	2.88M

SAVE THE DAY

Floppy disks have a safeguard on them called a *write-protect notch*. On the 5 ¼-inch disks this is a small notch cut out of the vinyl covering near the top right-hand corner. If you cover this notch with the little electrical-tape looking tabs that come in a box of disks, you cannot erase (accidentally or on purpose) whatever is stored on the disk until you remove the tape.

With a 3 ½-inch disk you don't have to fool around with messy tape. There is a little built-in shutter in the upper left-hand corner of the disk when you turn it around to look at the back of it. Move the tab with a mechanical pencil or pen. When you can see through the hole, you have write-protected the disk.

Unfortunately, hard disks have no such thing as a write-protect notch. You just have to be very careful not to erase anything that you might want.

The Eyes Have It

The video monitor is a very important piece of your computer equipment. With a really good monitor, you will not experience eyestrain, headaches or any eye-related problems. Just like your TV screen, monitors are measured diagonally (14 inches is pretty standard).

Resolution is measured in *pixels* (*PI*cture *EL*ements), which are the little dots on your screen, just like a TV. Other measurements for monitors include dot pitch (the smaller the better) and refresh rate (the higher the better).

If you are going to purchase a monitor, the best thing to do is to go to a computer store and look at all the monitors side by side, much like you do when you go TV shopping.

A good monitor with a high resolution can be pricey, but since we're talking about your eyesight here, this is not the place to be cheap.

The other half of this whole thing is the *interface card* that goes inside your computer. In this case, it would be the *monitor card*. The monitor card provides the translation between the monitor and the operating system and helps determine how sharp (or blurry) the stuff you see on your screen actually appears.

FOOD FOR THOUGHT

Some terms that you will hear nerds throw out are things like EGA, VGA, Super VGA and so on. Since you already know about pixels, table A.2 shows what those terms translate to:

Table A.2
Video Resolutions

Nerdspeak	Resolution	What It Looks Like
EGA	640x350	Blech
VGA	640x480	Pretty good
SVGA	800x600 or more	Now you're talking

The first number in the resolution column is the number of pixels across the screen, while the second is the number of pixels down the screen. Some SVGA video systems go as high as 1,280x1,024. Those not only have really sharp resolution, but you also might have to give up your first born to own one. Shop around.

Printing: Spreading the Word

Let's face it, a word processing program doesn't do you much good if you can't print out what you just spent hours composing. So we need to talk about printers for a moment. Your main choices are (drum roll)...

Laser

A laser printer provides the best quality of print. Laser printer prices are dropping like rocks, so once again, shop around. Decide on the features you absolutely have to have, because laser printers offer all sorts of features. Laser printers can print graphics, but graphics take up a lot of memory, both on your hard disk, in RAM, and to print (printers cannot use the computer memory for printing). So, just like your computer, the more memory the printer has, the bigger the pictures you can print and the better off you are.

Laser printer speed is measured in the number of pages it prints per minute (PPM). With a laser printer, you can also print both *portrait* and *landscaped*. Portrait means that the page is printed with the shortest side horizontal and landscaped means that the page is printed with the longest side horizontal. In other words, portrait is printed like this book, while landscape is sideways on the paper.

Ink Jet

Ink jet printers are really taking off. They print with a similar quality as laser, but slower. They are also measured the same way in speed (PPM) and the page can also be oriented either portrait or landscaped. Ink jet printers are a good alternative to laser printers; they don't print as sharply, but they don't cost as much either.

TRICK

If you are printing a *lot* of pages, look carefully at the cost per page for each kind of printer. While ink jet printers are cheaper to buy, they are typically more expensive to run. If your printing volume is high enough, a laser printer might be cheaper overall.

Dot Matrix

If you are very serious about your word processing, don't buy a dot matrix printer. The capabilities are much more limited and the quality is not as good as either a laser or ink jet printer. You have a choice of which way to orient your paper—as long as it's portrait. Many dot matrix printers do not support graphics, so look before you buy. Dot matrix printer speed is measured in how many characters per second it can print (CPS).

The Straight Fax

WordPerfect 6.0 has built-in fax capabilities, which is a really nifty bonus. But you do need a fax *modem* to take advantage of them. Modem stands for *MO*dulation/*DEM*odulation. What this means is that the modem translates the signals the computer speaks (digital) into a signal the telephone lines can understand (analog) and sends it over the telephone lines. The modem at the other end reverses the process.

Be careful when you go modem shopping. The rate the modem can transmit and receive data and the rate it can transmit and receive fax signals are often different. You might want to check with your favorite nerd about hooking up your modem.

Filing Cabinets, Drawers, and File Folders

Since you just bought WordPerfect 6.0, you'll want to start out right by organizing your files nicely so that you can find everything easily all the time, right? Right!

Actually, disk organization is a bit like the oil commercials where the guy says "Pay me now or pay me later." If you don't think about it and do a little planning ahead, you'll pay for it later when you spend hours searching for an important letter that you need, or end up erasing that same letter because you weren't paying attention.

Imagine that your hard disk is one giant closet. No drawers, no hangers, no nothing. Well, if you start filing your data without organizing it, that would be like throwing in the papers willy-nilly and you just end up with a mess. So, we'll wave our magic wand and (presto-chango!) turn the closet into a filing cabinet instead! There, that's nicer.

Now let's put some labels on the filing cabinet drawers. Hmmm... how about one called "WPDOCS" for your WordPerfect documents? What a concept! To do this on your hard disk, you create a *directory*, which is an area on your computer where you can group files (like a file drawer). When you installed WordPerfect, it asked you if you wanted your documents to go in a directory named WPDOCS, so that's probably already there.

So far you can see that a directory is like putting a label on a filing cabinet drawer. But now we need to organize the papers inside the drawer. That's like putting folders inside of each drawer and labeling those. The DOS equivalent is making *subdirectories* or a directory within a directory. You can make directories with WordPerfect; the actual commands to do that are covered in another chapter.

You might want to make several subdirectories in your WPDOCS directory. How about one called LET for letters, maybe another one called DOC for documents, or one called FORM for forms, REPORTS for reports, and so on. That way, you can file each type of document you create in its own directory and know just what you have.

Another way to organize your information is by document name. Unfortunately, you cannot store a letter on your disk and call it LETTER_TO_GEORGE_ABOUT_SPROCKETS. DOS limits you to shorter names, which can have no more than eight characters, followed by a period, followed by three more characters. The three characters are referred to as the *file extension*. Besides letters and numbers, you can use special characters, like **!@#$%^&*()-_=** in your file names. But those can be pretty cryptic, so we suggest you don't.

STOP!

Never, EVER use spaces in the names that you use for either directories, subdirectories, or file names. When you go to use them, they can't be. Can't be used, that is, because a space in the name just confuses the heck out of DOS.

A better way to use file names is to use something descriptive for the first eight characters and then standardize on the way you use the last three characters to classify the file by document type. So your letters might end in an extension of .LET or .LTR, a report in .RPT or .REP, and form in .FRM or .FM (you don't *have* to use all eight or all three characters).

The Last Word

No, this isn't the surprise ending. What we want to tell you is that there is no right or wrong way to organize your documents and files on your disks. What is important is that you *do* organize them.

Surprise Ending

OK, this is the surprise ending.

Symbols

A

D

X-Z